ON PHILOSOPHY, HISTORY, AND LITERATURE

Rudolf Steiner
(1904)

ON PHILOSOPHY, HISTORY, AND LITERATURE

Lectures at the Worker Education School and the Independent College in Berlin

Author's summary and summaries of thirty-four lectures,
held between 1901 and 1905.
With reports about Rudolf Steiner's activity
in the "Giordano Bruno Association," 1902.

TRANSLATION BY DANIEL HINDES
AND CLIFFORD VENHO

INTRODUCTION BY CLIFFORD VENHO

RUDOLF STEINER

SteinerBooks

CW 51

SteinerBooks | Anthroposophic Press
834 Main Street, P.O. Box 358
Spencertown, New York 12165
www.steinerbooks.org

Original translation from German by Daniel Hindes and Clifford Venho
Introduction by Clifford Venho

This book is volume 51 in the Collected Works (CW) of Rudolf Steiner, published by SteinerBooks, 2023. It is a translation of *Über Philosophie, Geschichte, und Literatur. Darstellungen an der Arbeiterbildungsschule und der Freien Hochschule in Berlin*, 1st edition, published by Rudolf Steiner Verlag, Dornach, Switzerland, 1983.

ISBN: 978-1-62148-321-2

Printed in the United States of America
by Integrated Books International

CONTENTS

Lecture Seven
DECEMBER 13, 1904

Lecture Eight
DECEMBER 20, 1904

Lecture Nine
DECEMBER 28, 1904

Schiller and Our Age

INTRODUCTION

CLIFFORD VENHO

THE LECTURES IN THIS VOLUME provide a unique glimpse into Rudolf Steiner's years in Berlin around the turn of the twentieth century. They are divided into two sections: part one consists of lectures given at the Worker Education School, founded in 1891 by the socialist Wilhelm Liebknecht (1826–1900) as a school for working-class people; and part two consists of lectures given at the Independent College, founded in 1901 by Bruno Wille and Wilhelm Bölsche.* The appendix contains documents related to Steiner's activity in the Giordano Bruno Association, also founded by Bruno Wille. This introduction will deal with Steiner's activity in the Worker Education School.

One might wonder how Rudolf Steiner, who was in many ways a critic of Marxist thought and was never a member of any political party, came to teach at an institution with direct ties to the German Social Democratic Party. It should be borne in mind that during Steiner's time there, the Worker Education School was not yet a training ground for political speakers and union leaders, though it later became this. Instead, it was a place where working people—who had generally ended their education around age fifteen or sixteen in order to work in factories—could further their studies in various subjects: economy, history, jurisprudence, natural science, and oration. Because of the long work days, courses were taught in the evenings from 9 to 11 p.m. With the rise of the workers' movement at the end of the nineteenth century, the school had received a fresh impulse, after struggling for some years. Many freethinkers of the day taught there, including

* Bruno Wille (1860–1928) was a liberal writer on religion, editor of *Der Freidenker*, and founder The Free People's Theater in Berlin. Wilhelm Bölsche (1861–1939) was a romantic lyricist, philosopher, critic, socialist, and novelist. He wrote a Faustian, monistic novel, *Revelations of the Juniper Tree.*

Wilhelm Bölsche. However, the post of history teacher had always proven difficult to fill. Students initially expressed interest in the subject, and many signed up for the history courses, but slowly numbers dwindled and teachers never lasted long.

In December of 1898, the school had to publish its programs for the following semester without having secured a history teacher. The school board approached a few candidates, but to no avail. Finally, the poet Cäsar Flaischlen told them to ask his friend Rudolf Steiner, a scholar who had worked on the Weimar edition of Goethe's works and who was currently the editor of the *Magazin für Literatur*. At the time, Steiner was, in the words of the dramaturge Walter Harlan, a "free-floating and unpaid scholar of God."* He was an unorthodox candidate, but the school board was desperate and approached him anyway. As Johanna Mücke describes in her account of Steiner's time at the Worker Education School: "We came to Habsburgerstrasse 11, where a friendly young gentleman received us and said, when we had made our request: 'Well, if you want me to teach history *in my own way*, then yes, I can do it.'"† In his *Autobiography*, Rudolf Steiner gives an account of his motivation for accepting the post:

> I made it clear to the directors that, if I took over the teaching, I would present history according to my own views of human evolution, not as interpreted by the Marxists, as was now customary in Social-Democratic circles. They nevertheless wanted me to give the courses. Having made this condition, it did not matter to me that the college was based on a Social-Democratic ideology by the elder Liebknecht. To me, it consisted of men and women of the proletariat; the fact that the majority of them were socialists was none of my business. The mental outlook of my students, however, was

* Quoted in Wolfgang G. Vögele, *Der andere Steiner* [The other Steiner] (Dornach, 2006), p. 85, and Peter Selg, *Rudolf Steiner, Life and Work, Volume 2 (1890–1900), Weimar and Berlin*, trans. Margot Saar (SteinerBooks, 2014), p. 192.

† Johanna Mücke and Alwin Alfred Rudolph, *Erinnerungen an Rudolf Steiner und seine Wirksamkeit an der Arbeiter-Bildungsschule in Berlin 1899–1904* [Recollections of Rudolf Steiner and his activity in the Worker Education School in Berlin 1899–1904] (Basel, CH: Zbinden Verlag, 1979), p. 14. [emphasis added]

> my business. I had to find a completely different way of expressing myself than I had become used to until then. To make myself understood to some degree, I had to find my way into their forms of concepts and judgments. . . .[‡]

When Steiner began teaching at the Worker School, the classes (and classrooms) were small. Less than fifty students attended his first course, "Intellectual Currents in the History of Modern Times from the Reformation to the French Revolution." Instead of presenting a Marxist interpretation of history, as was generally expected within the School, Steiner spoke about the spiritual movement initiated by Voltaire and Rousseau as a precursor of the French Revolution. Voltaire, with his free-spirited battle against any form of authority, and Rousseau, with his profound and persuasive writings on the free unfolding of the human personality, represented the spirit behind the Revolution. Interestingly, many years later, Steiner referred back to this spirit—which expressed itself more or less unconsciously in the motto "liberty, equality, fraternity"—when he sought to establish social threefolding after the First World War.

Steiner's approach was at first a surprise for the students, who had been schooled in Marxist thought and tended to view all spiritual matters as "byproducts" of material, economic processes. For them, it was questionable whether the spiritual striving of individual human beings could really be a driving force in history. Steiner knew the soul disposition of his students and the "inexpressibly tragic situation" that the proletariat's intense desire for knowledge had so far been "satisfied only through the grossest form of materialism."[§] But the materialistic ideas that had been absorbed by the workers from popular scientific literature and from Marxist writings contained "partial truths." Steiner therefore developed his approach on this basis:

> Had I merely ignored [the partial truths] and taught history from an idealistic perspective, the workers would have sensed that what I said did not agree with the partial truths they already knew. Consequently, I began with a fact that was comprehensible to my

‡ Rudolf Steiner, *Autobiography* (CW 28), trans. Rita Stebbing (SteinerBooks, 2005), p. 193.

§ Ibid.

> listeners. I showed why it makes no sense to say, as Karl Marx does, that economic forces dominated history prior to the sixteenth century. I also showed that economics did not assume a form as understood in Marxist terms until the sixteenth century and that this process climaxed in the nineteenth century. Thus I was able to speak quite factually about the spiritual ideals active in the preceding epochs of history, and I could show that more recently those impulses weakened in the face of material and economic forces. In this way the workers received ideas about knowledge capacities and the religious, artistic, and moral forces in history, and they ceased to regard them as merely ideological. It would have been useless to enter a controversy over materialism; I had to allow idealism to arise from materialism.*

Though Steiner's views were at odds with those generally held by the workers, his presence and teaching style were inspiring and drew them directly into the content of the lessons. Whereas other teachers usually held classes in the form of lectures, after which the students went home tired and more or less content, Steiner encouraged questions and lively debate after his presentations, taking the time to answer all of his students' questions patiently and objectively. The classes soon went to midnight or later.

Steiner began with less than fifty students, but within a few months he had around two hundred. In addition to history, he taught oration. He had a warm interest in all of his students, in their challenges, hopes, and longings. When correcting their work, he pointed out encouragingly the areas that needed improvement and he never hesitated to praise what was praiseworthy. The accounts of former students attest to the festive mood of his classes, which lifted all the participants above their narrow concerns and filled them with joy in learning.

Johanna Mücke describes one particularly memorable experience from that time:

> One conversation from the early years still stands vividly in my mind, which I overheard on a school excursion (because Herr Doctor also took part in it). Several young people walked alongside him

* Steiner, *Autobiography* (CW 28), pp. 193–94.

> and talked about their lives. One of them exclaimed animatedly: "Why is there so little happiness in life when everyone wants to be happy?" Herr Doctor replied: "Yes, but perhaps life is not there in order to make us happy!" "Yes, but why else?" said the young man, quite shocked. "Well, suppose life were there in order for us *to accomplish a task.*"
>
> These words were spoken very kindly but with such deep emphasis that we all went on in silence for a while, and they remained firmly in my memory, although I hardly understood them at the time.[†]

Despite Steiner's deep connection with his students, and their enthusiastic appreciation for him, the leaders of the school began to question whether Steiner should be a teacher there at all. He had made it clear that he would only teach in his own way and not along party lines. This was problematic for some of the more dogmatic directors of the school, who felt that Steiner's views went against the interests of the party. When Wilhelm Liebknecht (the founder of the school) was approached early on and asked his opinion as to whether Steiner should be permitted to continue teaching at the school, he responded: "They should be glad that they have such a good teacher. His political views need not concern them."[‡] But when Liebknecht died in 1900, the dogmatism and intolerance of the school directors grew steadily over the years and Rudolf Steiner was increasingly felt to be an unwelcome guest, despite his popularity with the students.

This situation was compounded by the fact that Steiner became General Secretary of the German Section of the Theosophical Society in 1902. Regarding his attitude toward the Theosophical Society at that time and his reasons for taking on a leadership role within it, he wrote:

> A large part of the membership fanatically followed individual leaders within the Theosophical Society. And they swore by the dogmas laid down by those very sectarian leaders. I was repelled by the triviality and dilettantism within the Theosophical Society. Only among the English theosophists did I find inner meaning that arose from

---

† Mücke, *Erinnerungen*, p. 18.

‡ Ibid., p. 20.

> Blavatsky, and this was still cultivated in the right way by Annie Besant and others. As for myself, I could never have worked as they did, but I found a spiritual center there with which it was possible to unite if one was serious about spreading spiritual knowledge in the deepest sense. Marie von Sivers and I counted less on the members of the Theosophical Society than on those in general who attended meetings with open hearts and minds when earnest spiritual knowledge was seriously cultivated.*

Steiner's decision to work within the Theosophical Society shocked the leaders of the Worker Education School. How could a theosophist be allowed to teach in their school? Steiner, for his part, made sure to send the first issues of the journal *Luzifer*, of which he was the editor, to the school's library so that there was no confusion about his views.

In order to discredit him and sow doubt among the students, the school board arranged a debate between Steiner and the Marxist Max Grunwald. The hope was that Grunwald would show the students the error of Steiner's views. Unfortunately for them, the opposite occurred. As one eye-witness described of the debate:

> It was a gigantic battle of spirits. Steiner was in rare form. He spoke dramatically, cowed his opponent with his wealth of knowledge, and spoke with such passion and fire that even his enemies were entranced. The little Grunwald, a struggling physician, had his work cut out for him. He was not stupid and people were usually in awe of his knowledge and ready wit. But he was already hopelessly lost in the first round.†

At the end, 12 of those present declared themselves in favor of Grunwald and 348 in favor of Steiner.

Steiner began to lecture throughout Europe and often had to postpone his classes at the Worker School to accommodate his touring schedule. This was seized upon as a justification for his dismissal from the school. The board claimed that Steiner no longer had any interest in the school, and because they could not oust him in the open,

---

* Steiner, *Autobiography* (CW 28), pp. 112–13.

† Quoted in Peter Selg, *Rudolf Steiner Life and Work, Volume 2 (1890–1900)*, p. 214.

they did it behind closed doors at a board meeting which Steiner was unable to attend. Johanna Mücke, dismayed by the underhandedness of the board and out of a sense of responsibility, decided to inform Steiner of the decision. He was not at all surprised and had been expecting his dismissal for some time. Many years later, in a public lecture, he remarked:

> And so I was thrown out—because I was not willing to teach the orthodox, dogmatic, and materialistic view of history—by those bigwigs; four people against six hundred of my students; four people who had never heard my lectures against six hundred students who had listened to me for years.[‡]

This was the tragic end of Steiner's time in the Worker Education School. The opposition he was later to face from many directions already showed itself in the duplicitous actions of the school board. Rudolf Steiner later wrote of the tragic fate of the worker movement:

> I have the impression that if more unbiased individuals had taken an interest in the workers' movement in those days, and if the proletariat had encountered real understanding, that movement would have developed very differently.[§]

Shortly after leaving the school, Steiner wrote in a letter to Marie von Sivers: "You know that my work in these circles was a mission for me. Something has been destroyed that I did not wish to see destroyed."[¶]

What was it that Steiner felt as a "mission" with respect to his working-class students? Was it, perhaps, a mission of awakening, of awakening in human souls a consciousness of the true nature and dignity of the human being? In the context of the Worker Education School, he primarily cultivated an "education through history," often referring to Hegel's words: "World history is the progress of humanity in the consciousness of freedom." Freedom and dignity were the two moral ideals that shone most brightly in his classes in the school.

---

‡ Lecture in Stuttgart, May 3, 1919, in *Neugestaltung des Sozialen Organismus* (GA 330), 2nd ed. (Dornach, CH: Rudolf Steiner Verlag, 1983), p. 161. Not available in English.

§ Rudolf Steiner, *Autobiography* (CW 28), p. 195.

¶ Selg, *Rudolf Steiner, Life and Work, Volume 2 (1890–1900)*, p. 215.

In a lecture on Roman history, he placed these ideals clearly before his students:

> We must see how this old Roman ruin is collapsing and how something came out of it under which the peoples had to groan for a long time. It begins with the call for freedom and ends with the suppression of freedom. It is the call declaring that everyone should respect each other as equals, and it ends with everyone being oppressed. It is strange that in our time historians have found themselves defending Caracalla because he gave so-called equality to the whole Roman Empire. As one of the most insignificant and harmful Caesars, he made those who were outside in the provinces equal to the Romans, but then he oppressed them all together! And this figure has been given the mantle of a champion of Roman freedom!
>
> When we see that the destiny of freedom can be like this, then I think we really gain from history what we can call a kind of education through history. Then we learn that there is a real rock, like Peter had—a rock based on the original founder, on which human development can really be built. This rock is and must be human freedom and human dignity. These can be suppressed at times, indeed as strongly suppressed as in the old Roman Empire by conditions that can be compared with few others. However, the education of the human being to freedom is given in history. We must remember this important fact: when power and violence ruled in ancient Rome at its peak, the foundation was at the same time undermined, and the whole structure collapsed. However deeply suppressed, it must be said of freedom that the following true saying applies to it, indeed arises from it:
>
> The old collapses, times change,
> And new life blossoms from the ruins.*

As the catastrophe of the First World War loomed on the horizon, it was to this "new life" that Steiner appealed—the new life slumbering in the souls of human beings, waiting to be awakened.

Steiner's activity in the school, like his later efforts for social threefolding, did not seem to change the political landscape of the time in a significant and lasting way. And yet, was it all in vain? Was the

* Lecture of July 19, 1904, on page 56 of this volume.

striving of the workers in the school in vain, given the unchanged social conditions?

Johanna Mücke asked Rudolf Steiner this question. His response was:

> You must make a clear distinction: for the improvement of social, organizational conditions, it means next to nothing because completely different laws apply; but for the development of individual souls, like any real striving, it means a great deal.[†]

† Mücke, *Erinnerungen*, p. 29.

ON PHILOSOPHY, HISTORY, AND LITERATURE

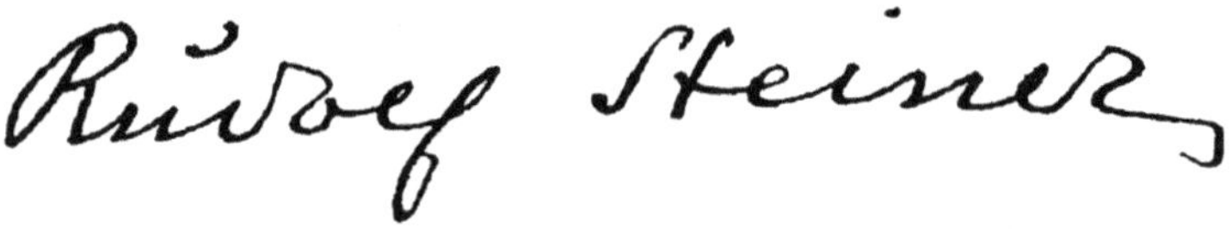

I

LECTURES AT
THE WORKER EDUCATION SCHOOL IN BERLIN

Views of the World and of Life from Ancient Times to the Present

Author's Summary. Summary of Ten Lectures, held in Berlin from January to March, 1901

1. The Greek Worldviews

Aristotle, whom the great medieval poet Dante called "the master of those who know," spoke the following beautiful words about the fact that man cannot stop at what his senses tell him about nature and about himself:

> All men naturally desire knowledge. An indication of this is our esteem for the senses; for apart from their use we esteem them for their own sake, and most of all the sense of sight. Not only with a view to action, but even when no action is contemplated, we prefer sight, generally speaking, to all the other senses. The reason of this is that of all the senses sight best helps us to know things, and reveals many distinctions. . . .
>
> All animals live by impressions and memories, and have but a small share of experience; but the human race lives also by art and reasoning.†

Hegel, in particular, has sounded the apparently self-evident yet highly important sentence: "Thinking makes the soul, with which the animals are also endowed, into a spirit."† The human being cannot help but ask many questions about the world and about himself. The answers that he, through his thinking, gives himself in response to these questions make up his "views of the world and of life." Angelus Silesius, a German thinker of the seventeenth century, aptly said that the rose blossoms simply because it blossoms. It does not ask why it blossoms.† The human being cannot live like that. He must inquire about the foundations of the world and of his own being. In the first place, the human being naturally puts his thinking at the service of practical life. With the help of thinking, he makes himself tools, machines, and devices by which he can satisfy his needs more perfectly than the animal can. Secondly, he wants to achieve something through his thinking that has nothing to do with practical utility. He wants to enlighten himself about things. He wants to recognize how the facts he encounters in life are connected.

The first ideas that the human being forms about the connections between things are religious. He thinks to himself that the events in nature are created by beings similar to himself. He imagines these beings as more powerful than he is. The human being creates gods in his own image. Just as he does *his* work, so he also imagines the world as a work of the gods. Gradually, however, scientific views grow out of the religious ones. He learns to observe nature and its forces. He can no longer be content with imagining these forces as similar to human forces. He no longer creates a god in his own image, but he forms thoughts about the connections between the phenomena of the world according to the image that observation and science provides.

Therefore, a thought-based worldview arises within occidental culture once natural science has reached a certain level. The first men of ancient Greece from whom we have inherited a worldview that no longer consists of religious conceptions were nature researchers. Thales, the first great thinker mentioned by Aristotle, was a nature researcher of great importance for his time. He was able to predict the solar eclipse that occurred on May 28, 585 BC, while the Medean and Lydian armies were facing each other at the Halys River. His contemporary, Anaximander, was a great astronomer.

If, in our time, the cultivation of the "views of the world and of life," which is taught as philosophy at our universities, does not enjoy any special reputation but is instead considered one-sided and superfluous academic book learning, it is because contemporary philosophers have mostly lost the proper connection to the individual sciences. Those who want to build up a "view of the world and of life" cannot stop at a single science. They must assimilate all the knowledge of their time, everything we know about the development of nature and culture. The entirety of all the sciences are tools for the philosopher. In view of the vast knowledge that has gradually become available, it is difficult today to form a comprehensive "view of the world and of life." What happens instead is that the teachers of views of the world and of life often deal with questions that do not arise from a true human need but are brought forward by their one-sided, traditional way of thinking.

A true "view of the world and of life" must deal with the questions that cannot be answered in any single science. For every single science has to do with a certain area of nature or of human life. The "view of the world and of life" must look for an interrelationship of thoughts in the knowledge offered us by all branches of science. Each individual branch of science also cannot be the concern of every single person; however, a "view of the world and of life" is of interest to all people. Not everyone can develop such a view because not everyone can study up on all sciences. But just as it requires considerable specific knowledge to build a table, knowledge that not everyone who needs a table can acquire, so, in order to build up a "worldview," it likewise requires a comprehensive set of tools that are not available to everyone. Anyone can make use of a table, but only those who have learned specific skills can build one. Views of the world and of life are of interest to everyone; however, only those who can obtain the requisite tools from all areas of science can and should build up a worldview and teach about it. The sciences are merely the tools of such views of the world and of life.

Kant posed the basic questions that produce in us the need for a worldview in the following way: "What can I know? What shall I do? What may I hope?"[†] Goethe expressed the matter more briefly and significantly by saying, "If I know my relationship to myself and to the external world, then I name it truth."[†] In fact, the human being wants to achieve nothing else through a view of the world and of life than an insight into the meaning of his own existence and how he is related to external nature.

According to Aristotle, the oldest Greek thinkers considered material substances as the origin of everything—that of which all things consist, from which everything originates, and into which everything finally passes away again. That is what their thought focused on. The seeds of living things developed in the moist earth. Thales[†] lived on an island, and he saw how countless forms of life develop in the sea.

It was obvious to him that water is the original material from which all things develop. This is how it came about that this early Greek thinker declared water to be the ground of all things. From water, he said, everything originates and in water everything changes. Anaximander took things one step further. He no longer trusted the senses as much as Thales. You can see water. But everything that can be seen turns into something else. This is how Anaximander thought. Water can become solid by freezing and gaseous by evaporating. The ancients considered steam and air to be the same thing. Likewise, they called everything solid earth. Solid water is earth, but it can change itself into liquid and liquid into air—so said Anaximander, following this logic. No specific material is therefore permanent. And so, he did not look for the ground of all things in a specific substance but in something indeterminate. By contrast, Anaximenes argued for a specific primal substance—namely, the air. He said, "Just as our soul, which is air, holds us together, so breath and air embrace the whole world."

Heraclitus[†] represents a much higher level of this type of worldview. The eternal change of all things is what impressed him above all else. Nothing remains; everything changes. Our senses deceive us when they tell us that something appears to be the same. I cannot step into the same river twice, because it is only apparently the same river when I step into it the second time. The water I touch, of which the river consists, is completely different water the second time. And so it is with all things. The tree of today is not the tree of yesterday. Other sap has moved through it, and much of what was in it yesterday has been excreted in the meantime. Heraclitus therefore sums up his conviction in the saying: "Everything flows." Therefore, the most restless element—fire—becomes for him the image of all coming into being and passing away.

Empedocles of Agrigento started from a completely different point of view. His predecessors had looked for a single, primal substance. He considered all four primal substances to be valid and equally significant. For him, earth, water, air, and fire all existed from the beginning. None of these substances can change into the other, but they can mix together in the most varied of ways. And by their mixture, all the different things in nature originate. Empedocles therefore no longer believed that a thing really comes into being and perishes. He believed that something appears to come into being when, for example, water and fire mix, and he believed that the same thing appears to pass away when water and fire separate again. Aristotle says of Empedocles: "According to Empedocles, the four primal substances are eternal, exist without coming into existence, and in various relationships combine to become one object or separate again from it."[†] Empedocles assumed forces prevailing between his four substances. Two or more substances unite if an attractive force prevails between them, and they separate if a repulsive force acts between them. These attractive and repulsive forces can, according to Empedocles, not only build up inanimate nature from the four substances but also the entire realm of living things. He imagined that, by means of these forces, animal and vegetable bodies naturally come into being. And because no discernable intelligence guides this coming into being, there arise, colorfully mixed up, practical as well as impractical living forms. Only the practical ones can exist; the impractical ones must perish. In this, Empedocles exhibits some similarity to Darwin's "struggle for existence." Darwin also imagines that in nature the practical and the impractical come into being and that the world appears to be purposefully designed only because in the "struggle for existence" the impractical is continuously defeated and must therefore perish.

Anaxagoras, a contemporary of Empedocles, did not believe it was possible to explain the purposeful order of the world from the mere working of mechanical natural forces. He assumed that a spiritual being, a universal cosmic intelligence, gives to things their existence and their order. He imagined that everything consisted of the smallest parts, the so-called *homoeomeria*, each type of which has different properties. The universal cosmic intelligence puts these original parts together so that they result in purposeful things and a harmoniously arranged cosmos. Because he put a universal cosmic intelligence in the place of the old folk gods, Anaxagoras was accused in Athens of renouncing the gods and had to flee to Lampsacus. In Athens, where he had relocated from his birth city of Clazomenae, he was in contact with Pericles, Euripides, and Themistocles.

Anaxagoras posited that the smallest parts, the *homoeomeria*, are the seeds of all things. He imagined them to be completely different from each other with a wide variety of properties. Democritus, on the other hand, conceived of these smallest parts as being differentiated by nothing other than size, shape, position, and arrangement in space. In all other respects, the smallest components of things, these atoms, he imagined to be equal to each other. According to this atomistic view, processes in nature can be nothing other than changes in the position and arrangement of the smallest parts of the body. If a body changes color, then in reality the arrangement of its atoms has changed. There is nothing in the world but empty space and the atoms filling it. There is no power that gives the atoms their order. They are in perpetual motion. Some move slower, others faster. The faster ones must come into contact with the slower ones. Through this, bodies clump together. Therefore, nothing comes into being through an all-pervasive intelligence or through universal reason, but only through blind natural necessity, which can also be called coincidence. Based on these convictions, the followers of Democritus understandably battled powerfully against the old folk gods. They were staunch deniers of the gods—atheists. You can see in them the forerunners of the materialistic worldviews of later centuries.

Parmenides and his followers tried to approach phenomena from a completely different angle than the thinkers mentioned so far. They assumed that our senses cannot provide us with a faithful, true picture of the world. Observing how everything is continually changing, Heraclitus came to the conclusion that there is nothing permanent, but rather that the eternal flow of all things corresponds to the true nature of being. Parmenides saw things in exactly the opposite way from earlier philosophers: because in the outside world everything changes, because externally everything comes into being and passes away, we therefore cannot obtain lasting truth by observing the external world. We have to understand that what this external world presents to us is only appearance, and we can only gain eternal, lasting truth through thinking itself. The external world is a deception of the senses, a dream. It is something completely different from what our senses would have us believe. We cannot arrive at the reality behind this dream, that which remains eternally the same, by observing the external world. That reality reveals itself to us only through thinking. In the external world, there is multiplicity and diversity; in thinking the Eternal Oneness reveals itself to us. It does not change but always remains the same. Parmenides expresses this in his didactic poem "On Nature." Now, we are dealing with a worldview that does not want to get the truth from the things themselves but tries to spin the origin of the world out of thinking.

If you want to understand the basic feeling from which such a worldview originates, then you must keep in mind that often thinking must indeed interpret and explain the perceptions of the senses in the right way in order to come to a satisfying thought. If we hold a stick in water, it appears broken to the eye. Thinking must look for the reasons why the stick appears broken. We get a satisfactory idea of the phenomenon only through the fact that our thinking explains our perception. If we look at the starry sky only with our senses, we can have no other idea than that the Earth is in the center of the universe and that the Sun, the Moon, and all the stars move around it. Only by thinking do we obtain any another idea. In this case, thinking gives us a completely different picture than sense perception. You can say truthfully that the senses deceive us in a certain regard. But the worldview of Parmenides and his followers is a one-sided exaggeration of this fact. For as perception supplies us with certain appearances that deceive us, so it also supplies us again with other facts by which we can correct the deception. Copernicus did not come to his view of the movement of the celestial bodies by spinning it out of mere thinking, but by bringing the one perception in line with the others.

In contrast to the views of Parmenides, there is another, older worldview. This one does not assume that the phenomena of the external world are a deception. Rather, through a deeper observation of this outer world, it wants to lead to the realization that in the world everything is based on a larger harmony, that in all things measure and number are innate. This view is that of the Pythagoreans.

Pythagoras lived in the sixth century BC. Aristotle says of the Pythagoreans that they turned to mathematics around the same time as the thinkers mentioned above were active and, in some cases, even before them.

> They first continued this and, being completely absorbed in it, they considered the beginnings in it also to be the beginnings of all things. They considered mathematics to be the ground of all things and to be found at the beginnings of all things. Since in mathematics the numberings of the things found in nature exist first, they believed to see in numbers much similarity to the objects of the external world in their process of becoming. Indeed, they saw more in numbers than they saw in fire, earth, and water, so they considered one property of numbers as *justice*, another property as *soul*, another as *spirit*, another as *time*, and so on for all other properties. Further, they found in the numbers the features and relations of musical harmony, so everything else appeared in its entire nature to be an image of numbers and numbers to be the primary thing in nature.[†]

Whoever can appreciate the importance of measure and number in nature will not find it surprising that such a worldview could arise. If a string of a certain length is plucked, a specific tone is produced. If the string is shortened in certain numerical ratios, then other specific tones are produced. You can thereby express pitch relationships as numerical ratios. Physics also expresses colors in numerical ratios. When two substances are combined into one substance, this always unfolds in such a way that a specific amount of the mass of one substance combines with a specific amount of the mass of the other substance in ratios which can be expressed in numbers. We can find countless such examples in nature of the role of number and measure. The Pythagorean worldview expresses this fact in a one-sided way by saying: Measure and number are the origin of all things.

All of the worldviews discussed so far contain a question. Nowhere in them does it come clearly to expression, because the thinkers obviously were of the opinion that it answers itself with the other questions they have asked. It is the question of the relation of the human being to the world. If Thales thinks all things originate from water, he also thinks the human being originated from the same source. Heraclites was of the opinion that the human being swims along with all other beings in the eternal river of things, and Anaxagoras thought of the human being as built up from his primordial particles. Anaxagoras and other atomists imagined that coincidence also had put together the human being from atoms. In Empedocles, something of the question first emerges: What is the human being's relation to the rest of nature? How can we recognize things? How is it possible for us to form conceptions of that which is nevertheless external to us? Empedocles gave the answer: Like can be recognized only by like. Because the human being consist of the same substances and forces as the rest of nature, he can also recognize them.

A number of thinkers have tackled this question in a completely different way and are usually overlooked. These are the Sophists, whose most significant personality is Protagoras of Abdera. They are usually considered to be people who played a superficial game with thinking, engaging in pointless disputation, lacking all seriousness in the investigation of truth. The way in which the reactionary comic poet Aristophanes ridiculed them in his dramas contributed a great deal to the popular opinion that has been formed about the Sophists. It may be that individual Sophists exaggerated the art of disputation. It may also be that among them there were some who were only concerned with splitting hairs and with foppish appearances; however, this does not apply to the most important of them. There were men among them who distinguished themselves through comprehensive knowledge in the most diverse fields.

Regarding Protagoras and Gorgias, it must be particularly emphasized that they were both outstanding politicians. The pupil of Prodicus of Ceos, Socrates himself, boasts that he was an excellent scholar who was particularly concerned with the ennoblement of language among his pupils. Protagoras expresses his basic view in the sentence: "Of all things the measure is Man, of the things that are, that they are, and of the things that are not, that they are not."[†] What can this sentence mean? One can say like Parmenides: Our senses deceive us. And one could go further than this and say: Perhaps our thinking also deceives us. Protagoras would answer: What does it matter to a man whether the external world is different from how he perceives and thinks it to be? Is he understanding the world for someone else and not for himself? Let it be how it may be for any other being. That is of no concern to him. His ideas need serve only him, and he should find his way in the world with their help. A person cannot want any other ideas about the world than those which serve him. Whatever is in the world—if he does not perceive it, he cannot care about it. For him there is what he perceives; what he does not perceive is not there for him. But this means that man measures things with the tools that his senses and his reason give him. Through his view, Protagoras gives the human being a firm position and security in the world. He frees the human being from innumerable anxious questions, which he throws out only because he does not dare to judge things according to their own nature.

It may be said that through the philosophy of the Sophists, the human being is brought into the center of the view of the world. That this happened at the time of Protagoras is connected with the development of public conditions in Greece. The social structure of the Greek city-states had loosened. This found its most significant expression in the Peloponnesian Wars of 431–404 BC. Previously, the individual was firmly enclosed in the social context, and community and tradition gave him the standard for all his actions and thinking. The individual personality had value and meaning only as a member of a whole. Under such circumstances, it would have been impossible to ask the question: What is the value of the individual human being?

The philosophy of the Sophists demonstrates tremendous progress after the Greek Enlightenment. The human being could now think of arranging his life according to his own reason. The Sophists went around the country as teachers of virtue. If you want to teach virtue, you must be convinced that traditional moral views are not binding and that the human being can recognize virtue through independent reflection. Socrates also lived out such a conception of virtue. He must be regarded as a disciple of the Sophists. Little is known about him. The accounts of what he taught are doubtful. What is clear, however, is that he was primarily a teacher of virtue like the Sophists. It is also certain that the way he taught was enrapturing. His teaching took the form of conversations in which he sought to draw out of the listener himself what that person recognized as the right thing to do. The expression "spiritual midwifery" is well known in relation to his teachings. He did not want to bring anything into the mind of the student from the outside. He believed that truth was in every human being and that a teacher only had to provide help so that this truth could come to light. If one takes this into consideration, it becomes clear that Socrates helped raise reason to its greatest height in every single human being. He always brought his students to the point where they could form the right concept of a thing. He started from the experiences of everyday life. One can consider, for example, what virtue is for the craftsman, what virtue is for the merchant, what virtue is for the scholar. It will be found that all these different kinds of virtuous life have something in common. This common feature is precisely the concept of virtue. If you proceed with your thinking in this way, you follow the so-called inductive process. You collect individual experiences to obtain a concept of a thing. When you have this concept, you can then define the thing, arriving at the definition of a thing. A mammal is a living thing with a spine that gives birth to living offspring. This is the definition of a mammal. The definition presents a characteristic—giving birth to living offspring—which is common to all mammals. Thus, Socrates acted as a teacher of sharp, clear thinking. This is his greatest merit. The Roman orator Cicero said of Socrates that he brought philosophy down from heaven to earth.[†] By this is meant that he made his observations especially about the human being himself and how he should live. That was above all close to his heart. That is why we see in Greece that those who strive for a worldview always ask what moral goals one should set for oneself.

This is quite apparent in Socrates' immediate successors. The Cynics, whose most important representative is Diogenes of Sinope, deal with the question of a *natural* life. How should one live so that one's life does not contradict the dispositions and abilities given by nature? The Cynics wanted to remove everything artificial and unnatural from life. It is therefore understandable that above all the greatest simplicity appeared to them as best. Their definition of *natural* is that which is a common need for all people. The proletariat came into its own in this conception of life. You can therefore understand why the so-called upper classes did not like this philosophy very much. After all, what the Cynics demanded was not in accord with artificially created needs. While originally the name "Cynics" was derived only from the educational institution—the Cynosarges—where the Cynics gave lessons, it later took on a negative connotation.

In addition to the Cynics, the Cyrenaics and the Megarian School were active at that time. They, too, were primarily concerned with practical life. The Cyrenaics sought to give pleasure its rightful place. If pleasure corresponds to the nature of the human being, then virtue cannot consist in eradicating pleasure within oneself but rather in not making oneself a slave to lusts. To the Cyrenaics, those who strive for pleasure but always in such a way that they remain master of their pleasures, are virtuous. Only those who become slaves to their passions are without virtue.

The Megarian School focused on Socrates' statement that virtue is teachable, that the perfection of thinking must also make one more virtuous. The most important representative of the Megarian School is Euclid of Megara.[†] To him, the good was an outpouring of the highest wisdom; therefore, he was primarily concerned with the attainment of wisdom. From this esteem for wisdom must have arisen in him the thought that wisdom itself is the original source of the world. If (so he thought) one rises to concepts through thinking, then one rises at the same time to the origins of all things. Euclid of Megara's worldview takes on a decidedly idealistic coloring. One must imagine the thought process of Euclid of Megara approximately in the following way: There are many lions. The substances of which these lions consist do not remain together. The single lion arises and passes away. It takes up substances from the outside world and gives them back to it. That which I perceive with the senses, that is the material. What is sense-perceptible about things therefore arises and passes away. Nevertheless, a lion that lived a hundred years ago has something in common with a lion that lives today. It cannot be the substances. It can be only the concept, the idea of the lion, which I grasp with my thinking. The lion of today and the lion of a hundred years ago are built according to the same idea. The sense-perceptible passes away, but the idea remains. The ideas embody themselves in the sense world always anew.

Plato[†] was a pupil of Euclid of Megara. He made his teacher's notion of the eternity of ideas his basic conviction. The sense world has only a subordinate value for him. The true things are the ideas. He who looks merely at the things of the sense world has only an illusion, a mirage of the true world. Plato's conviction is clearly expressed in the following words: The things of this world, which we perceive with the senses, have no true being; they do not remain. One can just as well call their whole being a non-being. Consequently, he who strives for the true cannot be content with the things of the sense world. For the true can only come from where the abiding element is. If you limit yourself to sense perception, you are like someone who sits tied up in a dark cave so that he cannot even turn his head and who sees nothing but, by the light of a lamp burning behind him, the shadows of the things behind him, and also his own shadow. The ideas are to be compared with the real, true things and the shadows with the things of the sense world. Even when perceiving himself, he who confines himself only to the senses recognizes only a shadow. The tree I see, the scent of flowers I breathe: they are merely shadows. Only when I raise myself through my thinking to the idea of the tree do I have that which is truly lasting and not a transient mirage of the tree.

Now, you must raise the question: What are Plato's thoughts on the relation of this world of ideas to the Greek conceptions of the gods? This relationship can by no means be discerned with perfect clarity from Plato's writings. He repeatedly speaks of gods; however, one could certainly argue that he merely wanted to lean on the Greek folk religion with such sayings. And one would not be wrong to view his designations of gods only as figurative clarifications. What Plato himself conceives as divinity is the primordial moving source of the world. One must imagine, in the sense of Plato, that the world consists of ideas and primordial matter. Ideas embody themselves in primordial matter continuously, and the impulse for this embodiment is given by God, the primal ground of all movement. At the same time, God is—for Plato—the good. This gives the world a great unified purpose. The good moves all being and happening. The highest laws of the world thus present a moral world order.

Plato wrote down his worldview in the form of conversations.

Throughout the ages, his method of presentation has been the object of admiration within the development of Western culture. Plato came from a noble family in Athens. From reports, we know that he was predisposed to daydreaming. He became the most faithful and sympathetic student of Socrates, attached to his master with unconditional veneration. After the execution of his teacher, he went to Megara to study with Euclid of Megara. Later, he undertook great journeys to Cyrene in Libya, to Egypt, to Greater Greece (that is, the Greek colonies in southern Italy), and to Sicily. In 389 BC, he returned to Athens. Subsequently, he made a second and third trip to Sicily. After returning from his first Sicilian journey, he founded his school in Athens, from which many of the most important thinkers of that time emerged. In Plato's writings, one can observe a gradual change of outlook. He adopts ideas that he finds in others. In his first writings, he stands entirely on the foundation he formed as a student of Socrates. Later, Euclid of Megara had a strong influence on him, and during his stay in Sicily, he became acquainted with the Pythagoreans. In Egypt, he appropriated various Oriental concepts. This is why his worldview does not appear to be cast from a single mold. He incorporates subsequently discovered ideas into his original views. We may count among these his doctrine of the transmigration of souls. The soul already exists before the body. It is subject to embodiment—that is, its connection with matter is regarded as a kind of punishment that it must suffer for a guilt contracted in its pre-earthly being. However, the soul embodies itself not only once but repeatedly. Plato connects this view with the idea of universal world justice. If everything were to end with one life, the good would be at a disadvantage compared to the bad. Instead of this, the evil committed by the soul in one life must be atoned for in another. Only when all guilt has found its expiation in different lives can the soul return to the realm of ideas from which it originated.

The human soul does not form a unity in connection with the body. It is divided into three souls. The lowest soul is that of sensory life; it is responsible for the nourishing and reproductive instinct. Plato calls the middle soul the willpower in the human being. Personal courage and bravery are based on it. The highest soul is the purely spiritual one; it is responsible for the highest knowledge. It is native to the realm of ideas. It is the real immortal part of the human soul. Plato connects his concept of immortality with Socrates' idea that teaching consists only of a kind of midwifery. If this is so, then all thoughts awakened in the human being must already lie within him. They lie within him because he had them already before his birth, for the soul existed before birth. Therefore, in life he remembers only those thoughts which were already in him before birth.

Plato's view of the state is likewise connected with his doctrine of the soul. Even the state is the embodiment of an idea, and when it is perfect, the state is an embodiment of the image of human nature. The individual soul forces are represented in the state by the different classes. The highest soul is represented by the rulers, the middle soul by the guardians who are there for defense, and the lowest soul by the craftsmen. Plato's *Republic* is a communistic state, but it has a strictly aristocratic class structure. For the two upper classes, Plato recommends the abolition of marriage and property. The upper classes should be a monastic community with a communistic distribution of goods. The entire education of youth should be the task of the state, except for the physical care of infants, which is to be provided by the family.

Plato's most important student is Aristotle of Stagira in Thrace. He became Plato's pupil at the age of eighteen, but he soon went his own way. In 343 BC, Aristotle became the tutor of Alexander, the son of King Philip of Macedonia. When Alexander undertook his Asian conquests, Aristotle went back to Athens and opened a school there.

The relation of Aristotle's worldview to that of Plato can be illustrated by the following comparison. Plato's ideas are completely foreign to the matter in which they are embodied. They are like the idea of the work of art that lives in the head of the artist and that is then molded into the material. This material, the marble of a statue, is something completely separate from the artist's idea. Aristotle, on the other hand, does not think of the relationship of ideas to matter in this way. For him, the idea lies in the matter itself. It is as if a work of art did not receive its idea from the artist, but rather gave itself its form through a force inherent in the material. Aristotle called the ideas inherent in a substance the "forms of things." In the sense of

Aristotle, there is, for example, no idea of the lion separate from the substance. This idea is in the substance itself. There is, according to Aristotle, no matter without form and no form without matter. A living being develops from the embryo in the mother's womb into its completed form because the form is active in the living substance and works like a force inherent within it. This force or form is already present in the first development of a living being but is not yet externally visible. It is, as it were, still dormant. But it develops so that the substance takes on the form that already lies within it as a dormant force in the beginning. In the beginning of things, there was only external, formless matter. The power of the substance still slumbered completely within it. There was a chaos with an immeasurable power slumbering in it. In order to awaken this force so that the chaos formed itself into the manifold world of things, a first impulse was necessary. Therefore, Aristotle assumes a first mover of the world, a divine world cause.

If the idea—or in Aristotle's terminology, the form—lies in each thing itself, then you cannot, as Plato does, regard things as mere mirages and shadows and raise yourself with your thinking into a completely different world. If one wants to attain the true, one must turn precisely to the sense-perceptible things themselves and bring to light the essence lying within them. Therefore, thinking observation itself gives enlightenment about the world. Because Aristotle was convinced of this, he turned his attention above all to observation. He became thereby a pioneer of the sciences. He cultivated the individual natural sciences in as comprehensive a way as was possible for his time. He is acknowledged as the "father of natural history." From him, for example, we have subtle and inspired investigations into the development of living beings from the germinal state on. Such investigations were connected with his conceptual worldview in the most natural way. For example, he had to be of the opinion that in the egg the whole living being is already present, only not yet in an outwardly visible way. He says to himself: If a living being arises from the egg, then it must be this living being itself that works its way into existence in the egg. If we look at an egg, it basically has a double being. First, it is as it appears to the eye. But it also contains an invisible being, which will appear only later in the full-grown bird.

Aristotle extends this view to the whole of nature. Only when he gets to the human being does he stop. The whole human being is already in the human egg, even the soul, insofar as it carries out its lower activities, which can also be carried out by the animal. But it should be different with the human spirit, which carries out the higher activities of thinking. This spirit is not yet in the human germ. If the germ were left to itself, it could only reach the level of an animal being. A thinking spirit would not arise. Something else is needed for this—namely, the moment the purely animal development of the human being has progressed far enough, a higher creative power must step in and create the spirit in the body. In human development, everything happens in a natural way until a certain moment when the body is far enough advanced that it can accommodate the spirit. Then, when this has happened, when through natural development the body has formed all the organs the spirit needs for its purposes, then the spirit is carried into its bodily dwelling place. Aristotle thinks of the human spirit-soul as having come into being in time, not through the same forces that gave rise to the body but through a higher influence. It must be emphasized, however, that the organs that serve the spirit have arisen through the development of the body. Therefore, when the spirit makes use of the eye in order to form thoughts about what is seen, it does so only within a body that first developed an eye for this purpose. Aristotle cannot speak of immortality in the sense of the spirit continuing to exist after death in the same sense as it does before death. After all, in death its organs perish. It can no longer perceive. It is no longer in any connection with the world. Therefore, one must not claim that Aristotle imagines immortality as if the spirit leaves its body like an earthly prison and continues to exist with the same familiar qualities. Rather, it is deprived of all the properties that it has in its earthly existence. It then indeed leads a kind of shadow existence like the Greek heroes in the underworld. And of this life in the underworld, Achilles made the famous statement: "Better a day laborer in the light of the sun, than a king over the shadows."[†]

With such a view of the spirit, Aristotle had to regard moral action as something this spirit carries out with the help of the animal soul. The animal part of the soul has arisen naturally. If this part acts alone—that is, if one follows animal instincts and passions alone—then one cannot be virtuous. One will only become virtuous when the spirit takes hold of the animal instincts and passions and gives them the right measure. The animal nature in man would in all matters do either too much or too little. The person who merely follows his passions is either foolhardy or cowardly. The spirit alone finds the right middle between foolhardiness and cowardice—namely, prudent bravery.

With regard to the state, Aristotle professes the view that the commonwealth must take into account the needs of all its members. It is part of human nature to live in a community. One of Aristotle's sayings is: "He who wants to live for himself alone must be either a god or an animal. . . . But man is a political animal."[†] Aristotle does not assume a form of state that is right for all people; rather, in each individual case, he finds the form of state best suited to the needs of the people in question. In any case, he imposes on the state the duty to care for the younger generation. Education is thus a matter of the state, and the purpose of education appears to him to be the formation of virtue.

Whoever wants to understand ancient Greek culture in its uniqueness must not forget that this culture was built on the foundation of slavery. The educated among the ancient Greeks could pursue their form of education only because it was afforded to them by a great legion of slaves. Even the most advanced Greek could not conceive of culture without slavery. Therefore, even Aristotle sees slavery as a necessity of nature. He simply takes it for granted because he believes that many people are so constituted by their whole nature as to be entirely unsuited to full freedom. It must not be overlooked, however, that the Greek was concerned with the welfare of his slaves, and Aristotle, too, speaks of the master's obligation to care conscientiously for his slaves and to respect the human dignity in them.

Aristotle has dominated Western education for more than a millennium. For many centuries, people were not concerned with the things of nature themselves but with Aristotle's opinions about these things. His writings were accorded perfect authority. All scholarship consisted in explaining the writings of the ancient sage. Moreover, these writings were only available in a very imperfect and unreliable form for a long time, and, therefore, the most diverse opinions were attributed to Aristotle. It was only through the Christian philosopher Thomas Aquinas that the writings of the "master of those who know"[†] were produced as a reasonably reliable text. Until the twelfth century, moreover, people dealt almost exclusively with one part of Aristotle's thought—his logical investigations. It is true that Aristotle was particularly groundbreaking in this field. He established the art of thinking correctly (i.e., logic) in such a way that even Kant at the end of the eighteenth century was of the opinion that logic had not made any essential step forward since Aristotle. The art of deducing many truths from one truth in the right way by appropriate conclusions of thought—this Aristotle masterfully brought into a system. Since scholarship in the Middle Ages was less interested in expanding the human mind through the observation of nature than in supporting the truths of revelation through logical proofs, this scholarship was particularly interested in how to deal with the doctrine of thought.

What Aristotle had really taught was clouded soon after his death by the interpretations that his successors gave to his views and by other opinions that joined his own. We see in the next centuries after Aristotle the appearance of three worldviews: Stoicism, Epicureanism, and Skepticism.

The Stoic School was founded in Cyprus by Zeno of Citium (342–270 BC). The school takes its name from the colorful hall of columns (the Stoa of Attalos) in Athens, where its teachers held their classes. Public life in Greece had become even more relaxed since the days of the Sophists. The individual stood more and more for himself. Private virtue increasingly took the place of public virtue in the center of thought. The Stoics considered the highest human achievement to be perfect equanimity in life. If one can be hurled into inner turmoil by desires and passions, one cannot be granted such equanimity. One is driven every which way by lust and desire without being able to feel satisfied. Therefore, one should reach the point of being independent of lust and desire and lead only such a life as is regulated by wise insight. The Stoics thought the world originated from a kind of primeval fire. They believed that from the fire everything emerged and that into the fire everything returns. Then from the fire the exact same world renews itself. The world exists therefore not once but innumerable times in completely the same way. Every single process has already existed infinitely often and will return infinitely often. This is the doctrine of the eternal return of all things and processes, which in our day Friedrich Nietzsche has reintroduced in exactly the same fashion. Such an explanation of the world agrees perfectly with the moral doctrine of the Stoics. For if everything has already existed, then the human being cannot create anything new. It is therefore natural to find the highest moral wisdom in the equanimity toward everything that must necessarily come.

The Epicureans saw the goal of life in the satisfaction afforded by the pursuit of pleasure and happiness in a rational manner. It is unreasonable to pursue petty pleasures, for these must in most cases lead to disappointment, even unhappiness. It is equally unreasonable to spurn the noble, high pleasures, for they lead to the lasting satisfaction that constitutes one's happiness in life. The whole of Epicurus' view of nature shows that he is concerned with lasting satisfaction in life. Above all, a correct view of the power of judgment is considered important so that we can find our way in life through thinking. The senses do not deceive us, only our thinking can deceive us. If the eye sees a broken stick submerged in water, the eye does not deceive us. The real facts are such that the stick must appear broken to us. The deception arises only when our thinking forms a false judgment about how it is that the stick appears broken. Epicurus' view found numerous followers in late antiquity, and many Romans striving for edification sought satisfaction in it. The Roman poet Lucretius Carus gave it a perfect expression in his ingenious didactic poem, "On Nature."

Skepticism is the worldview of doubt and mistrust. Its first significant proponent was Pyrrho, a contemporary of Aristotle, but at that time, he made little impression. Only his followers found supporters for their opinion that human cognitive powers are not sufficient to gain an idea of reality. They believed that one can only express human opinions about things. Whether things really behave as our thinking tells us is beyond us, and nothing can be decided about that.

The manifold attempts to arrive at a worldview through thinking had led to such diverse and contradictory ideas that by late antiquity, people had come to distrust all sense perception and all thinking. In addition, there were ideas, such as those of Plotinus, that the sense-perceptible world was only a dream or a mirage. Such ideas were now combined with certain Oriental thoughts that preached the nothingness and worthlessness of life. From these components, Neo-Platonism was built up in Alexandria in the centuries of late antiquity.

The most important proponents of this doctrine are Philo, who lived at the time of Christ, and Plotinus. Philo draws the consequences for the moral life from the teachings of Plato. If reality is a delusion, then virtue can only consist in turning away from this reality and in directing all thoughts and sensations to the only true reality, which he sought in God. What Plato had sought in the world of ideas, Philo believed to find in the God of Judaism. Plotinus subsequently does not seek to reach this God through rational cognition, for rationality can only refer to the finite and the transient. He seeks instead to come to the eternal primordial being through inner enlightenment, through ecstatic immersion in the depths of the soul. Through such immersion, one comes to the primordial being who has poured itself into the world. This world is only an imperfect outpouring, a derivative of the original being.

2. The Worldviews of the Middle Ages and of Modern Times

With the advent of Christianity, something completely new appears in the development of worldviews in the Occident. Rational thinking is pushed aside by a completely different authority—revelation. Truth does not come from thinking but from a higher power that has revealed itself to humanity. This now becomes the common conviction. It is belief in facts of supernatural importance and disbelief in reason that constitutes the essence of Christianity.[†] The confessors of the Christian doctrine do not want to believe in their thinking but in sense-perceptible events through which the truth has revealed itself. "What has happened from the beginning, what we have heard, what we have seen with our eyes, what we ourselves have beheld, what our hands have touched of the word of life . . . what we have seen and heard we report to you, that you may have fellowship with us." So says the first Epistle of John. And Augustine says: "I would not believe the Gospel if I were not moved to do so by the authority of the Catholic Church."[†]

What Christ's contemporaries saw and heard, and what the Church through tradition preserves of such events, now becomes truth. No longer is what one achieves through one's thinking considered as truth.

In Christianity, we encounter, on the one hand, the religious thought-world of Judaism and, on the other, the ideas of the Greek worldview. The religion of Judaism was originally a national-egoistic one. God chose his people for earthly power and glory, but this people had to experience the most bitter disappointments. They had come into captivity and subservience to other nations. Their hopes for the Messiah arose from the fact that they expected their God to deliver them from their shame and humiliation. This humiliation they attributed to their own sinfulness. Ideas of turning away from the life that led to sinfulness emerge here. One should not cling to this life that leads to sin; one should rather turn to God, who will soon bring His kingdom to this earth and free people from shame. Jesus was filled with such ideas. He wanted to speak to the poor and oppressed, not to those who cling to the treasures of this life. The Kingdom of Heaven, which is coming soon, will belong to those who lived in misery before. And Jesus envisioned the kingdom of heaven as being close at hand. He did not refer people to a spiritual hereafter but to the fact that in time, and soon, the Lord would come and bring glory to humanity.

Already through Paul, and then even more through the teachers of the first Christian centuries, a connection between the teachings of Christ and the ideas of the later Greek philosophers took the place of naive faith. The temporally near kingdom of heaven thus became the beyond. The Christian faith was reinterpreted with the help of ideas from the Greek worldview. From this reinterpretation, from this collaboration of originally naive ideas with other traditional views, the dogmatic content of the Christian doctrine developed over the course of time. Thought entered completely into the service of faith. It became the servant of revelation. The whole Middle Ages worked to support the revelation with the help of thinking. Augustine, the Church Father, is an example of how thinking and revelation worked together in the first centuries. Thomas Aquinas is an example of how this happened in the Church in a later age.

Augustine says to himself: Even when we experience doubt, the fact remains that we are thinking. The thinking person himself must be there; otherwise, he could not doubt. When I doubt, I think; therefore, I exist because my reason exists. And, in reason, certain truths reveal themselves to me. But my reason never recognizes all truth but always only individual truths. These individual truths can only come from the being in whom all truth exists, from God. A divine being must therefore exist. My reason proves this to me. But my reason gives me only parts of the truth; in revelation lies the highest truth.[†]

Thomas Aquinas is a comprehensive thinker who assimilated all the knowledge of his time in an amazingly perceptive way. One must not imagine that this Christian philosopher was hostile to the knowledge of nature and reason. Nature was for him one source of truth; revelation, however, was the other. In his opinion, everything in the world comes from God. Natural phenomena are also an outpouring of divine being. When we study nature, we research with our thinking the deeds of God, but we cannot penetrate to the highest deeds of God with our weak human thinking. According to Thomas Aquinas, we can still prove with our reason that there is a God; however, we cannot learn anything from reason about the nature of God, about His Trinity, about the redemption of humanity through Christ, about the power of the sacraments, and so on. We are informed about these things by revelation through the authority of the Church. It is not because these things have nothing to do with reason. Rather, Thomas thinks the human being cannot reach them through reasoning because human reason is too weak. A more powerful faculty of reason could therefore also comprehend the revealed truths. This view is presented in the scholasticism of the Middle Ages.

German mysticism took a different path than scholasticism to reach truth. The most important mystics are: Meister Eckhart, Johannes Tauler, Heinrich Suso, Paracelsus, Jakob Boehme, and Angelus Silesius. They are the forerunners of more recent worldviews insofar as they did not start from an external authority but wanted to search for the truth in the human soul and in the phenomena of nature. No external Christ can, in their opinion, show the human being the way to his goal; only the spiritual forces within the human being can do this. "The physician must go through the exams of nature,"[†] says Paracelsus, pointing out that the source of truth is in nature itself. Angelus Silesius emphasizes that the divine being is not outside the things of nature but that God is in nature. He expresses in beautiful sentences how nature itself is the divine and creates as the divine: "I know that God cannot live a moment without me; if I perish, He must needs give up the ghost."[†] God has no life apart from objects but only in objects. Jakob Boehme's worldview is also completely pervaded by such an idea.

It is clear that Scholasticism always sought to establish a harmony between reason and revelation. This could not be done without a highly sophisticated logic, without the most subtle conclusions. The mystics wanted to free themselves from such conclusions. Logical subtleties seem to them an impossible foundation on which to base knowledge of the highest thing we can know. Rather, the highest must reveal itself clearly and directly in nature and in the human mind.

Luther also began from similar feelings. He was less concerned with what mattered to the mystic. He wanted to save divine revelation above all from the contradiction of reason. He tried to achieve this, in contrast to the scholastics, by saying: Reason has no right at all to decide in matters of faith. Reason should deal with the explanation of phenomena; it has nothing to do with the truths of faith. The revealed word is the source of faith. Reason has nothing in common with this faith; faith is not reason's concern. Reason cannot refute faith, nor can it prove faith. Faith stands firmly for itself. When reason approaches religious truths, there is only vain bickering and gossip. That is why Luther reviled Aristotle, on whose teachings the scholastics had relied when they sought to give a foundation to faith through reason. He says: "This God-cursed Aristotle is a true devil, a ghoulish slanderer, a wicked sycophant (slanderer), a prince of darkness, a beast, an ugly deceiver of mankind, almost devoid of all philosophy, an open and acknowledged liar, a lecherous goat."† You can see what we are dealing with. Aristotle had wanted to reach the highest truths through human thinking; Luther wanted to secure these highest truths once and for all before engaging them through reason. That is why he also calls reason "the devil's whore, which can do nothing but blaspheme and profane what God speaks and does."† We see Luther's ideas continuing today in the same form, even if modern theology spreads a progressive cloak around them. In the much-praised *Essence of Christianity* by Adolf Harnack, we read:

> Science is not able to give meaning to life. . . . Religion, namely love of God and neighbor, is what gives meaning to life. . . . Jesus' real greatness is that he led people to God. . . . The Christian religion is eternal life in the midst of time.

Shortly after Luther appeared on the scene, reason, which he reviled, achieved one victory after another. Copernicus established his new view of the motion of the heavenly bodies. Kepler established the laws by which the planets move around the sun. Galileo looked out through his telescope into unmeasured celestial spaces and thus gave nature the opportunity to reveal a wealth of facts on its own. Through such advances, natural science had to gain confidence in itself as well as in reason. Galileo reflects the feelings that lived in a thinker of that time. One no longer felt that working in the sense of Aristotle meant clinging to what he had asserted long ago with his limited knowledge. This is what the Middle Ages had done. Now one wanted to create in the spirit of Aristotle by directing one's attention to nature as he had done. Galileo spoke words of wisdom in this regard: "You're always dealing," he says, "with your Aristotle, who cannot speak. But I tell you that if Aristotle were here, he would either be convinced by us, or refute our reasons and teach us better. . . . Philosophy is written in that greatest book which is continually open before our eyes. I mean the universe, which cannot be understood unless one has first understood the language and learned the signs in which it is written."[†]

Giordano Bruno[†] is one of the representative spirits of this flourishing thought who was able to build up an explanation of the world on the basis of the observation of nature but who nevertheless completely adhered to the traditional dogmas without demonstrating how one could be united with the other. If human thinking were not to deny itself, were not to be pushed into a completely subordinate position, it had to tread in a new way the path that had already been sought by the Greek worldviews. It had to seek out of itself to penetrate to the highest truths.

René Descartes (Cartesius)[†] was one of the first to make an attempt. His way has much in common with that of Augustine. Descartes also started from the doubt of all truth. He said to himself: Even if I can doubt everything, I cannot doubt that I am. I think when I doubt; if I did not think, I could not doubt. But if I think, then I am. "I think, therefore I am" (*cogito, ergo sum*)—that is the famous principle of Descartes. From this basic truth, Descartes seeks to ascend to higher knowledge. He says to himself: Anything I see as clearly and distinctly as "I myself am" must also be equally true. And now a peculiar phenomenon occurs to him. The Christian ideas of God, soul, and immortality, which a centuries-long education has inculcated in occidental humanity, Descartes believes to find in his faculty of reason as truths just as certain as the knowledge that he himself exists. These essential components of pre-existing theology reappear as supposed truths of reason.

We even find in Descartes the old conception of the soul. He thinks of this soul as an independent spiritual being that only makes use of the body. We have met such an idea in Aristotle. The animals, according to Descartes, have no trace of a soul. They are automata. The human being has a soul, its seat being in the brain, and interacts with the soulless body through the pineal gland. We see with Descartes an endeavor, which is also present in the Scholastics, to want to prove by reason the "highest truths" transmitted by tradition. Only the Scholastics openly admit that they want this, while Descartes believed he drew all proofs purely from reason itself. Descartes thus apparently proved from reason what came only from religion.

This disguised scholasticism prevailed for a long time. In Germany, we have in Leibniz and in Wolff[†] its most important representatives. Leibniz saves the old conception of the soul by considering all things to be independently animate beings. These do not come into being and do not pass away. He also rescues the conception of God by ascribing to it the property of bringing all beings into a harmonious interaction. Again and again, the old religious ideas appear as alleged truths of reason. This is also the case with Wolff. He distinguishes between truths of the sense world, which are gained by observation, and higher knowledge, which reason draws from itself. But these higher truths, seen in the clear light of day, are nothing other than the old truths of revelation acquired through distortion and filtering. Little wonder, then, that reason, in proving these types of truths, rested on highly questionable concepts that could not stand up to closer critical scrutiny.

Such a critical examination of the evidentiary process of human reason was undertaken by the English thinkers Locke and David Hume, and the German philosopher Immanuel Kant.[†] Locke examined the human faculty of knowledge and claimed that we can come to knowledge only by observing the processes of nature itself. Hume then asked about the nature of this knowledge. He said to himself: If I observe today that the heat of the sun is the cause of the heating of the stone, have I a right to say that it will always be so? If I perceive a cause and then an effect, may I say that cause will always and necessarily have this effect? No, I am not allowed to do so. I see the stone fall to the earth and perceive that it makes a cavity. I cannot claim that it *has* to be like that, that it could not be different. I see certain processes and become *accustomed* to seeing them in a certain context. Whether such a connection really exists, whether there are laws of nature that can tell me something real about the connection of things, of that I know nothing.

Kant, who had lived in the ideas of Wolff's worldview until maturity, was shaken in all his convictions when he got to know the writings of Hume. He had not doubted before that reason could prove eternal truths. Hume had shown that even in the case of simple truths, there could be no question of proof, but rather we accept everything we believe out of habit. Could there really be no eternal truths? Kant asked himself. There must be. He did not wish to doubt that the truths of mathematics, for example, must always and necessarily be true. Nor did he wish to doubt that a statement such as "every effect has a cause" must be eternally valid. But Hume convinced him that these findings could not be eternally true if we had gained them from outside through observation. For observation can only tell us what has always been but not whether this must always be so. Kant found a way out. He said: How they appear to us does not depend at all on the things in nature. It depends solely on ourselves. I am organized in such a way that for me "twice two must be four." I am organized in such a way that for me every effect must have a cause. Therefore, what happens externally, within the "thing in itself," is of no consequence to me; it may be the case that "twice two is three," another time that "twice two is five"; none of this can reach me. I can only perceive that "twice two is four." Consequently, everything appears to me in such a way that "twice two is four." I can only link an effect to a cause, and everything appears to me as if effects were always linked to causes. I am unable to know whether within the "thing in itself" causes are also connected with effects. It is as though I were stuck with blue-lensed glasses. The things outside may have certain colors, but I know in advance that everything will appear to me in blue-colored tones. Therefore, I do not know how the "things in themselves" are; I only know how they appear to me. Because God, immortality, and the freedom of the human will cannot be observed at all, are not visible phenomena, human thinking, reason itself, cannot determine anything about these things. They do not concern reason. But do they therefore not concern the human being at all? This Kant asks himself. His answer is that they do indeed concern the human being deeply. But one cannot understand their existence; one must believe in them. I know that I should do my duty. A categorical imperative speaks in me: Thou shalt. Therefore, I must also be able to do it. At least I have to believe that I can. And for this belief, I need another. I myself cannot give the necessary weight to the fulfillment of my duty. I cannot arrange the world in such a way that it corresponds to what I must regard as the moral world order. Therefore, there must be a God who determines this moral world order. He also gives my soul immortality so that it can enjoy the fruits of its duties in eternal life, which can never be granted to it in this transient, imperfect life. You see that with Kant everything that can never be reached by knowledge reappears as faith. Kant achieved by different means something similar to what Luther had been aiming for in his way.

Luther wanted to exclude from reason the objects of faith. Kant wanted the same thing. His faith is no longer Biblical faith; he speaks of a "religion within the limits of mere reason." But cognition and knowledge should be limited only to sensory phenomena; concerning the objects of faith, they should have no say. Kant has rightly been called the philosopher of Protestantism. He himself has best described what he thinks he has achieved with the words: "So I had to abolish knowledge in order to make room for faith." Knowledge, then, in Kant's sense, has to do only with the subordinate world that gives no meaning to life; what gives meaning to life are objects of faith, which no knowledge can approach. Whoever wants to save faith can do it with the weapons of Kant's worldview. Knowledge has no power—in the sense of this view—to decide anything about the highest truths.

In many of its currents, nineteenth-century philosophy is under the sway of Kantian ideas. One can so conveniently use these ideas to clip the wings of knowledge; one can deny the right to have a say about the highest things. One can say, for example: What does natural science want? It can give only subordinate wisdom at best. Kant, whom we like to call the great reformer of philosophy, has proved once and for all that knowledge is limited, subordinate, and that it cannot give meaning to life. Contemporary worldviews, which rely on such self-distortion of knowledge, have not even penetrated to the standpoint of scholasticism, which at least felt obliged to bring about a harmony between knowledge and faith. Du Bois-Reymond even clothed this point of view in scientific garb in his famous lecture "On the Limits of the Knowledge of Nature."[†]

3. Modern Worldviews

Another philosophical lineage, which reaches up to the present, takes its starting point from Spinoza. He is a thinker who has an unconditional trust in human reason. What can be known, like mathematical truths, reason accepts as its knowledge. And the things of the world stand in just such a necessary connection, like the links of a calculation or like mathematical figures. Everything spiritual as well as everything physical is governed by such necessary laws of nature. It is a childish idea to believe that an anthropomorphic, all-knowing providence arranges things. The actions of living beings, the actions of the human spirit, are subject to the laws of nature just like the stone that falls to the earth according to the laws of gravity. It is a mistake to believe that a creative power has created any beings according to certain purposes. One is mistaken if one believes, for example, that a creator gave horns to the bull so that it could push. No, the bull got his horns according to laws just as necessary as those that govern the movement of a billiard ball when struck. He has horns by nature and therefore he pushes. One can also say: The bull does not have horns so that he can push, but he pushes because he has horns. God is in the sense of Spinoza nothing but the natural necessity inherent in all physical and spiritual phenomena. When the human being looks out into the world, he sees God; when he thinks about processes and things, the divine world order presents itself to him and is nothing but the natural order of things. In the sense of Spinoza, one cannot speak of a dichotomy between faith and knowledge. For there is nothing except nature. The human being himself belongs to this nature. Therefore, when he looks at himself and at nature, everything of which it is possible to speak makes itself known to him.

Goethe was also imbued with this worldview. He, too, sought in nature itself what earlier views had sought in a world "beyond." Nature became his God. He did not want to know anything about any other divine entity.

> What kind of God would it be who would only push from the outside, who would let the universe run on his finger in a circle! It is his purpose to move the world within, to nurture nature within himself, himself within nature, so that what lives and weaves and is within him never misses his power, never misses his spirit.[†]

This is Goethe's view. Nature is God to him, and nature also reveals God. There is no other revelation. There can be no other entities to be reached only by faith besides the entities of nature. Goethe never wanted to have anything to do with the Kantian distinction between faith and knowledge. He believed that everything the human being can desire in regard to truth can also be achieved by the contemplation of nature and of the human being himself. That is also the conviction of the thinkers who in the beginning of the nineteenth century endeavored to develop their worldviews. This is also the conviction of the thinkers in the second half of the nineteenth century who wanted to build a worldview out of the insights of natural science. These latter thinkers (for example, Haeckel) are of the opinion that the laws of nature that they investigate are not merely subordinate things but that they truly represent that which gives meaning to life.

Johann Gottlieb Fichte[†] places the human being's own I at the center of his reflections. What have earlier worldviews done with this I? They have lifted it out of the human being and made it a god. Thereby the anthropomorphic creator of the world came into being. Fichte leaves all such conceptions of God alone. He seeks out consciousness where it alone can really be found, in the human being. Something that was worshipped as God in former times, such a spiritual being, Fichte finds only in the human being. Thus, when the human being seeks the relationship between spirit and world, he does not have to deal with a connection between "God and the world" but only with an interaction of the spirit—which is in him—with nature. This is the meaning of Fichte's worldview. Everything that has been attributed to Fichte—claiming he had wanted to assert, for example, that the individual human being creates nature out of himself—is based on a very myopic interpretation of his work.

Schelling† then continued to build on Fichte's ideas. Fichte wanted nothing other than to eavesdrop on the human mind when it forms its ideas about nature. For no God gives him these ideas; he forms them alone. The question for Fichte was not how God but how the human being finds his way in the world. On this foundation, Schelling built the view that we can look at the world from two sides—from the outer side when we look at physical processes, and from the inner side when we look at the spirit, which is also nothing other than nature. Hegel then went one step further. He asked himself: What is it, then, that our thinking actually reveals to us about nature? If I explore the laws of the heavenly bodies through my thinking, does not the eternal necessity that prevails in nature reveal itself in these laws? What do all my concepts and ideas give me? Nothing exists but what is outside in nature itself. The same entities are present in me as concepts, as ideas, as rules. All existence in the world is present as eternal, iron laws. If I look inside myself, I perceive concepts and ideas; if I look outside myself, these concepts and ideas are the laws of nature. In the individual human being is reflected as thought that which rules the whole world as law.

One misunderstands Hegel if one claims that he wanted to spin the whole world out of the idea, out of the human head. It will one day have to be counted as an eternal disgrace of German philosophy that it has misunderstood Hegel in this way. It would never occur to anyone who actually understands Hegel that Hegel wanted to spin anything at all out of a mere idea. Marx really understood Hegel, in a productive sense.† That is why Marx looked for the laws of economic development where they alone can be found. Where are these laws to be found? To this question, Hegel answered: Where the facts are, there are also the laws.† An idea is only to be found with the facts one is seeking to understand through this idea. Whoever investigates the facts of real life thinks in a Hegelian manner. For Hegel believed that rather than existing in abstract thoughts, the things themselves lead us to their essences.

In the same way, contemporary natural science proceeds in the spirit of Hegel. Contemporary natural science, whose great foundational work is Charles Darwin's *The Origin of Species* (1859),† looks for the laws of nature in the realm of living beings, just as one does this also in lifeless nature. Ernst Haeckel† summarizes the creed of this natural science in the words: "The magnet that attracts iron filings, the powder that explodes, the water vapor that drives the locomotive . . . they work just as much by living force as the man who thinks." This natural science is convinced that the laws that reason extracts from things are revealed at the same time as the essence of these things. There is nothing left for a faith that is supposed to give life its meaning. In the 1850s, courageous minds, such as Carl Vogt, Jacob Moleschott, and Ludwig Büchner,† tried to reassert the view that in the things of this world their essence is also completely and utterly revealed through knowledge. Today it has become fashionable to attack these men as the most narrow-minded heads and to say of them that they had not seen the actual riddles of the world at all. This is only done by people who themselves have no idea what questions can be raised in the first place. What did these men want other than to explore nature in order to gain the meaning of life from nature itself through knowledge? Deeper minds will certainly be able to extract even deeper truths from nature than Vogt and Büchner; however, these deeper spirits will have to do it using the same methods of cognition as they. For one always says: You must seek the spirit, not the raw material! Well, the answer can only be given by Goethe: The spirit is in nature.

To the question of what any God separate from nature might be, Ludwig Feuerbach has given the answer by showing how such a conception of God is created by the human being in his image: "God is the revealed interior, the expressed self of man; religion is the solemn unveiling of man's hidden treasures, the admission of his innermost thoughts, the public confession of his secrets of love."† What the human being has within himself, he puts out into the world and worships it as God. The human being does the same thing with the moral order of the world. This can only be refined by him in connection with his equals. But he then imagines that it is set over him by another, higher being. In a radical way, Max Stirner† grasped the essence of such entities that the human being creates for himself and then sets over himself like higher powers, calling them a spook or ghost. Stirner demands the liberation of humanity from such ghosts.

The path that frees us from these ghosts was only begun by the worldviews built on a natural-scientific basis in the second half of the nineteenth century. Other worldviews, such as, for example, those of Arthur Schopenhauer and Eduard von Hartmann,† are again only relapses into outdated ideas. Schopenhauer, instead of the whole human I, made only a part—the will—the divine being. Hartmann treated the I in like manner after removing consciousness from this I. By this means, he came up with "the unconscious" as the original ground of the world. It is understandable that from such presuppositions these two thinkers had to come to the conviction that the world was the worst imaginable. For they have made the I the primal origin of the world after having removed reason from it, either completely or partially. Earlier thinkers of this kind first idealized the I—that is, they endowed it with even more reason than exists in the human being. Thereby the world became an organization of infinite wisdom.

The truly modern worldview can no longer absorb anything of old religious ideas. Its basis was already expressed by Schiller when he characterized Goethe's view of nature in a letter to him: "From the simple organization you ascend, step by step, to the more intricate one, in order to finally build the most intricate of all, the human being, naturally from the materials of the whole building of nature."† If the human being wants to let his existence emerge from something, he can only let it emerge from nature itself. The human being is formed out of nature according to eternal, iron laws; however, he is not yet in any way already present in nature—neither as God nor as any other sort of spiritual being.

All conceptions that imagine nature as animate or spiritualized (for example, Paulsen, among others) are relapses into old theological ideas. The spirit has come into being and has not developed out of nature. This must be understood first. Then thinking can form a view about this spirit as developed within the natural order. Only such a worldview can speak of a real freedom. I have shown this in detail in my *Philosophy of Freedom* and in my book *Views of the World and Life in the Nineteenth Century*.† A spirit that had developed out of another spirit would have to receive its moral aims and purposes from the latter, from the spirit of God or of the world. A spirit that has developed out of nature sets itself the purpose and aim of its existence and gives itself its destiny.

A true philosophy of freedom can no longer say—as does Adolf Harnack†— that knowledge is not able to give meaning to life. It rather shows that the human being has come into being by natural necessity and that he, however, has not received a predetermined meaning. It is up to him to give himself a meaning. The old worldviews stand with the old economic orders, but they will also fall with them. The economically liberated human being will also be free as an enlightened and moral human being. When the economic order will bring to all human beings an existence worthy of the human being, then they will also make a worldview of their own that will completely liberate the spirit.

William Shakespeare

BERLIN, MAY 6, 1902

According to the famous writer Georg Brandes,[†] Shakespeare must be counted among the German classics. Shakespeare had become known again in Germany in the middle of the eighteenth century especially through Lessing.[†] Schlegel and Tieck[†] provided an excellent translation of his works. If one considers the extraordinary influence that Shakespeare had on Goethe, Schiller, and on the whole development of German literature, one must agree with Brandes' statement.

A whole legend has been formed about Shakespeare; whole libraries have been written about each of his works. Scholars have read all sorts of things into his works. Finally, a number of writers have regarded the non-scholarly actor as incapable of producing all the thoughts they find in Shakespeare's works. They have conceived the hypothesis that it was not the actor of the Globe Theater, William Shakespeare, who wrote the works that bear his name, but some eminent and highly learned man, such as Lord Francis Bacon of Verulam.[†] They believe Bacon was the actual playwright who merely borrowed the actor's name because of the low estimate of literary activity in those days. These assumptions are based on the fact that no manuscripts in Shakespeare's hand have been found. Then the assumptions became based on a notebook discovered in a London library, in which they sought to find individual passages corresponding to certain passages in Shakespeare's works, and so on.

But the works themselves are a testimony to Shakespeare's authorship. His dramas speak of the fact that they are written by a man who knew the theater in the most exact way and had the finest understanding for the effects of acting.

If Shakespeare himself did not organize an edition of his works, it was only because that was a general custom of the time. None of his dramas were printed during his lifetime. The plays were anxiously guarded against becoming known through printing. People were supposed to come to the theater to see the plays there, not to read them at home. All that could be produced at that time were pirate prints, which were recorded during the performance with the help of the then emerging stenography; therefore, they contained not the authentic text but manifold distortions and errors.

These partial gaps and errors have led individual researchers to claim that Shakespeare's works, as they exist, are not special works of art at all but that they were originally composed quite differently. One representative of this view is Eugen Reichel,[†] who sees in the writer of the Shakespeare dramas the representative of a certain worldview. On the other hand, the fact remains that these dramas, as they are, make an extraordinary impression. In works that we certainly know are distorted (such as *Macbeth*), we see this captivating effect. Proof of this was provided by the performance of *Henry V* at the opening of the Lessing Theater under the direction of Neumann-Hofer, which made a tremendous impression despite the absurdly shoddy translation and inept staging.

Shakespeare's dramas are first and foremost character dramas. It is not primarily in the plot but in the magnificent development of the individual characters that the tremendous interest of these poems lies. This is precisely because the playwright places a human character before us and allows the character to unfold, portrays him in all his thinking and feeling as a single personality.

This artistic development, which reached its perfection in Shakespeare, was only possible through the preceding cultural development of the Renaissance period. Only through the higher valuation of the individual personality resulting from this Renaissance culture was Shakespeare's character-driven drama possible. In the earlier Middle Ages, we see even in Dante, despite his strong personality, basically the expression of Christian ideas as they then appeared. The generic Christian type of Dante's time was imposed over the individual and personal element. This lay in the general conception of that age.

The Christian principle had no interest in the individual personality. Only gradually did interest in the individual emerge under the new approach.

The fact that Shakespeare's fame spread so quickly proves that he found an audience that had a great interest in theater and that had a rich sense and understanding for the portrayal of character that Shakespeare offered them. Shakespeare was interested precisely in this portrayal of character; he was far from developing an ethical or moral idea for his audience. The idea of tragic guilt, for example, with which Schiller believed he had to burden his hero in order to justify his downfall, was completely absent from Shakespeare's mind. He lets events unfold as natural processes unfold, one logically arising from the other but not influenced by the idea of guilt and atonement. It would be difficult to prove a concept of guilt in this sense in one of Shakespeare's dramas.

Shakespeare was also not concerned with the representation of an idea, not jealousy in *Othello*, not ambition in *Macbeth*. No, he wanted to portray the specific character of Othello, Hamlet, Macbeth. That is why he was able to create such great characters—because he did not weigh his characters down with theory. He knew the stage from the ground up; he knew how a process was effectively presented. It was precisely he, as a practitioner, who could develop a process so that it carried the listeners away. There are no dramas in all of world literature that are as thoroughly conceived from the point of view of acting. This settles the authorship question in favor of the actor Shakespeare as the author of these dramas.

Shakespeare was born in Stratford in 1564. His father was a wealthy citizen, and he attended the Latin school in his hometown. Legends have cropped up about his youth; it is claimed that he was a poacher and led an adventurous life. All this has also been asserted against Shakespeare's authorship, and yet all of this experience has benefited his poetry. The very fact that he, although well educated, was spared from actual study ensured him the possibility of facing things much more freely and impartially, of seeing them unencumbered by the clutter of book learning. It is precisely the adventurous nature of the playwright that accounts for some of the greatest merits of his works.

The bold flight of imagination, the abrupt change of events, the passion and daring—all this speaks of a man who had also experienced the vicissitudes of fortune and who must have led an eventful life.

After the financial circumstances of his father deteriorated, Shakespeare came to London in 1585. He began his career at the theater in the most menial job imaginable. He kept the horses of theatergoers while they attended the performance. Later, he was promoted to the position of overseer of a number of such horse boys until he finally found a place on the stage and was allowed to play his first major role in 1592.

Now his fame soon spread as an actor and playwright. With it, his wealth grew, so that in 1597 he could already buy a house in Stratford. He became a very wealthy man, especially after becoming co-owner of the Globe Theater.

The dramas of Shakespeare's first period—*Love's Labor's Lost* and *As You Like It* as well as some of the histories—are not yet so essentially different from other dramas of the same period, such as those created by Marlowe[†] and others. These early plays did not yet possess Shakespeare's full power of expression because their purity and naturalness were still impaired by a certain artificiality of language in accordance with the fashion of the time. Gradually, the great character dramas followed—*Othello*, *Hamlet*, *Macbeth*, *King Lear*, *Julius Caesar*, *Coriolanus*—and established Shakespeare's enduring fame. From a number of his later works, some biographers and writers infer bleak experiences and adventures that the playwright must have undergone at the time to lead him to a bitter view of life. However, such an inference is very difficult to justify in Shakespeare's case precisely because he, more than any other playwright, takes a back seat to his characters. It is not his own opinion that he expresses through the mouths of his characters; rather, he lets them think and act according to their own character.

It therefore seems idle to ask what Shakespeare himself thought about various questions. Not Shakespeare but Hamlet broods over being or not being. He is frightened by the spirit of the father, like Macbeth by the witches on the heath. Whether Shakespeare believed in witches, in ghosts, whether he was a believer or a free spirit, does not come into consideration here at all. He asked himself the question: How must a ghost or a witch present herself on the stage in order to have the effect on the audience that I intend? The fact that the effect of Shakespeare's characters has remained the same to this day proves precisely how well he answered this question.

It must not be forgotten that the conditions of our contemporary theater are not particularly favorable to the effect of Shakespeare's dramas. The importance attached today to the setting, to all kinds of accessories, the frequent changes of scene—all this impairs the effect of the character's portrayal, which remains the main thing. In Shakespeare's time, when a change of scene was simply indicated by an unhung panel, when a chair and table sufficed to furnish a royal palace, the effect in this respect must have been considerably greater.

For a modern playwright, so much of the performance depends on all the props and scenery. Today the playwright usually prescribes the furnishings of the rooms down to the last detail so that in a bad performance the effect fails completely. Shakespeare's dramas, on the other hand, have a powerful effect even in the worst performances.

One day, when we again look more to the essentials than we do today, the effect of Shakespeare's art will become ever mightier through the power of his character portrayal, which has remained unsurpassed through the centuries.

On Roman History

BERLIN, JULY 19, 1904

We have seen† that about eight hundred years before the Christian era, an empire spread out from Rome that originally took its starting point from a kind of priestly kingship. We have seen how this priestly kingship then changed over the course of about two-and-a-half centuries into a republic. Then, we see the Roman state spreading through five centuries over a part of the world. Roughly seven hundred years before Christ's birth in Rome, we see a reigning king who is clothed at the same time with the highest priestly dignity of that time. This office has been preserved. The bearer of this office, to whom the royal dignity belonged in earlier times before there were secular kings in Rome, was called *pontifex maximus*. During the rise of the Roman state, we see a *pontifex maximus* standing at its head. We then see how the dignity of the *pontifex maximus* gradually declines so that only the priestly forms remain to him. We see that the *rex*, the king, still exists but is only a shadow of the original personality. Now we see the republic expanding more and more. In the time when Christianity is founded in the East, we see in Rome again a personality having all authority, all power in his hands: Caesar Augustus.† He finds it appropriate, necessary at that time, to transfer to himself, among other offices of the Republic, the dignity of *pontifex maximus*. Thus, at the beginning of the Christian era in Rome, we again have the *pontifex maximus* with the highest power. But this is a *pontifex maximus*, a high priest, whose power is not based on the priesthood but solely on his temporal power.

A few centuries later (about five hundred years), we see this temporal power of the Roman ruler completely destroyed. Next, we see again a *pontifex maximus*, a high priest, a Roman bishop, the later Pope, who again carries the dignity of the *pontifex maximus*. Around the year 800 AD, the ruler who is most mentioned,† who ruled those who overthrew the secular *pontifex maximus* in Rome, received the secular royal crown from this *pontifex maximus*. He completely subjugated the secular rule to the priestly rule, to the priestly power. And now begins the Roman Empire, the Holy Roman Empire.

We see a transformation taking place in history. We see that the only thing that has remained, that has continued to grow, is the dignity of the head priest in Rome. All around, changes of world-historical importance have taken place which one must also survey from a higher point of view in order to understand completely.

We will have to ask ourselves above all: How did this transformation take place in the time we are now examining, when Christianity began at the beginning of our era? How did it come about, on the one hand, that a worldly ruler had complete dominion over the world of that time and that this tremendous power was completely destroyed shortly thereafter? How did it happen that the people on whom this power was based ceased to play a role, to exercise power? How is it that five hundred years after the beginning of our era, the Roman emperorship was destroyed and that in Rome, the Roman priest sat as a prince with as much power over souls as the Roman emperor, Caesar, once had in a worldly sense?

There are two great currents that bring this about—two currents with an importance that few in history possess. On the one hand, it is the spread of Christianity from the East, and, on the other hand, it is the wandering wars of the Germanic tribes. The Roman Empire is threatened from two sides—in a spiritual sense from the East and in a worldly sense from the North. Everything that used to make up the greatness of the Roman Empire was no longer there in a certain respect. But something else was there. The outer forms of this Roman empire had remained. What had remained was that which constituted the actual significance of this Roman empire, that which originally determined the greatness of the Roman world empire. The Roman thinking, the Roman worldview with regard to external institutions, had remained. We will see to what extent these were preserved. It is true that all former content had been driven out of this empire, but the mere form, the external attire had remained. Poured into this form was something else—namely, Christianity, which now appears in the same form as the Roman emperorship. That on which the rule of the Romans was based had been destroyed by the Nordic peoples. This is a peculiar story because at least as much remained of the Roman empire as perished. What remained of it is told by the history of the Catholic Church; what remained of it is told by what we can experience every day. Go into a courtroom and see how charges are brought, how they are defended, and how justice is meted out. That is Roman law. This law was created in Rome and still exists today. We live in institutions that are completely permeated by the views of this Roman Empire. Everything we still think about law, property, and ownership, about family relationships, and so on can be traced back to the old Roman Empire, even though the people from whom all this emerged lost their external power and significance in world history five hundred years after the birth of Christ.

We have described the spread of Rome over the globe; we have seen how Rome extended its rule from this center of the world into all known lands that came into consideration at that time. We have also seen on what basis it was possible for Rome to become so powerful. We have considered the Roman people in each stage of their development. We have seen also how, out of the entirety of their circumstance and the whole character of this people, the means developed that led them to their world domination. At the same time, we have seen how the decline of the Roman world dominion had to come out of this very same way of being. This is so closely connected with their origin that we have to use the same thoughts that we used when we spoke of the origin. We have seen that Roman land ownership, acquired in immeasurable greed, increased wealth immeasurably and, on the other hand, produced a poverty that likewise grew immeasurably. Consequently, we see luxury and wealth, on the one side, and discontent, on the other.

We have also seen the basis of all that made Rome great. We have seen what it meant to be a Roman citizen. We have to enter into that mindset. We have seen how the *cives*, the Roman citizens, had their interest in the state, how every Roman citizen felt called to have a say, to participate, and how the voice of the individual came into consideration. This is expressed in the way Rome was governed, in the way all the offices were conceived so that the power to govern was in the hands of the entire citizenry. Those who administered the empire during the republican period were only administrators of civic power. They were entrusted with their office for a period of one year (or sometimes longer). A Roman citizen believed that what the *praetor* did was actually for his benefit and that the *praetor* did it only as his representative. The Roman considered the *consul*, the *quaestor*, the *praetor* as substitutes.[†] And on what was this based? It was based on the fact that the shortest possible election periods were introduced so that essentially no one ever held office for a lengthy period. There was nothing other than trust between those who were elected and those who voted. There could be no distrust between a ruling personality and the people. Incidents could occur during the short reign of a tribune,[†] but, on the whole, this government was built entirely on trust.

It was a delegated power, and the Roman understood this. He understood that he was the master while the other, to whom the government power was transferred, only acted as a representative. This is evident from the way the Roman was a member of a legally-minded people. Only in later times did things change somewhat. Ask an educated person today—they may even be very educated—what the legal difference is between the term "property" and the term "possession." These are two terms that come from Roman law. I am convinced you can go far and wide, even among people who have studied quite a bit, and they will hardly be able to tell you the difference. If you had asked a Roman peasant, he would certainly have known the difference between property and possession. Just as in the Middle Ages one learned the Ten Commandments, so every Roman boy learned the twelve tables of the law in school. The Romans were a people devoted to law, and law was second nature to them.

Now, Roman rule extended over immense areas and many provinces. You can imagine that such a state structure as we have just studied can only hold together as long as it does not exceed a certain size. When the many provinces were conquered, this could no longer be so. The difference between the original Roman state and the provinces appeared. Roman citizenship was denied to the provinces. The provinces had no rights, and the people were subjugated. This goes hand in hand with the other stages of development, with the expansion of large landholdings and the related problems of inheritance. It goes hand in hand with the emergence of an enormous proletariat. The rise of the proletariat is connected with the fact that the old army of citizens was gradually transformed into an army of mercenary troops recruited by individual leaders, such as Marius[†] and the like. We see that next to the old Roman citizenry, a kind of military power developed that was controlled by those who could win the favor of this military power. We further see that people like Gracchus[†] are trying to stop the fall of the Roman Empire by creating a kind of middle party. I have already described the Gracchan movement to you. Now, it is still important that the younger Gracchus wanted to create a middle party. This party was to consist of people who had been senators and had left. It was a kind of knighthood. It was this knighthood that had been envied by the proletarians.

Now something very special had happened in Rome at the time when Caesar's power was emerging. This knighthood was to form a power against the large landowners, against the so-called Optimates. The old agrarian laws were to be renewed. No one should have more than five hundred acres of land, at most two hundred and fifty acres for adult sons, and at most for a family a thousand acres. The other land was to be given to this middle class in the form of smaller estates. In this way, it was believed that a middle class would be created between the large landowners and the proletariat. But this failed because the proletariat had become suspicious and because it did not want to tolerate a party between itself and the actual owners. The middle party had also then joined the Optimates. So now we have the proletariat, on one side, and a kind of ordering party, on the other. This has emerged in recent times. The republican forms of power had passed very gradually, almost unnoticed, into the power of the Caesars. Octavius,[†] the first Roman emperor, began as a republican ruler, and he gradually rose to supremacy. It was quite by necessity that Octavius-Augustus' peculiar breadth of power emerged from those

Roman conditions. He simply continued the old Roman structures and had all the offices gradually transferred to him. That he was able to assume all these offices simultaneously and indefinitely as a kind of autocrat came from the fact that the difference between the conditions in Rome itself and those in the provinces had become so great.

The provinces had long been governed in a kind of aristocratic manner. The Roman citizens were not at all opposed to this. They felt themselves to be Roman citizens, and they were not at all concerned that those outside in the provinces should have the same rights as they enjoyed. They accepted the fact that from Rome a kind of absolute governmental power developed over the provinces. In particular, Roman autocrats transferred to themselves all the so-called proconsular powers over the provinces; therefore, it came about that the first consuls were rulers of a very unique type and power. Within Rome, they knew to maintain the limits of power that had been transferred to them as in earlier times, but outside of Rome, they ruled the provinces in the name of the state. This is how Roman autocratic power developed with the agreement of the Roman citizenry. Then, during the Caesar period, the following occurred. By means of absolute power over the provinces, the Caesars had appropriated all of the tax-collecting institutions and the entirety of military power; therefore, they were able to draw enormous revenues from the provinces. In addition to the Roman state treasury, a kind of imperial treasury developed. From Octavius' power, the Roman-Caesarian autocracy developed in the following way: It was the Roman citizens who agreed to do everything that had to be done in the provinces by no longer using the Roman treasury. These expenditures were often things that had become necessary. Even these could no longer be paid for out of the state treasury. The income did not flow into the state treasury but into the treasury of the Caesars. In this way, it happened that the Caesars could raise themselves to be seen as a sort of benefactor. The Caesarian authority and power developed, and all other offices had to sink down to the level of shadow offices. From within, the power of the Roman Caesars conquered the power of the Roman state. Basically, we can say that only the first emperors were true Romans. We can say that later, there were essentially no real Romans sitting on the throne of the Caesars. These were people who had been elected in the provinces, and who, like Hadrian and Caracalla,† were able to seize power. From the periphery, Rome was led to absolutism. Thus, by a kind of inner necessity of development, what had been distributed among the Roman citizens passed into the hands of autocrats. It now becomes quite natural that the whole Roman system of law and related concepts is transferred to the one central point. What was formerly done by the Roman citizens is now done by individual officials, not only in the provinces but also in Rome itself.

Something is happening here that one must understand if one wants to understand the age correctly. If we look back for a moment to Greece and to Rome in the time of the old kingship, we will see everywhere a direct relationship of the rulers to the ruled. No matter how this relationship of trust was formed, it was a natural relationship stemming from the earlier times we described in the last historical consideration. The rulers were recognized by the ruled so that people believed in them. In principle, the one who ruled had to acquire certain qualities, especially in the older priestly states. There, nobody believed in divine powers that hovered beyond the world. They did believe in a kind of divinization of the human being because they looked for the principle of development in the human being. The priest-king in Rome was recognized only if he had acquired the spiritual and moral qualities of the gods, if he had developed inwardly. One could develop oneself to be a kind of deified person who deserved veneration. It was not a relationship of subservience but of trust. Anyone who really knows about these things must take this view. It was based on something that was always there in the heart, and it continued to grow in the Republic.

Because of the way Roman law developed, it was capable of completely erasing this personal, living relationship of ruler and ruled. It was inclined to replace the personal with an abstract, conceptual relationship. If you could go back to those times of Rome, you would see that he who sat in judgment as *praetor* in Rome, even if he had the law of the twelve tables before him, could still do something based on trust through personal insight. Something still depended on the personality. That became quite different later. Later, the whole legal system gradually became a purely abstract system of thought. All that mattered was to interpret the law according to its paragraphs by logical acuity. The jurist should be a mere thinker, a merely logically-trained man. Thinking was the only thing that mattered. Nothing of the immediate life should flow into it—nothing of the soul and nothing of personal influence. Only the letter of the law was to be followed. The law was interpreted more and more according to the letter. Only officials handled the letter of the law outside in the provinces, and later also in Rome. There, it was a question of studying the paragraphs and deciding the case—removed from every immediate aspect of life—only by means of thoughts that tended toward sophism. The whole way of thinking that expressed itself in administration and government had assumed a character that treated entire institutions as computational examples. This you must grasp, and then you will understand what it means to say that the whole of Roman life had been transformed into a system of dogmas. The Roman state, which had created law out of the free decisions, out of the very soul of its citizens, had gradually transformed that law into dogmas.

At the time of the emergence of Christianity, personal government was no longer considered valid, only written law. It was a real state of legal dogmatism. The Caesars could move about freely. All that mattered to them was forcing the whole state into a legal system that could be tightly controlled from a central point. The whole Roman state was gradually dogmatized. We see it divided into smaller areas headed by legal administrators. These areas were again grouped together into dioceses. We see the Roman state gradually taking on a form that later appears in the division adopted by the Catholic Church. It was not Christianity that created these forms; this was done entirely according to the template of the Roman dogmatized state.

Christianity was transplanted from the East into this state, the nature of which you now understand. Of course, we must deal with personalities; however, we cannot deal with individual Roman emperors. This story is also fundamentally quite boring. It is perhaps enough if we mention Caligula—Mr. "little boots."[†] But one thing is important. We have to realize what happened to or from the Roman culture. This Roman culture had something that reminds one of the culture of another time. I would like to describe to you a personality who is typical, representative, and who can be cited here for comparison—that is, Lucian.[†] He came from Asia and introduced a very special light. He tells us about himself in a remarkable work, "The Dream." I mention this not because it is a significant literary product but because it is characteristic of the mindset of the Roman Empire at that time.

Two female figures appeared to him in his dreams—one was art, the other was education. Art demanded that he strive for hard work. Education demanded nothing of the sort. He only needed to acquire a few tricks of the trade, such as how best to persuade people. In ancient Rome, talking meant as much as writing newspapers does today. He said to himself, Why should I follow in the path of Phidias or Homer? I'll remain a poor fellow. He followed the second figure and became an itinerant speaker, a speaker of a very peculiar kind, a speaker with no educational foundation. Education at that time meant to speak to the people without knowing anything, without having studied seriously, just as one writes in the newspaper today. This is how he went out into the world. Now, we see how he talks about religion and politics, how he appears as a personality of whom history reports nothing, but who was able to lift speech in a conversation, as in an editorial, up to heaven. Everywhere he was active in this way. He came as far as France, was a personality without a backbone, without inner content or substance. This was the nature of education in the great Roman Empire of that time. These were the educated. The ones who had a core, like Apollonius,[†] a contemporary of Lucian, could not rise to any position of importance. That was quite impossible at that time. But the whole empire sighed. It was the discontent and immorality from which they suffered. I cannot describe to you those kinds of cruel and immoral amusements. A third of the year was spent in gladiatorial games, in bullfights, or in shows of the most boisterous kind. And this became more and more widespread. On the one hand, we have extreme luxury, and, on the other hand, we have indescribable poverty and misery.

Now you see how it happened that in this Roman empire, an

element spread increasingly, an element that differed from all the others in its earnestness and profundity. That was Judaism. The Jews could be found everywhere in the Roman Empire at that time. It would be quite unhistorical to believe that at that time the Jews were limited only to Palestine. In the whole of North Africa, in Rome and in France, everywhere you find the Jews already spread at that time. Their religion was still much more substantial than what the education of the Roman time offered. It existed alongside the currents of lower spiritual forms. Through the fact that the Romans came to rule the whole world, they spread also the cults, the sacrificial acts, and the holy acts of the different provinces. In Rome itself you could see Persian, Arabian, and Egyptian services. This resulted in a tremendous externalization.

In the Roman Caesar era, religion reached such a degree of superficiality that it cannot be compared with anything earlier. The priest of earlier times was a kind of initiate, having overcome everything of a lower nature within himself. He was also called a divinized personality. This was achieved in the various schools of different lands. To the extent that this dignity was previously exalted—it was one of the most sacred of antiquity—it was now lowered. It was so that the Roman Caesars were revered as so-called initiates, even divinely worshipped. Lucretia attained even divine veneration because with her, prepared by external actions and training, an initiation had been carried out.

But this was completely external. When Augustus assumed the title *pontifex maximus,* he assumed externally everything that had formerly been the inner sign of the priests. Because it had lost all connection with its origin, it had also lost all meaning and the right relationship.

This was the situation in Rome at the time when it received a complete renewal of the religious view from the East. We do not need to describe the inner content of this renewal of the religious view but only its outer forms because we are not presenting a history of religion but a general history. Above all, a religion of wisdom was transplanted. The first propagators of this Christian religion were indeed the most learned, the deepest, and the most significant men of that time. Standing on the firm ground of this learning, they looked up to the founder of Christianity. If you read them—Clement of Alexandria, Origen, and so on—you will see what wisdom they attained in the scholarship of that time. They put all of that at the service of this new idea. They were trying to achieve nothing other than a complete renewal of religious feeling, linked at the same time to a penetration of the whole human being.

Now, imagine that while in Rome everything had become superficial, all religiosity was wrapped around Caesar like a cloak, and all discussions of religion were mixed with mockery (as in Lucian), the religious element was to be renewed not through anything of a worldly nature but purely out of the innermost depths of the human being, the human heart. And the religious element is renewed in such a way that deep, learned men are put into the service of this idea. It was so—this must not be misunderstood—that the representatives of earliest Christianity were not ordinary members of the masses but the cleverest people of that time. This spread with lightning speed because the whole religion had nothing of asceticism, nothing of otherworldliness about it. Ordinary people in the midst of everyday life took it up. Everything that had been perceived as Roman, everything that had led to luxury and well-being in Rome, was foreign to the core of this religion. You can see what was understood and grasped by the whole human being, by the ordinary person, through this rapidly spreading confession if you read the description of the Christian principle in Tertullian,[†] who says: We Christians know nothing that is foreign to human life. We do not withdraw from everyday life. We want to bring something to the human being as he is every day, we want to represent the world. We want to enjoy what is in the world. Only we want nothing to do with the debaucheries of Rome.

To show how these Christians lived together where the Roman Empire had not yet destroyed the markets, I need only quote from the Acts of the Apostles, not as a sermon and not as an admonishing word:

> All the believers were one in heart and mind. No one claimed that any of their possessions was their own, but they shared everything they had. With great power the apostles continued to testify to the resurrection of the Lord Jesus. And God's grace was so powerfully

> at work in them all that there were no needy persons among them. For from time to time those who owned land or houses sold them, brought the money from the sales and put it at the apostles' feet, and it was distributed to anyone who had need. Joseph, a Levite from Cyprus, whom the apostles called Barnabas (which means "son of encouragement"), sold a field he owned and brought the money and put it at the apostles' feet.[†]

This is not a sermon. This is a description of what was intended and what was also realized many times. This was what was opposed to the life of the Roman state. This was one reason why Christianity was introduced with such speed and why Christianity so quickly entered the hearts of those who had nothing to hope for. Not only did they hear that there was no dogma, it was the living word, the living work, that they felt.

The one who spoke, spoke what he knew and had recognized as truth. He could say it today in one form and tomorrow in another. There was no established Christian dogma. It was the attitude, the inner life, that held this Christian community together. That was what the first Christians preached. It was also why, in the early years of Christianity, people freely discussed the truth back and forth. There is no freer discussion, no freer debate than that which was present in the early days of this Christianity.

Only little by little is there talk of violence. The important thing to consider—which then later leads to violence, which leads to the emergence of the dogmatism of Christianity in the first place—is the fact that the Roman Empire was dogmatized. The whole Roman Empire was transformed into a dogmatic system. One could not grasp anything other than matters of the intellect, nothing other than stiff, abstract dogma. Thus, it happened that the first Christians were persecuted, that they became, nevertheless, more and more important, and that, in the end, after Constantine's proclamation, the Caesars and the Constantines themselves were forced to recognize the Christians.[†] But how did they recognize them? They let them grow into the Roman state, into that which was filled with the dogma and temporal power that were founded in the Roman state. For this, Christianity had to put all its influence at the disposal of the Roman rulers, and the original structure went over into the bishoprics and dioceses.

It is not surprising that in the year 325, the Nicaean Council turned out the way it did.[†] At that time, the two currents of Christianity were still opposed to each other in the presbyters Arius and Athanasius.[†] Athanasius was completely educated in the Roman spirit. Arius believed in the gradual development of the human being. He saw it as unlimited and he called it divinization. Man can resemble God; that is true Arianism. This was opposed by the Roman dogmatist Athanasius, who said: "The divinity of Christ must be raised above all that is connected with humanity to the abstractness, the otherworldliness of the dogmatism that gradually developed in the Roman Empire."[†] Arian Christianity turned into Athanasian Christianity, and the latter won. What was important for the Roman Caesar? Later, he himself converted to Christianity—not to Athanasian Christianity but to Arian Christianity. He knew, however, that Athanasianism could at least seemingly support the old Roman Empire.

Christianity was to become a support for the Roman Empire. This was the important question that was decided at the beginning of the fourth century.[†] At the same time, however, this was the epoch of world history when the Germanic tribes had become more and more powerful, and it was no longer of any use to support the old Roman Empire through transformation and remodeling. It was swept away by the Germanic tribes. We will talk about this next time, how the Germanic tribes overthrew the old Roman Empire.

Then, we still want to show how the Roman Empire remained a power even in its death throes. It had the task of transforming the doctrine of Christianity in such a way that this doctrine took on a political form and was suitable to be the bearer of a political system. Powerful, however, was the idea that at that time the leading Christians knew how to extract from the original Christianity. It was *power* that they added to the idea of the Roman Caesar and to the transformed Christianity. The resulting political system was so powerful that when the Germanic tribes were destroying the old Roman Empire, when the Germanic territories were spreading more and more, the supposedly most important ruler of the early Middle

Ages, Charlemagne, received the imperial crown from the hands of the Pope, the *pontifex maximus*. Such were the effects even when little remained of the old Roman Empire. You see how peculiarly the destinies of the world are interlinked. You see that we must know above all that we are dealing with a political power throughout the Middle Ages because the Roman idea of the state flowed into the original Christianity. Actual Christianity was not inserted into the Roman idea of the state. It was always the case that, in monasticism, Christianity rebelled against the political form of Christianity. Another idea is related to this. It is an idea that is difficult to grasp because it was not based in the original Christianity at all. You do not find anything of monasticism in original Christianity because that kind of isolation, of withdrawal from the world, was quite foreign to it. To anyone who took Christianity seriously, the form, the political form, was foreign, so such a person withdrew to the monastery in order to be true to the religion of Christianity. Everything that has asserted itself as such associations, as monasticism, through the centuries—even if it degenerated because the Catholic Church wanted to suppress every such attempt—that was a living outcry of Christianity against political power. Thus, we have the development of power.

Now, we still have to recognize what significance the Germanic element has in this time, to recognize what role Christianity plays in the Germanic element. We also have to recognize what is developing out of the old Roman Empire. We must see how this old Roman ruin is collapsing and how something came out of it under which the peoples had to groan for a long time. It begins with the call for freedom and ends with the suppression of freedom. It is the call declaring that everyone should respect each other as equals, and it ends with everyone being oppressed. It is strange that in our time historians have found themselves defending Caracalla because he gave so-called equality to the whole Roman Empire. As one of the most insignificant and harmful Caesars, he made those who were outside in the provinces equal to the Romans, but then he oppressed them all together! And this figure has been given the mantle of a champion of Roman freedom!

When we see that the destiny of freedom can be like this, then

I think we really gain from history what we can call a kind of education through history. Then we learn that there is a real rock, like Peter had—a rock based on the original founder, on which human development can really be built. This rock is and must be human freedom and human dignity. These can be suppressed at times, indeed as strongly suppressed as in the old Roman Empire by conditions that can be compared with few others. However, the education of the human being to freedom is given in history. We must remember this important fact: when power and violence ruled in ancient Rome at its peak, the foundation was at the same time undermined, and the whole structure collapsed. However deeply suppressed, it must be said of freedom that the following true saying applies to it, indeed arises from it:

> The old collapses, times change,
> And new life blossoms from the ruins.†

History of the Middle Ages up to the Great Inventions and Discoveries

Foreword by Marie Steiner to the First Edition (1936)

The transcript of these lectures on the history of the Middle Ages given by Rudolf Steiner in the Worker Education School in Berlin faithfully and accurately reproduces their content, even if somewhat condensed. The lectures show in what sense Dr. Steiner wanted to see history treated, and represent the groundbreaking prelude to what emerged from his complete works as a new science of history. Their spiritual scope—which brings out the background of earthly events from deeper sources than we are accustomed to—is already announced in this condensed overview of widely divergent historical events.

These freely spoken lectures were entrusted to the configuration of soul that emerged in working-class circles. They were geared toward what the listeners could follow with understanding out of their well-trained and alert intelligence. They did not serve any party program but opposed in the most eminent sense the dogma of a materialistic conception of history. Therefore, they were considered heretical by the leading personalities in the school, who did not demand freedom but, as they expressed themselves, "a reasonable compulsion"!

This led to Rudolf Steiner's dismissal from teaching in the Worker Education School, despite the general support of the students who wanted him to continue teaching. There were many letters from workers who had recognized in what way Rudolf Steiner had wanted to serve them. They were grateful that finally one had come who trusted them to have other interests than the struggle for bread, who had spoken to them from the spirit, presupposing such a striving also in them and thus appealing to their best powers.

We are indebted to Miss Johanna Mücke for the transcription of these lectures.

Lecture One

BERLIN, OCTOBER 18, 1904

Goethe said that the best thing about history is the enthusiasm it arouses, which stirs one to similar deeds.[†] In a certain deeper sense, all knowledge and all cognition can only receive the right value if it ventures out into life. It is necessary to go far back in history to find the causes of later developments. Just as, in order to understand individual branches of the external development of human culture (such as the building of bridges and roads) we must keep in mind that these are the fruits of the achievements in the individual sciences—physics and mathematics—so, too, in genuine history, we see everywhere the fruits of earlier events. What is expressed in our life reaches back to distant times.

We have considered the beginnings of culture, tracing its development through Greek and Roman times. In this view of history, we are approaching the present. Now we are going to look at a period of time which many people do not like to consider, which they would like to erase from history—the dark Middle Ages. We are standing before an important period of history: Barbarian peoples, who know nothing of morality and art, appear on the scene of history. These tribes of peoples are displaced from their homelands in modern-day Russia by Mongolian peoples, and they migrate far to the west. We will follow the struggles and destinies of these peoples. Then our path will lead us on to the discovery of America, to that point in time when the Middle Ages and modern times merge. We view the time of great inventions and discoveries, when that invention appeared which probably had the most profound significance of all—the invention of the printing press. This is the time when Copernicus gave us a new view of the world. This human development has led from the migration of peoples to the discoveries of modern times.

It is far more difficult to prove the connection between cause and effect in history than in chemistry and physics, for here cause and effect are often far apart.

Only today do we consider tolerance of different religious confessions as a demand of the times, a necessary cultural condition. Yet already in the third century before Christ in India, there was such a mutual respect and tolerance of the most diverse creeds, as evinced by a monument of King Ashoka.[†] The Christian attitude that appeared in the later Roman Empire had its effect throughout the Middle Ages; however, its causes lie neither in the Roman Empire nor in Germania but in a small lost sect of the Jewish people in Palestine: the Essenes. Given the relatively large syllabus, not every point in time can be treated in detail now. In a sense, a charcoal sketch must first be drawn, the lines of which are then to be further elaborated upon. We must first understand what flows to us from the Middle Ages if we want to understand what effect this period must have for us. An outstanding Roman writer, Tacitus, has preserved for us in his *Germania*[†] a picture of those tribes which had settled in what is now Germany. He describes them as individual tribes, alike in terms of their language, and, while they regarded themselves as different peoples, to him as an outsider, they appeared very similar. He found out what they had in common and gave them the common name *Germania.*

If we now examine the folk soul of these Germanic peoples, we encounter the difference between them and the Greeks and Romans. In the formation of these mental characteristics, it is a question of an important time difference. Greek culture with its incomparable art marks a special point in the development of humanity. Before the conquest by the later invading Hellenes, we saw an ancient people approximately equivalent to the later Germanic peoples—namely, the Pelasgians, who lived in a community of free people. After the immigration of the Hellenes, we found the two strata of the population: conquerors and conquered, the contrast of free and unfree. Out of migration and conquest came Greek rule. From this it follows that only a small part of the population had a share in the goods of the culture. Out of this situation, the low valuation of work results; even artistic work was unworthy of the free Greek citizen. Greece perished because of this low esteem for work. This culture of the Greeks, unrivaled in many respects, was a culture that was only possible under conquerors. The Roman character was formed during conquest, and the history of the Roman Empire is a history of continuous conquests. When it could conquer nothing more, it perished.

The Germanic character was formed in all its essential elements before the conquest and it has not allowed itself to be subjugated by contact with other peoples. Its development has stood firm in the face of struggles. Thus, we see the formation of the national spirit taking place with the Greeks after, with the Romans during, and with the Teutons before the great historical battles. If we want to consider these traits, we will have to distinguish these groups of peoples in Central Europe more precisely. Three peoples come into consideration. In Spain, France, Ireland, and Southern Germany, we find first the ancient Celts. They are driven out of most of their homes by the Germanic tribes. From the east, the Slavs advance and push the Teutons further. We find among the Germanic peoples, who are surrounded by the other two peoples, a strong mixture with Celtic and Slavic blood. This mixture of the Germanic with the Celtic and Slavic element also affects the whole culture of the Middle Ages.

If we go back to distant times, the great, strange culture of the ancient Celts reveals itself. Active, energetic, spiritually stimulated, inclined to revolutionary impulses—this is how the Celtic blood shows itself even in later times. Great poetry, songs, and scientific ideas are owed to the Celtic peoples. The Celts were the inspiration for the sagas that were worked on by German poets in the later Middle Ages—Roland, Tristan, Parsifal, and so on. This strange people has almost disappeared after being pushed further and further to the west and being mixed with the Germanic tribes.

The Germanic character shows as its main characteristics bravery, wanderlust, and a strong feeling for nature. Domestic and martial virtues, practical efficiency, and activity directed to usefulness develop in them. The main occupations of the Germanic peoples are hunting and cattle breeding. The Teutons[†] have a few simple poems that are borrowed from an older people. The Germanic character remains unchanged in its basic characteristics from barbarian primeval times. Within the Germanic element, the driving forces of opposite development emerge. A strange transformation takes place within the Middle Ages. Greece had developed its high art and Rome its legal life and the concept of the state. The simple legal views of the Germanic peoples were based on completely different premises.

In Rome, property relations, especially with regard to land, were the decisive factor. The complicated legal concepts of the Roman state originate from the effort to bring harmony between the free citizens and the owners of the land. All the struggles between the plebeians and the patricians, the struggles of the Gracchi, even the party struggles of the later Republic, were struggles for the right of the free citizen against those who were also in possession of power through land ownership. Formally, every Roman citizen had the same right to the state. Yes, even in the later times of emperorship, the emperors nominally possessed the right to the state, uniting the right of all free citizens in their person and exercising it in their place.

Such elaborate concepts were foreign to the simple legal views of the Germanic peoples. The special value of the free citizen was not legally recognized. What developed out of these views was the law of the fist, the law of the strongest. The powerful consisted of those who could assert their right by their strength. At first, it was physical power that asserted itself. Everyone had to submit to the stronger force. But the fruit of what had prepared itself in the Germanic age emerged later as the right of the free personality, conditioned by nothing but self-acquired ability.

This is expressed in the founding of cities. This culture of cities, which arose in the eleventh century throughout the whole of Western Europe, is a significant phenomenon. From what did the cities originate? Cities emerged from the fact that those who felt oppressed by their landlords were looking for a place where they could enjoy undisturbed what they owed to their activity and their personal skill. The free citizen of ancient Rome was based on a title that came with certain rights. In the Middle Ages, it was not a title of citizen that was valid but only what a person attained to. In the battles that the cities fought with the nobility and knights for their freedom and independence, nothing else is expressed than the struggle of the free personality. It was not like that in ancient Greece, nor in ancient Rome. It was a significant transitional stage.

What was the reason behind people coming together in cities? At first, it was material interest and the desire to be free from oppression; therefore, the activity was also initially directed toward benefit and material acquisition.

Also from the urban culture—but for a different reason—in Italy, on the scene of an ancient dying culture, there emerges the formidable poet-personality of the Middle Ages—Dante. In the Germanic cities, practical inventions were first developed (such as the compass and gunpowder) up to the momentous event of the invention of the printing press. All this, which leads to a complete transformation of conditions, was born out of what had been practically achieved. This may seem very far-fetched at first glance, but, as already emphasized, cause and effect are far apart in history. Let me explain with an example:

In 1846, František Palacký, the Czech historian, in his work on the Czech people in the fifteenth century,[†] drew attention to the reform movements of the Middle Ages, to those movements which, long before the so-called Reformation, attempted to reorganize the Church. He draws attention especially to the Hussite movement,[†] which he treated with great sympathy because he himself took an active part in the revolution of 1848. He characterizes in a very peculiar way what has formed in the hearts of those in the urban culture. It is a characteristic common to the Celtic, Germanic, and Slavic tribes. We understand it when we look at the sagas and songs of these peoples. They differ from ancient Greek and Roman sagas in that they describe what the human heart can suffer and what can redeem it.

This is the sense of the tragic. Among the Greek and Roman peoples, the hero of the saga was the one who won outwardly, not the one who sustained his soul. The heart of the people was always with those who were outwardly favored by fortune. It was different with the Germanic peoples. The heart of the Germanic and Slavic peoples beats for the heroes who perish outwardly but maintain their soul.

They live in the soul, in the spirit. Heroes like Siegfried and Roland or the king's son Marko[†] are celebrated in the poetry of these peoples. Not the outer victory of these heroes but their courage in suffering and downfall, their unbowed spirit, is celebrated. Everything takes a back seat to the rights of the spirit and the soul. In imperial Rome, we see bravery, the consciousness of right. In Greece, art flourishes. The life of the soul meets us with the Teutons. They had no images of their gods. Unlike the Greeks, they do not make glorious images of their divine figures in sculptural form. Their soul worked on the images of their gods; deep inside the mind, the German formed his god.

The idea of the Reformation also arose from this people's disposition. These people demanded to be involved in what their faith should be. One hundred years before Luther, Wycliffe[†] had initiated a Reformation movement in England. The spirit of the people demanded that they take the Bible into their own hands. The Hussite movement also came from this spirit. Already in the early Middle Ages, there were beginnings in this direction. Emperor Henry II,[†] of Saxon descent, to whom the Catholic Church later gave the name "the Saint," demanded an *ecclesia non romana*. Milíč,[†] the underappreciated scholar who languished in the dungeon of Prague, wrote his book on the Antichrist. The Roman Church with its external organization was the Antichrist for him. What emerged in such demands and movements, the detachment from external constraints, the inner deepening, Palacký claims for the Slavic people. He sees the idea of humanity, as expressed by Herder,[†] in the brotherhoods as they developed on Bohemian soil. It lies deep in our people to regard an informal organization as an ideal.

It was neither after nor during conquest that the Germanic peoples formed their national character. The trait that lay in them before that time has been preserved through this stage and has finally developed into this ideal. The idea of freedom was formed during the Middle Ages in spite of all the oppression, in spite of all the counter-currents that make up what is called the Dark Ages. Even though the Middle Ages may seem to many today to be a dark time, what developed in the Middle Ages was what the poets later sought—the consciousness of freedom for which the eighteenth century found little more than the definition, for which one fought bitterly in the nineteenth century, and toward which today's struggle is directed.

We must free ourselves from the coercive relationships in which people are still bound today. The awareness that each person is the same in terms of the feeling of freedom has become more and more widespread. People have understood that legally a person cannot be a slave, not a bondsman. Legally, one feels free today. But another form of unfreedom has been preserved—the material one. Unfree in ancient Greece were the oppressed, the conquered, the slaves. In ancient Rome, unfree was the person who did not belong to the bourgeoisie, the person who had no part in the state. In the Middle Ages, people were unfree through physical violence. All these forms have not been able to survive; only economic bondage has survived.

The striving for full liberation of the personality is becoming more and more evident. The ancient Greek attached importance to the nobility of the race; the Roman attached it to the nobility of the person. With the Teuton, the value lay in the power and strength of the person. The modern person attaches importance to capitalism, to the appearance of possession. This development points to the fact that, more and more, the barriers which restrain the personality from the outside will fall. Then the ground will be free for the new ideal. History teaches us that the free human being acquires a new value out of the spirit. The person who fulfills the ideal will be the one who is freed from all these forms of oppression. Once freed from the heaviness of the earth, he can direct his gaze upward. Only then will the words of Hegel ring entirely true: History is the progress of humanity toward the consciousness of freedom![†]

Lecture Two

BERLIN, OCTOBER 25, 1904

The picture of Central Europe changed considerably from the first to the sixth century AD. This change consisted in a complete replacement of the peoples who lived in the valleys of the Vistula, Oder, and Elbe rivers; therefore, it is very difficult to get a picture of these peoples, to learn something about their customs and their way of life. One must resort to a peculiar method to find a picture of those peoples. In Tacitus' descriptions in the *Germania*, we get a picture of the region at that time. We do not have any other documents from that time and we must refer to the sagas of the northern Germanic tribes to supplement our ideas. Something very significant for the Roman's view of the conditions of that time is what Tacitus says about these peoples. He is of the opinion that they are the original inhabitants of that country because he cannot imagine that other peoples could have turned to these inhospitable regions. He names those tribes of people who live on the Rhine, on the Lippe, on the Weser, on the Danube, and in Brandenburg; only these are known to him. He describes their unique traits and calls their common features "Germanic." The people felt themselves to be many different tribes and they are called by the most diverse names during the battles with the Romans. Only a few names have survived into later times, such as the Suevi, Lombards, Chatti, Frisians, and so on.

They originally derive from Tuisto [the legendary divine ancestor of the Germanic peoples], to whom they pay divine tribute in their war songs. The son of Tuisto was Mannus, after whose three sons they name their main tribes: Ingaevones, Istvaeones, and Irminones. If we compare this description of Tacitus with the myths of another

Aryan people, we find in the sacred Sanskrit language of the Indians the same designation—*Manu*—for superhuman leaders. This points us to a tribal affinity. Indeed, we can trace the same deities among all the Indo-European peoples. Tacitus tells us that the hero of the Greek myth, Hercules, was also worshipped by the Germanic peoples and was called Irmin by them. We know that among the southern Indo-Germanic tribes there lived a legend that found an artistic form in Greece—the legend of Odysseus. Tacitus describes a cultic site near the Rhine that was dedicated to Odysseus and his father Laertes. So we see that the culture of the Germanic peoples around this time was related to the culture we find in Greece in the eighth and ninth centuries BC. Later, we see in Greece the formation of a culture that remained at a lower level in Germany.

All this points to an original relationship. Those peoples who later lived in Germany, Greece, and Russia probably had their former homeland north of the Black Sea. From there, one tribe migrated to Greece, one tribe to Rome, a third tribe to the west. The original culture of all these peoples has been preserved in this form among the Germanic peoples and was further developed among the Celts.

Tacitus tells us nothing of the customs and traditions of this strange people. We are limited to the legends and songs, which were later summarized in the older and younger Edda in Iceland. In these tales lives that which has been produced by this people. Tacitus tells us further of the customs of the Germans at their popular assemblies (which we have to imagine as consultations of very small communities). To these, all men of the district gathered. The deliberations were held with beer and mead, and it is said that the old Germans made their decisions in the evening while drunk, but then, in the morning, these decisions were revised when they were sober again and only then were they considered valid. As we learn from the *scholia* to the *Iliad*,[†] the same custom existed with the Persians. We must therefore conclude that there exists a relationship of all these peoples branching from an original Aryan[†] trunk.

The Germanic peoples of the north evince great similarity particularly in their peculiar forms of religion. In their basic character, they are similar to those of the south, but they nevertheless show a far greater harmony with those of the Persians. According to the view of the northern Germanic peoples, there were originally two kingdoms separated by an abyss—a kingdom of fire called *Muspelheim* and a kingdom of ice called *Niflheim*. Through the sparks that flew from *Muspelheim*, the first race of giants arose in the abyss. Ymir was the most outstanding of the giants. Then there arose a cow, Audhumbla, who licked the ice, and from it a strong human form emerged. From this form came the gods Wotan, Wili, and We, whose names mean reason, will, and mind (*Gemüt*). This second family of gods was called the Aesir. Their origin was derived from the elder of the giants.

An important linguistic connection emerges, for the gods of the Persians were called by an almost identical name, Asuras, which points to a relationship among all these peoples. A further important reference is found in an old Persian incantation, or incantation-poem, which is handed down to us. It points to changes in the soul of the people, to old gods who have been deposed and displaced by others. The worship of the Devas is renounced; the worship of the Asuras is invoked. We see here a resemblance between the Devas and the giants, who were conquered by the Aesir.

Furthermore, the northern Germanic legend tells how the three gods found an ash tree and an alder tree on the seashore and created the human race from them. The Persian myth also describes the human race emerging from a tree. With the Jews, we find echoes of this myth in the account of the Tree of Life in the Garden of Eden. Thus, we see traces of the same mythical conceptions from Persia across Palestine to Scandinavia.

We have shown a common, basic character among certain peoples. Once again, differences arise between a more southern and a more northern branch of the common main trunk. The Greeks, the Latins, and the Indians belong to the southern branch, and the Persians and the Germanic peoples belong to the northern branch. Let us see, then, what kind of peoples we are dealing with at this point in the Germanic lands. They appear to us in such a way that we must believe they have preserved traits that the Greeks and Italians had long since shed—namely, the Greeks *after* and the Romans *during* the conquest of their respective empires, while these northern peoples had developed their essential traits and characteristics *before* that conquest. It was the original characteristics that these peoples had preserved. They had not passed through that intermediate stage which those southern peoples had passed through in the meantime. We are therefore dealing with the clash between a people who remained conservative and a related people who had, however, reached the height of culture.

At the time of the emergence of Christianity, which was to be of such importance for them, the Germanic peoples stood at that level of culture which we find described among the Greeks in Homer. They had not participated in the progress in culture and morals that lies between the two stages. In the first century AD, Tacitus describes the Germanic peoples of the borderlands on the Danube, the Rhine, and the Lippe. These peoples are characterized by wanderlust, love of freedom, and a fervor for hunting and war. Domestic affairs were in the hands of the women. Now we encounter here a morality and a form of society that had long since disappeared among the Greeks and that could only be preserved where the individual members of a tribe were still bound to each other by blood relations—hence the many tribes. With those who were conscious of their descent from the same family—for they were regulated families, not hordes—tribal kinship developed from the individual families. Therefore, the wars they fought were almost always wars against unrelated strangers.

Toward the end of the fourth century and on into the fifth, we now see all these peoples forced to leave their homelands to look for new ones.

The Huns broke in, and the epoch of the migration of peoples began. With it dawned the knowledge of the peoples living further east: the Alans, the Gepids, and so on, especially the Goths. This people, divided into Western and Eastern Goths, had already accepted Christianity. It is this people that is of particular importance to us by the nature of their conception of Christianity. While the people who later spread Christianity from west to east—the Franks—imposed it by force on other peoples, the Goths were full of tolerance. The high level of culture they had already reached is shown by the fact that we owe to a bishop of the Goths, Ulfilas or

Wulfila, the first translation of the Bible, the so-called *Silver Codex*, which is preserved in Uppsala.

These Goths, whose Christianization had come from the East, were not such Christians as those whose conversion came later from the West; they were not like the Franks who at the time of Charlemagne imposed Christianity on the Saxons by force of arms. They were not Athanasian but Arian Christians.[†] All these eastern Germanic tribes professed the Arian faith, a faith that was declared heretical and persecuted by the followers of Athanasius at the Council of Nicaea.

The Arian Christians assumed that God resided in every human breast; therefore, the Goths believed in the divinization of the human being as shown to humanity by Christ, who had gone before them. This belief was connected with a profound education of the mind. The Goths were extremely tolerant of all other religious views. Between the two Christian religions, so different from one another, no understanding was possible. Given that absolute tolerance was a characteristic of these Goths and that they did not seek to impose their faith on others, we can see the difference between their approach and the way in which, for example, Charlemagne and Clovis (the followers of the Athanasian creed) exploited Christianity for political purposes.

The Arians saw in Christ a human being, highly developed above all others, but nonetheless a human being among fellow human beings. Their Christ belonged to humanity and dwelt in the human breast. The Christ of the Athanasian Christians is God Himself, enthroned high above humanity.

Athanasius was victorious, and the development of culture was significantly influenced by this.

The Germanic tribes were surrounded by foreign peoples: in the south and west by the Romans and Gauls—Celtic-Germanic peoples—while from the east there was a continuous influx of new peoples. The first Christian Germanic tribes had known nothing but absolute tolerance. The Frankish Christians brought a compelled Christianity. This led to a change of the whole cultural disposition. The further development of European culture was significantly influenced by the development of this portion of the Germanic tribes.

A profound change in legal relations had gradually taken place. To a certain extent, peace and a sense of permanent settlement came at the end of the fifth century. Due to the continued influx of people from the east, larger communities were formed out of the previously mentioned peoples, who were constantly interacting with each other and of whom only a few had retained their original names—Chatti and Frisians and so on. The dissolution of the old blood ties had created another motive for togetherness. Blood was replaced by the bond linking the human being to the land he cultivates.

Tribal affiliation became synonymous with local affiliation. The village community came into being. The individual members of the community were no longer bound to each other by the consciousness of a community based on blood but by the sense of belonging to the land. This led to a transformation of property relationships.

Originally, everything was common property. Now the distinction between common property and private property begins to emerge. But, for the time being, everything that can be common property is indeed still common property: forest, pasture, water, and so on. Then an intermediate stage was formed between common and private property, the so-called *Hufe*.[†] The use of this half-private, half-common property was subject to the decisions of all the free inhabitants of a so-called *Hufe*, or commune. In those earlier times, almost all the inhabitants of the commune were free.

This contrasts sharply with actual private property: weapons, implements, garments, gardens, livestock, and so on—that is, everything that the individual had acquired personally. This restricted character was expressed in the fact that private property was closely connected with the person of the owner. Therefore, the dead person was given his weapons, horses, dogs, and so on, to take with him to the grave. An echo of this old usage continues today at the funeral of a prince when his medal, crown, and so on are carried after him, as well as his horse.

The old Germanic peoples share this custom in common with another people, the Chinese: one gives the dead those objects that belonged to them personally to take to the grave, although today people are content with paper models.

We see what had developed from certain conditions: a transition from the tribal community to the village community. From this example, we can understand further transformations. We understand why Tacitus does not speak of the Aesir, but of Tuisto and his son Mannus. He speaks of peoples who have not yet come to the stage of village community. The Aesir gods belong to a higher level of culture. Other peoples came from the north and brought with them ideas that had developed there. These were now suited to the higher level of culture reached in the meantime. How far does the human being go with ideas as they meet us in Tuisto, in Mannus? He remains with the human being; he does not go beyond himself. It would have been fruitless to introduce the worship of Wotan among these tribes. The worship of Wotan goes out into the universe; the human being seeks his origin in the lap of nature. Only at the later stage of culture could the human being rise to these religious ideas. He has become settled; therefore, he understands the connection with nature. We have seen how the primitive culture of the more southern Germanic peoples is influenced from the north and how high cultures had developed in the south among related peoples during the same time.

We will continue to examine the conditions under which the southern cultures then pour over the Germanic peoples. An interesting overview presents itself to us—a profound original kinship of the various peoples, an inner connection that determines their nature. We then see external influences that change the character. Thus, cause and effect appear before us.

From the past we can learn to understand the present. Eternal changeability dominates not only nature but also history. How could we look to the future with confidence if we did not know that the present also changes, that we can shape it how we see fit, that here too the poet's words are fulfilled:

> The old collapses, times change,
> And new life blossoms from the ruins.[†]

Lecture Three

BERLIN, NOVEMBER 1, 1904

We need only mention one of many indicative facts in order to see what sweeping changes took place in the fifth century. The Visigoths we find at the end of the fourth century east of the Danube; a century later, the map shows them in Spain. Just as this people moved from one end of Europe to the other, so too did many others. They moved to lands where they encountered other cultures and adopted other customs.

We must look back to the previous historical epoch to understand the change brought about in one hundred years in Central Europe. If we follow the reports of the Romans, we find warlike tribes along the Rhine whose main occupation, apart from fighting, is hunting. Further to the east, we find agriculture and animal husbandry among the Germanic tribes, and still further to the northeast, we find tribes living by the sea, whom the Romans describe as if they were something quite dark and misty.

It is said that this people worshipped the sun and that they believed that the sun goddess came out of the sea. Of the people who lived in these regions of the Margraviate of Brandenburg, the Semnones, it is said that their worship was characterized by its bloody sacrifices. It was not humans but animals who would have been offered to the gods, but the sacrificial service would have carried a cruel character that distinguished it from the other tribes. Still, many other things would have to be described from this time.

Then follows a relatively quiet period at first.

Gradually, the individual tribes crossed the borders of the Roman Empire. In the third century, the Burgundians were the first to advance against the Roman Empire in the southwest, and, further north, the Franks invaded Gaul. Further to the east, along the Danube, other Germanic peoples advanced against the empire. Thus, the Romans, with their highly developed culture, had to defend themselves against those peoples. We find here a great difference in cultural levels. Among the Germanic peoples, a barter economy still prevailed everywhere, while among the Romans, a developed monetary economy prevailed. Trade among the Germanic peoples was merely barter. Trade with money was not yet known. It is significant to note how in France—among whose population so much Celtic blood is found—a fully-developed monetary economy was introduced after the Roman conquest, but this was again displaced by the conquest of the Germanic tribes with a barter economy. We see the clash of highly developed culture with barbarian tribes.

Then the Huns break in. In 375 the first clash takes place, beginning with the Ostrogoths, who had their residence on the Black Sea, and the Heruli. They are pushed to the west, and the Visigoths are also forced to leave their homes. Where should they go but to the Roman Empire, which they overran to the Danube. The Roman Empire was already divided into an Eastern and Western Roman Empire, the former with Byzantium and the latter with Rome as its capital. The Eastern Roman ruler assigned residences to the Visigoths, which, however, they had to fight for in the battle of Adrianople. In those regions, Ulfila wrote his translation of the Bible. Soon, they had to continue their migration because Slavic peoples were pushing them further to the west. Under their king Alaric, they conquered Rome and founded the Visigothic empire in Spain in the fifth century.

The Ostrogoths followed them and also tried to establish residences in the territory of the Roman Empire. The Germanic tribe of the Vandals conquered Spain and then sailed to Africa, where they founded a Vandal kingdom in the area where Carthage had once stood. From there, they assailed Rome with raids. The whole character of this upheaval of peoples is that in all the parts that formed the new shape of Christian Rome, these Germanic peoples forced their way in. From this kind of conquest, new formations of a very peculiar nature emerged.

In the territory of the former Gaul, a powerful empire was formed—the Frankish Empire. For centuries it left its mark on the whole of Central Europe. It was here that what is usually called "Roman Christianity" was formed. Those other peoples who subjugated parts of the Roman Empire in rapid victory, the Goths and the Vandals, soon disappear completely from history. In the case of the Franks, we see a mighty empire expanding over Europe. What are the reasons for this?

To discover these reasons, we have to take a look at the way these tribes extended their empire. It happened in such a way that one to two thirds of the territory they invaded was distributed among the conquerors. The leaders received large tracts of land, which they now put to use for their own gain. The subjugated population, some of whom had become slaves or serfs, was used for work. This is what the Visigoths did in Spain and the Ostrogoths in Italy. You can imagine that under the already existing conditions, where the population lived on a higher cultural level, this practice found great difficulties and could not be maintained in the long run.

It was different in Gaul. There were large forests and uninhabited areas. Here, too, the conquered territories were distributed, and large portions fell to the leaders. Here, one was not forced into already existing conditions; there was the possibility of expansion. The leaders here became large landowners and rulers over the subjugated tribes, but the conditions made it possible that this happened without too much coercion. In the times before the migration of peoples, the members of a tribe had been essentially equal. Freedom was a common, Germanic good, and in a sense, each was his own master, responsible to no one, on his own land. This independence and power of the leaders was now extended because so many people had come to depend on them.

As a result, they were able to protect themselves better, and small owners placed themselves under the protection of the larger ones. This created a protective relationship of the powerful over the less powerful. The many small feuds led many small landowners, who could not defend themselves well enough, into a relationship of dependence on the more powerful. They pledged allegiance in case of war, and others ceded parts of their property or paid interest to the patron. Such dependents were called vassals. Others were given ownership of an estate by the large landowners for their service in times of war: a fief. The more powerful one became the feudal lord, the other the vassal. In the most natural way, certain property relations were formed.

The conquests of the Goths had no lasting effect. Those peoples who had pushed their way onto cultured soil came to nothing; their power was soon broken. It was different in Gaul. Here, where large areas were still to be cleared, the invasion of new masses of people could only be welcomed in the interest of culture. In the empire of the Franks, powerful individuals were unrestrained in the formation of the character of their folk.

The Goths, Vandals, and all the Germanic tribes that had come into already developed economic areas were wiped out. In the case of the Franks, we have independence from the economic substructure. The Franks imposed their character on the subsequent period—namely, also through the fact that the Christianity they had formed found fertile ground to spread freely as well. While the Visigoths were originally Arian Christians, other ideas were inculcated into their character. Under the economic preconditions foreign to the Visigoth's nature, there developed what can be regarded as the pressure of material conditions. It was not so with the Franks. It was within the Frankish tribes that the Church became a large landowner. Unperturbed by material conditions, these abbots, bishops, priests, and scholars could devote themselves to the service of religion. Purely as it arose from the essence of the feeling of these people did the peculiar culture of this Christianity take shape. The spiritual aspirations within the free Frankish peoples were promoted by the influx of the Celtic element. The Celts, whose fiery blood again broke through, became the teachers and leaders of the less spiritually vital Franks. From Scotland and Ireland, Celtic monks and priests came in great numbers to preach their faith in the Frankish Empire.

All this made it so that Christianity at that time was not a reflection of external conditions but could develop on free soil, unrestrained by material pressures. The conditions of Central Europe were determined by Christianity. All the knowledge of antiquity was thus preserved by Christianity for the Germanic peoples. Aristotle gave the spiritual core that Christianity sought to grasp. At that time, there was no dependence on Rome. Christian life could develop freely in the Frankish kingdom. Plato's world of ideas also found its way into this spiritual life. This happened especially through Scottish and Irish monks, above all through Scotus Eriugena in his work *On the Division of Nature*,[†] a work that marks a height of spiritual life. Thus, we see how spiritual life is shaped unperturbed by external circumstances. The spiritual currents take on their character precisely where they are independent of economic conditions. Later, when the material pressure expands, the spiritual currents retroactively take on the character of these conditions, but then the currents themselves flow into these conditions and influence them again.

Several small kingdoms formed the empire which we know as that of the Merovingians and which only later came under the power of one individual.

After what has been described to you, you will realize that the more southern Christianity must have been different from this Frankish Christianity with which it was later mixed. Frankish Christianity was relatively independent and could use political conditions in its favor. The more that Roman rule was pushed back, the larger became that part of the clergy which emerged from the Franks, whose education lagged far behind that of the other clergy; however, the learned priests and monks were all Celts.

Over the course of these centuries, the most diverse peoples were gradually mixed together. The invasion of the Huns had given rise to these changes. While within the actual cultural currents what has been described here was taking shape, great external struggles had taken place. But what we call the development of culture was not essentially touched by these external struggles.

The Huns had advanced far to the west. If we are not blind to what ancient sagas proclaim, we know: They had reached as far as southern France. In the old heroic poem that has been handed down in Latin, the Walthari song,[†] it is told how the nobility of the Germanic tribes, the Burgundians and Franks and so on, had to give hostages to the

Huns, including Walthari, the son of the prince of the Germanic tribe that ruled in Aquitaine. This heroic song tells of the deeds of Walther, Hagen, and Günther. The invasions of the Huns continued, disturbing the Germanic peoples far to the west, until at last, the Franks, Goths, and what was left of the Roman people formed a power that opposed the Huns in the Battle of the Catalaunian Plains in 451. This was the first blow to the rule of the Huns, a rule that weighed heavily on the peoples but did not leave a lasting impression.

The Huns were a people so foreign to the European peoples in customs and traditions that the whole nature and form of the Huns is described as something quite strange. The important thing was that this people formed a compact unit. A submissiveness to their king Attila, which increased to the point of idolatry, made them appear irresistibly frightening to the other peoples. After the Battle of the Catalaunian Plains, this power received its final, decisive blow through Leo the Great, the bishop of Rome, who confronted Attila and persuaded him to go back. Psychologically, this event is understandable. Leo knew the power that Attila exerted on his people. But Attila, with all his power, did not know what was confronting him—Christianity; therefore, he yielded to it.

The rule of the Huns thus remained an episode; what came from the west had much more lasting effect. After Attila's death in 453, the power of the Huns soon disintegrated again; the rule of the Goths, Gepids, Vandals, and so on was also impermanent. They found themselves enclosed in predetermined conditions and could not preserve their own character. In contrast, the culture of the Frankish Empire proves to be faithful to the character of the Frankish tribe, and we can see how this people develops powerfully. Later, however, we also see how this tribe forcibly compels others to accept Christianity. We also see that there is nothing more suitable for shaping material culture than Christianity; all kinds of cultural formations receive their character from external Christianity. Because these formations can freely preserve their character, they provide the framework for loose entities in which spiritual life can develop: thus, the spiritual economic communities arise in the monasteries and so on. In time, however, a disjointedness of spiritual and economic culture develops. Because of the fact that Charlemagne's empire makes itself a Christian empire but spreads Christianity by force, it puts itself in contradiction with the spirit of Christianity. Soon Christianity does not accord with economic life. The conditions of economic life are felt to be oppressive, so the free cities come into being.

This is the development of spiritual and material culture in broad strokes. The interrelationships are presented to you in their actual meaning. Only when the spiritual currents no longer coincided with the material conditions did this disproportion find its expression in the emergence of a purely material culture—the city culture. Out of material interest, these economic formations arose. The population, which could not endure in the countryside, pushed into the cities to find protection and security there, and we see the emergence of new economic formations that were to assume the most far-reaching significance. You see kingdoms coming into being and passing away and new structures taking the place of old ones. You also see that we can only understand the organism of these structures if we recognize how the first authoritative empire, the Frankish Empire, was formed. Without being forced into preexisting conditions, but rather developing where there was room for free expansion, the essence of this tribe developed and its rule was able take shape.

Not only thoroughly mixed together but newly formed were the tribes that had been driven from their homes by the great migration of peoples. Some had completely disappeared from history, and others took their place. The great transformation had taken place not only from the outside but much more in the deepest core of their character. We see at the beginning of the epoch of the migration of peoples the different Germanic peoples asking the question of their destiny. For the Goths, who had chosen a tolerant Christianity, this question meant annihilation. For the Franks, who were confronted with this question under different, freer, more favorable conditions, it meant the development of power for centuries to come. Was this development for the good of the whole? We will see in due course.

Lecture Four

BERLIN, NOVEMBER 8, 1904

It is a common preconception that human development proceeds in a regular, successive course and that the unfolding of historical events never makes any leaps. Gradual and successive progress is development. This is connected with another preconception—namely, that nature makes no leaps. This is said again and again, but it is incorrect for nature as well as for history. Nowhere in nature do we see things making progress without leaps, especially when it is a matter of enormous progress. Nature's course is not gradual; rather, from small processes important results arise, and the most important things happen by leaps. One could enumerate many cases in which nature progresses in such a way that we can observe a transition of its forms into their opposite.

In history, this is particularly important because we have two such events of significance that first prepare themselves gradually, then subside, but nevertheless signify a leap forward: first, the founding of the free cities at the beginning of the Middle Ages, and second, the great inventions and discoveries at the end of the Middle Ages. History advances more rapidly at the turn of the eleventh and twelfth centuries. New forms of society develop from the old and from the fact that many people leave their homes and settle in the cities. Such cities with new living conditions, orders, rights, and constitutions emerge throughout Germany, France, England, Scotland, and on into Russia, and Italy. Then, at the end of the Middle Ages, we find the great discoveries: the sea voyages to India, America, and so on and the globally significant invention of the printing press. All this shows us what radical change is brought about by the burgeoning of the new scientific spirit through Copernicus.† Thus, two decisive points are given. If one wants to look meaningfully at the Middle Ages, these two events must be placed in the proper light. One could say that everything points to these great events. They look like leaps, but such events prepare themselves slowly and then burst forth with the force of an avalance. If we follow them further, it will gradually become apparent how these two events prepared themselves in the life of the Germanic peoples. We shall see through what circumstances the Frankish people were granted that power, that influence over the shaping of European conditions. For this, we must understand the character of this people, the necessary transformation of social relationships and the powerful impact of Christianity in the fourth century. These two things signify a change in the life of the Germanic peoples. They condition the development of the Middle Ages. It would be useless to follow all these migrations of the Germanic peoples—to see how Odoacer dethroned the last Western Roman emperor, how the Goths were driven out of Italy by Emperor Justinian, how the Lombards took possession of northern Italy—for we always see the same relationships unfolding.

In southern regions, where the Germanic peoples find firmly established political and economic conditions, the peculiarities of these peoples have disappeared. They have lost all significance. We no longer hear of Goths, Gepids, and so on. They have disappeared except in name. In contrast to this, the Franks had arrived in not-yet-consolidated, free conditions where there was no other serious claim to landownership. Through this political configuration, the Franks became the influential people.

Now we have to see how in this Frankish kingdom the entity developed that we call the Merovingian kingdom. It was nothing other than the many small kingdoms that formed in the most natural way. The Merovingians remained as victors, having overcome the others originally equal to them. All these kingdoms had formed in the following way: some small tribe migrated, subjugated the inhabitants, and distributed the land so that all members received smaller and larger free estates. Thus, all such territories were founded on landownership. The most powerful received the largest territory. For the cultivation of the land, a large number of people were needed; these were taken from the population, and, to an extent, prisoners of war were also made to work. The power relations were formed only through this difference between the smaller and larger landowners. The greatest landowner was the king. His power was based on landownership; that is the characteristic. The legal relations developed from these power relations, and it is interesting to observe how the legal relations develop on this basis. However, we find among the old Germanic tribes their customary rights that had developed in earlier times into which we no longer have any insight. In the case of the smaller tribes, all the people gathered to pronounce justice; later, the tribesmen met only on the first of March to deliberate on their affairs. Now, however, the large landowner was unaccountable to the others for what he did on his territory. True, we find a conservative adherence to the old legal customs among the various tribes. We find them preserved for a long time especially among the Saxons, Thuringians, Frisians, and among the Cherusci (whose tribe survived longer than is generally believed). It was different where large estates developed, because the owner, being unrestricted in his territory, also became unaccountable. He had the power to exercise jurisdiction, police power. From unaccountability, a new legal status developed. If another committed an offense, he was held responsible. If the unaccountable individual did it, the same offense was considered a right. What was wrong for those who lacked power was right for the powerful. They had the possibility of transforming might into right.

Now consider that in this way, especially in the northwest, the Franks were able to further expand their power and conquer large areas. At a time when there was always war, the less powerful were dependent on the protection of the powerful. There arose the feudal and vassal system, which produced a selection of the most powerful. There arose the way of transferring certain rights through treaties. The large estates, including the royal estate, acquired special legal relations that could be transferred by the king or the owner to others. Jurisdiction and police power were transferred together with the land. The royal right and the right of the small vassals were created. As a result of such a transfer, we see a powerful officialdom developing, not on the basis of salary but on the basis of landownership. Such lords of the court were supreme judges. In the beginning, they still had to consider the rights of powerful tribes, and they were obliged to respect ancient rights. But gradually this relationship became an absolute magistracy, so that subsequently in the Frankish Empire a kind of official nobility was formed alongside the kingship. The nobility grew to be the rival of the kingship. First it was dependent, and then it became a powerful rival. Already in the sixth century, the rivalry between the royalty and the official nobility developed more and more strongly in the Frankish Empire, and the Empire attained the greatest importance.

The original ruling dynasty that emerged from the great landowners, the Merovingians, is replaced by the Carolingians, who originally belonged to the official nobility. They formed the mayor of the palace, the majordomo, of the first ruling dynasty, which was overthrown by the rivalry of the official nobility. In essence, it was large-scale landownership that established the balance of power here, and the most powerful moral current, the Church, had to initiate its rule through this detour of large-scale landownership.

The characteristic feature of the Frankish Church is that at first it is nothing but a number of large estates. We see bishoprics and abbeys emerging, and vassals who would otherwise be under the protection of large landowners but now come under the protection of the Church in order to receive fiefs from it. Thus, alongside the secular landowners, spiritual landowners were formed. This is why we perceive so little depth and so little science, and why what we find there in Christianity in terms of spirituality is essentially the result of foreign influences. Not within the Frankish people but through members of the Anglo-Saxon and especially the Celtic peoples of the British Isles do we find success in creating that mighty stream which then poured eastward. In the British Isles, eminent scholars who were pious monks worked in earnest on this deepening. Here real work has been done, as we see in detail in the revival of Platonism and its union with Christianity. We see mysticism, dogmatism, but also enthusiasm and inspirited feelings emanating from this region. From here come the first converts: Columbanus, Gall, and Boniface,† the converters of the Germans. These first missionaries, because they had nothing but the spirituality of Christianity in mind, are not inclined to adapt to the conditions of the Frankish tribe. They are the driving force and have their main influence among the eastern Germanic tribes, especially Boniface. Therefore, in the Frankish Empire at this time a growing influence from Rome is taking hold. Now we have to see what formerly had a determining effect. Here we have two heterogeneous elements that adapt themselves to each other: the rough strength of the Germanic peoples and the spiritual teachings of Christianity. It seems wonderful how these tribes adapt themselves to Christianity and how Christianity transforms itself in order to adapt to the nature of the Germanic peoples. These emissaries work differently than the later Frankish kings who spread Christianity by force of arms. It is not forced into their souls as something foreign: places of worship, sacred customs, and persons are preserved so that old institutions are used to pour forth the new content. It is interesting how the old becomes the clothing, while the new becomes the soul. We have from that time, from the Saxon tribe, an account of the life of Jesus: they took the form of Jesus, but all the details were attired in Germanic fashion. Jesus appears as a Germanic prince, and the intercourse with the disciples resembles a tribal gathering. This is how the life of Jesus is depicted in *Heliand*.[†]

Ancient heroes are transformed into saints. Festivals and cultic customs become Christian. Much of what people today consider to be the sole property of Christianity was imported at that time from pagan customs. In the Frankish Empire, on the other hand, we must see that the Franks saw in Christianity nothing more than a means of fortifying their power relations. A Frankish law book[†] begins with an appeal to Christ, who loves the Franks above all other peoples.

These are the ways in which these two world-historical currents grow into each other. During the period when the British missionaries represent the moral influence of Christianity, the influence of the Roman Church increases significantly. Based on what had been prepared here, the Frankish kings sought affiliation with the papacy. The Lombards occupied Italy and unsettled the bishop of Rome. They were Arian Christians. This caused the Roman bishop to turn to the Franks for help, but at the same time, he offered his influence to the Franks. Thus, the Frankish king became the protector of the pope, and the pope anointed the king. Hence the Frankish kings derived their special position, the special splendor of their dignity, from this sanctification by the pope. This was a reinforcement of what the Franks had seen in Christianity. All this took place essentially in the seventh century. Through this alliance between the papacy and the rule of the Franks, the later coronation of Charlemagne was slowly being prepared. So, we see powerful social and spiritual changes taking place. But this alone would not have led to that event which I called one of the most important, a material revolution—the founding of cities. For something was lacking in the Frankish-Christian culture, although efficiency, spirit, and depth were there.

Not present was what one calls science, purely external science. We followed only a material and a moral movement. That which was present in science had come to a standstill and remained at the level at which it stood at the time of the first contact with Christianity. Just as the Frankish peoples had no interest in improving their simple agriculture and did not think of developing it scientifically, so the Church sought only to extend its moral influence. Primitive agriculture did not offer any special difficulties that would have led to the development of physics, geometry, and technology, as in Egypt. Everything here was simpler, more primitive—just as the already existing monetary economy had been replaced again by a barter economy.

Thus, European culture needed a new infusion, and one does not understand it if one does not appreciate this infusion. From the East, from whence Christianity once came, from Asia, this new culture arrived through the Arabs. The religion that was founded there by Mohammed is simpler in its religious content than Christianity. The inner content of Mohammedanism is essentially based on simple monotheistic ideas that are limited to a basic divine being whose nature and form one does not particularly investigate or fathom but to whose will one surrenders faithfully. Therefore, this religion is made to call forth a tremendous trust in this will, which leads to fatalism and a willingness to surrender. Therefore, it was possible that in a few human lifespans, these tribes extended the Arab rule over Syria,

Mesopotamia, North Africa, and up into the empire of the Visigoths in Spain. Already at the turn of the seventh to the eighth century, the Moors spread their rule there and put their own culture in place of that of the Visigoths.

Thus, something completely new and different is flowing into European culture. In the spiritual, religious field, this Arab culture has only a simple content, which established certain powers in the soul; however, it did not acquire many ideas and did not particularly engage the spirit. This spirit was not filled with thinking about dogmas, about angels and demons and so on. The spirit was not filled with that but with what the Christian-Germanic tribes lacked at that time—external scientific interest. We find here all the sciences, such as medicine, chemistry, and mathematics, being advanced. The practical spirit, which had been brought to Spain from Asia, now found activity in sea voyages and so on. It was brought over in a time when a science-less spirit had founded its empire. The Moorish cities became places of serious scientific work. We see there a culture that can only be admired by those who know of it, of which Humboldt[†] said: "This breadth, this intensity, this sharpness of knowledge is without precedent in cultural history." These Moorish scholars are full of vision and profundity, and they not only adopted Greek science, as the Germanic peoples did, but modelled it. Aristotle also lived on among the Germans, but among the Arabs, the true Aristotle as the father of science was revered with great vision. It is interesting to see how that which was modelled in Greece, the Alexandrian culture, lived on there. Thus, we have touched on one of the most peculiar and remarkable currents in human intellectual life. The Arabs provided the foundations for objective science. This first flowed from there into the Anglo-Saxon monasteries in England and Ireland, where the old energetic Celtic blood lived. It was curious to see what a lively intercourse was initiated between them and Spain, and how there, where profundity and the ability to think existed, science was revived through the mediation of the Arabs.

It is a strange phenomenon when we see further that the Arabs, who at the beginning took possession of the whole of Spain, were soon outwardly defeated in the battle of Poitiers in 732 by the Franks under Charles Martell. But the spiritual power of the Arabs remains invincible, and just as Greek education once conquered Rome, so Arab education conquered the West, confronting the victorious Germanic tribes. When science that is needed to expand the field of vision for trade and world business comes into being and urban culture develops, we see how Arab influences assert themselves here and completely new elements flow in and try to adapt themselves to the old ones.

Walther von der Vogelweide† shows that someone who followed these conflicting currents in the Middle Ages with an open mind could become confused. The poet saw how the Germanic peoples strove for external power, and he saw an opposing current emanating from Christianity. I would ask you to note that Christianity only later took on the form which then attached to it. In Walther von der Vogelweide, we see transformed into sentiment what flowed through the Middle Ages, in the wistful description:

> I sat one day alone
> Cross-legged upon a stone,
> With elbow resting on my knee,
> And chin and cheek reflectively
> Supported in my hand,
> And tried to understand
> Why we are called on earth to live.
> And little comfort could I give
> How three things we should cherish
> So that not one might perish:
> Honor and worldly wealth are two,
> Harm oft from each to other grew;
> The third is Heaven's grace,
> Which takes the foremost place.
> In one shrine would I set the three.
> Alas! it nevermore may be
> That honor and wealth shall dwell,
> With Heaven's grace as well,
> Together in one heart again;
> All roads and paths from them are ta'en;
> Falsehood in ambush lurks;

Violence vaunts its works;
Justice and peace are wounded sore;
If these two be not quickly healed,
the three will never prosper more![†]

Let us then see how difficult it became for the people of the Middle Ages to unite these three things in their hearts and how they caused the great battles that tore the Middle Ages apart.

Lecture Five

BERLIN, NOVEMBER 15, 1904

If you pick up any of the usual textbooks or any of the other common representations of the period of the Middle Ages we are now going to discuss—the eighth or ninth century—the personality of Charlemagne will occupy an extraordinary amount of space. You will understand little of what actually constitutes the significance of this age if you follow these conquests and deeds of Charlemagne in this way. All this was only an outward expression of much deeper events in the Middle Ages that present themselves as the interplay of many significant factors. If we want to look at these, we must touch upon things we have already discussed in order to shed light on them.

If you remember the description of European conditions immediately after the migration of peoples, when the Germanic peoples settled here and there, you will have to think of the fact that these peoples had brought their old institutions, customs, and traditions to their new homes and there continued to develop them. In doing so, we see that they preserved a peculiarity: a kind of social order consisting of the distribution of private and common property. They originally lived in small social associations, village communities, and then later formed *Hundertschaften* (communities of one hundred) or districts. In all of them, there was common property in everything that lent itself to being common property: forest, meadow, water, and so on. Only what a single individual could cultivate, the individual plot of land, the *Hufe*, was assigned to the private family and became hereditary. Everything else remained common property.

Now, we have seen how the leaders of such tribes were assigned larger territories during the conquest and how certain power dynamics arose as a result, especially in Gaul where much land was still unclaimed. For the cultivation of these lands, partly the members of the former population and partly the Roman colonists or prisoners of war were used. As a result, certain legal relationships developed. The large landowner was unaccountable for what he did within his property. He could not be held responsible for what he decreed. Therefore, he could enact legislation and police measures for his property. We do not meet a unified kingship in the Frankish realm; what is called the Merovingian Kingdom was nothing other than such a large estate. The Merovingians were one of the large landowning families. Originating from private-law relationships, their dominion extended further and further through the struggle for existence. More and more new territories were included. The large landowner was not a king in the sense in which this has been understood since the thirteenth and fourteenth and even the sixteenth century, but private relationships of power were transformed into legal relationships.

He transferred certain parts of his territory to others, less fortunate—because he could not cultivate everything himself—and with them his rights. This was called "under immunity"—that judicial power that had grown out of unaccountability in such circumstances. In return, the person concerned had to pay taxes and follow the king into war. In such an expansion of property relations, the Merovingian dynasty emerged as the victor over others. We must adhere to the formula: the old Frankish Empire emerged from purely private relationships of power.

Again, the transition from the Merovingian to the Carolingian dynasty, from which Charles Martell came, happened in the same way, out of the same circumstances. The Carolingians had originally been administrators of the domains of the Merovingians but had gradually become so influential that Pippin the Short succeeded in putting the foolish Childeric into a monastery and deposing him with the help of the Pope. From him came his successor, Charlemagne. In this brief account, we can only touch upon the external events, for they have in any case no particular significance. Charlemagne warred against the surrounding German tribes and extended certain dominions. One cannot yet call this empire a state. He waged long battles against the

Saxons, who held on to the old village constitution, the old customs, and the old Germanic faith with great tenacity. The conquest took place after protracted wars that were waged with extraordinary cruelty on both sides.

With such tribes as the Saxons, a certain personality stood out in particular, and he then became a leader. This time, it was a leader with large properties and a strong army, Widukind, whose bravery offered the fiercest resistance.[†] He was overcome with the greatest cruelty and had to submit to the rule of Charlemagne. What does such rule mean? It means the following: If Charlemagne had left, nothing special would have happened. Such tribes, which had to be baptized by the thousands, would have continued to live in the same way as before. The means of establishing a relationship of power here was the form that Charlemagne gave to the Church. By means of the power of the Church, these territories were subjugated. Bishoprics and monasteries were founded and were granted large estates previously owned by the Saxons. The bishops and abbots took care of the cultivation; in this manner, the Church took over what otherwise had been secular rights protected by immunity. The Church thereby became a judicial power. If the Saxons did not comply, they were forced to by new incursions of Charlemagne. The same thing happened as in the western Frankish Empire: the smaller landowners could not maintain control as individuals; therefore, they gave what they had to the monasteries and bishoprics to receive it again as a fief.

The one relationship is thus that large land holdings belonged directly to the Church, as with the newly founded bishoprics of Paderborn, Merseburg, and Erfurt, which were cultivated for the bishops by their subjects. Those who still had land holdings of their own took them in fief and had to give ever greater dues to the dioceses and abbeys concerned. This is how the rule of Charlemagne was established here, and a balance of power was established with the help of the great influence attained by the Church, of which he was the overlord.

Charlemagne extended his power to other areas. In Bavaria, he succeeded in breaking the power of Duke Tassilo, putting him in a monastery and thus including Bavaria in his dominion. The Bavarians had allied themselves with the Avars, a people that can be described as descendants of the Huns. Charles remained victorious in this struggle and fortified a strip of land as a frontier border against the Avars—the Avar March, the original land of today's Austria. In the same way, he also created a frontier against the Danes.

Against the Lombards, who were troubling the Pope, he fought in Italy like Pippin had. He remained victorious and once again established a dominion there. He also tried against the Moors in Spain. Almost everywhere he remained victorious. We see the Franconian rule being established over the European world of that time, which we cannot call a state. It merely contained the germs of future state power.

In such newly acquired areas, counts were also appointed who exercised judicial power. In areas where Charlemagne held his court in alternation, the large landholders known as the counts palatine† held court in secured castles called *Kaiserpfalzen*,† and they received certain levies from the surrounding territories. However, proceeds not only from land but also from judicial power fell to them. If someone had been murdered, the *Gau-* or *Pfalzgrafen* (the regional count or count palatine), invoked a public court. A relative or someone closely related to the murdered person brought the case to court. At that time, a certain *Wehrgeld* (blood money)† could be paid for murder, which was different for free and unfree men. Part of this sum was paid to the family of the murdered person, part to the *Gau-* or *Pfalzgrafen*, and part to the royal central treasury. For supervision and common affairs (those related to taxes and defense), landgraves (counts who had jurisdiction over a territory) who traveled from one country to another were employed as ambassadors without particular functions.

Under these circumstances, what could be called the contrast between the new landed nobility and the serfs arose. This includes those freemen who were still personally free but who had become heavily dependent because they had to pay large tax sums and serve in the army. These conditions became more and more acute. Secular and ecclesiastical holdings expanded more and more, and soon, in the tenth, eleventh, and twelfth centuries, we see how the people are heavily dependent. We already encounter smaller uprisings and revolts as a foreshadowing of what we know as peasant wars. In the process, material culture developed greater and greater productivity.

Before the migration of the peoples, many Germanic tribes had not yet practiced agriculture but had earned their livelihood through cattle breeding. Now they developed more and more in the area of agriculture. Mainly oats and barley were cultivated, but also wheat, flax, and more. This is the main thing that had given meaning to the older culture. Actual handicrafts did not exist at that time; they developed only under the surface. Weaving, dyeing, and so on were mostly done in the house by women. Blacksmithing and goldsmithing were the first crafts to emerge. Trade was even more insignificant.

Actual cities developed from the tenth century onwards. A historical event is thereby prepared; however, what started from these cities—trade—had no importance at that time. At most, Jewish merchants traded valuables with the East. Trade practices were almost non-existent, although Charlemagne had coins minted. Almost everything was traded in barter, in which cattle, wares, and such things were exchanged.

This is how we must imagine the material culture of those regions, and now we will understand why the spiritual culture also had to take on a very specific character. All that we imagine as spiritual culture did not exist in these regions, neither among the free nor among the bonded. Hunting, warfare, and agriculture were the occupations of the landowners. A symptom of this is that not just the peasants but also landowners—princes, dukes, kings, even poets (if they were not clerics)—could rarely read and write. Wolfram von Eschenbach[†] had to dictate his poetry to a cleric and have it read to him, and Hartmann von Aue[†] boasts that he could read books as a special talent. With all those who took care of worldly affairs, there was no chance of their being able to read and write.

Only in the innermost sanctuaries of the monasteries was the cultivation of science and art pursued. All others were dependent on what was offered to them by the instruction and preaching of the clergy. This conditioned their dependence on clergy and monks; it meant the sovereignty of the Church.

When today we find what is described as the "Dark Ages," the persecutions of heretics, witch trials, and the like, we must be clear that we are dealing with conditions that begin only in the thirteenth century. In earlier times such things did not exist. The Church did not exercise any rulership other than that over the large secular estates. Either the Church went hand in hand with the secular rule, was only a member of it, or it endeavored to use it to educate people in Christian knowledge and theology.

Until the stream of the spiritual influence of the Arabs came, everything spiritual was cultivated only in the monasteries. What the monks did in there was something that was completely unknown in the world outside. Outside, all that was known was preaching and a kind of spiritual instruction that took place in primitive schools.

The rule of the Church was also promoted by the fact that the clergy themselves carried out all the tasks that required knowledge. The monks were the master builders, they decorated the churches with pictorial works, and they copied the works of the classics in elaborate writing. Even the higher officials, the chancellors of the emperors, were for the most part monks.

Now let us examine what happened in the monasteries. One form of education that was cultivated there in the monasteries was Scholasticism, and a later one was mysticism. This Scholasticism, which flourished until the middle of the fourteenth century, accomplished something tremendous. It was able to produce a strictly-trained thinking, at least in one class. This is the great difference from what came later. There were hard tests to pass. No one could get ahead without hard tests in the absolutely logical training of thinking. Only he who could really think logically could participate in the spiritual life. This is not respected today. In fact, it was this logical-consequential thinking which, when the Moorish Arabic culture came to Europe, allowed this science to encounter trained thinking. The forms of thinking with which science works today are found in Scholasticism. There are very few forms of ideas that do not originate from Scholasticism.

The terms with which the sciences of today still operate, in fields like chemistry, medicine, and philosophy—key concepts like subject and object—were established then. A training of thinking, to a degree not otherwise found in world history, was practiced there. Today's sharp thinkers owe what in this era flows in the channels of their minds to this training of thinking, which was cultivated between the fifth and fourteenth centuries in Scholasticism. Now someone may consider it unjust that the great masses of ordinary people at that time had nothing of all this; however, the course of world history does not go according to justice and injustice but follows the great law of cause and effect. Thus, we see two currents running strictly side by side here: first, the external material culture with its utter absence of any sort of scientific approach and, second, a finely sculpted culture among a few within the Church. Yet the city culture was based on this strictly scholastic way of thinking. The men who brought about the great turnaround came from it: Copernicus was a canon, and Giordano Bruno was a Dominican monk,† among other examples. Their education and that of many others, their formal training, was rooted in this spirit of the Church. It was not powerful people, not bishops and rich abbots but simple monks who propagated science, poor monks who lived at that time and who often felt the pressure of the powerful.

As the Church allied itself with external powers, it had to materialize; it had to resort to making its doctrine and whole being more worldly. In the oldest times up to the twelfth century, there was nothing more sublime, more solemn for the Christian than Communion. It was supposed to be a grateful memorial sacrifice, a symbol of the internalization of Christianity. Then came a turn toward the worldly and with it came the development of a lack of understanding of such high, spiritual facts, especially of the festivals. In the nineth century, in the land of the Franks, at the court of Charles the Bald,† lived a very important Christian monk from Ireland, Scotus Eriugena, in whose book *On the Division of Nature*† we find a wealth of spirit and profundity, though admittedly not of what the twentieth century understands as science. He had to fight against a hostile direction in the Church. He defended the old doctrine that Communion was the symbol of the supreme sacrifice. Another, material conception existed and was protected by Rome—that bread and wine were actually transformed into flesh and blood. Under the influence of the ongoing materialization, the present Communion dogma emerged, but it became official only in the thirteenth century.

Scotus had to flee to England and was murdered in his own monastery by his fraternal monks at the instigation of the Pope. These are struggles that take place not within the Church but through the intrusion of secular influence. You see, spiritual life was limited to a few and remained unrevealed to the great masses which came under ever-increasing pressure from secular and clerical landowners. Under these circumstances, discontent grew greater and greater. It was unavoidable that discontent would accumulate in the people who were dependent on two sides. Out in the countryside, on the farms, new causes of discontent kept arising. It is little wonder that the small towns, which already existed on the Rhine and the Danube, grew larger and larger, and new ones were formed by the exodus of those who could no longer stand it in the countryside. The reason for the transformation of such conditions was the outflow of a population thirsting for freedom.

It was a purely material cause from which urban culture arose. The spiritual culture remained untouched for the time being. Many cities also developed around the bishoprics and monasteries. From the urban culture arose everything that established trade and commerce in the Middle Ages and later brought about completely different conditions. The need for a direct realization of the human personality gave rise to the founding of cities. This was a mighty step on the way to freedom, just as, according to Hegel, history is nothing other than the education of humanity to freedom.[†]

If we continue to follow the history of the Middle Ages, we will see that this founding of urban culture is not a small but a great step forward on this path.

Lecture Six

BERLIN, DECEMBER 6, 1904

The history of the Middle Ages is extraordinarily important to consider because we are dealing with a period which we can already research better, in which we can trace human development from its simple origins up to the emergence of what we call nation-states. In addition, we have here an interweaving of the most manifold factors. Under simple conditions, a complete cultural structure establishes itself: Christianity. From a state of barbarism, we increasingly see the growth of what appears as the flowering of the Middle Ages, what we know of as inventions.

Among these peoples, who were intermixed through the migration of peoples, we see emerging by way of a complicated detour that which is today called "science." The Middle Ages had a great inheritance. Of what we have come to know as Greek culture, nothing remained but some traditions going back to Plato, as seen through the lens of Christian theology. On the other hand, a powerful inheritance from the time of the Roman Empire had remained: the mighty structure of a state with its administration and judicial system in a uniformity and comprehensiveness such as had never before appeared in the history of the world and such as we do not find in the entire Middle Ages. Only in the modern age, which otherwise imagines itself to possess so much freedom, do we encounter such an extension of state power. This, combined with that other idealistic cultural movement that had gradually permeated and absorbed the Roman Empire, came to peoples who had nothing of any similar education and were in addition uprooted by the migration of peoples. All these tribes of peoples—Goths, Heruli, Lombards, Franks, Saxons, and so on—were something completely different. They had completely remained in the infancy stage of political development compared to the Romans. They led a kind of natural life, limited to hunting and warfare, without fixed law and order. A great transition now took place in the conditions and views of these peoples who lived together in small associations.

What held these individual tribes together? It was the memory of some ancestor who had given the name to the tribe and the memory of powerful families who had distinguished themselves in ancient battles or in the conquest of the new land and had supplied the tribe with what are called counts, princes, and dukes.

This transition is now expressed in the fact that people love common ground. They begin to place more value on the commonality of landownership than on consanguinity—relationships of blood.

Tribal affiliation is replaced by what we call village community. The entire material life is based on the land. Trade and commerce do not yet exist, and what these people need by way of goods is produced by women, young people, and slaves. The largest part of the population did not know anything other than agriculture and frequent wars. They had no idea of what we call culture today, no idea of what we consider the first requirement of it—reading and writing. Charlemagne is credited with the fact that he made an effort to learn to read and write in his old age. All that had been available in the way of education was in the possession of the Roman population in the areas that had been conquered. From them came the civil service, hence the influence of Roman legal ideas. This was the case in the western regions; it was different in the east. There, in the present German territories, the original Germanic nature had kept itself free from these influences. The unbroken strength of the Thuringian and Saxon tribes was something of significance for all of the Middle Ages.

The only thing that brought education here was Christianity. But actual science, such as mathematics, natural science, and so on, was not included in this education. Christianity brought moral and religious education. The merit of Christianity was that it added moral and ethical concepts. Especially within the most privileged Franconian tribe, the influence of the clergy, especially of the visiting, learned Celtic monks, was very great. With this tribe, which was led by the favor of circumstance to become a free country where it could live out its peculiarity in still largely uncultivated areas, we see best how this transformation takes place. The transformation from smaller to larger communities occurred here. Counts and princes conquered ever new territories, and enfeoffed[†] small owners with parts of their property. As a result, the power of the large landowners spread more and more. A kind of jurisdiction and constitution arose from the transfer of originally purely private legal relationships. What originally drove the Irish and Scottish monks was the holy zeal of faith, the thought of working for the salvation of humankind. All this changed. The ideology of the Franks could only understand Christianity as a means of power.

Charlemagne in particular used the Church to expand his territory. Any bishop he appointed was mostly destined to be an instrument of his rule. In the beginning, the Church was led only by zeal of faith, by real conviction. Later, under the influence of external force, it sought to gain a relationship of political power for itself. Thus, the bishop was first a serving member of the Church but later became a ruler and landowner. This is how the Middle Ages appear to us at the time of Charlemagne, but we must not speak of Charlemagne's empire as we speak of empires today. The possession of vast estates creates the opportunity to transfer landownership to others. New territories were conquered and resulted in new opportunities to increase a ruler's power through further transfers. This is how counts as court officials came into being. Manorial courts with imperial counts, or if appointed by bishops, administrators called *Vögten* (stewards), take the place of the old *Gaugericht*.[†]

Here and there we still have independent tribes that held on to their old rulers and their self-chosen courts.

Such was the situation at the death of Charlemagne, and it remained so under his son Louis the Pious. We see the following from his relationship with his three sons Lothar, Pippin, and Louis: He divides his kingdom among them as if it were a private possession. And when he fathers another son from a second marriage and makes another division, his elder sons rise up against him, defeat him in the battle of Lügenfeld, and force him to renounce the throne so as not to allow their property to be diminished. By this example, we can clearly see what the nature of the state at that time was all about. We also see what a false picture is given by what is usually told in history about that time. The battles that took place at that time were purely private disputes, and the actual masses of ordinary people were indeed disturbed and troubled by the maneuvers of armies during such campaigns. However, for the progress of humankind, all these battles in the post-Carolingian period have no real significance.

But what was of real importance was the contrast that had developed between the Frankish Empire and the empire that encompassed Germany and Austria. In the Western Empire, a struggle had gradually arisen between the secular nobility and the ruling ecclesiastical power. The educated clergy supplied what had formerly been taken from the remnants of the Roman population: the higher court officials, the clerks in the courts, and so on. They all possessed a completely uniform education, which came out of the monasteries. Beside this educated clergy, there was a large uneducated mass which was completely dependent on the educated clergy. The entirety of education of that time emerged from what was taught in the monastic schools. Christian theology comprised seven sciences—three lower and four higher.[†]

Out in the countryside, we see a people only engaged in war and agriculture; in churches, schools, and among officialdom lives that which comes from the monastic schools. Here in the clerical schools, these sciences are taught. The three lower ones were: Grammar, Logic, and Dialectic. Grammar was the doctrine of language. Logic, the doctrine of thought, was preserved in the same form as in ancient Greece in the monasteries of the Middle Ages until the nineteenth century, while today it is considered superfluous. Logic was then followed by Dialectic, which has completely disappeared from the stock of today's science. Medieval education rested in dialectics, which had to be learned and mastered by everyone who wanted to achieve something in the intellectual life. Dialectics is the art of defending a truth against attacks in a proper way. The laws of reason must be known in order to be able to do this. It was not possible to work with fake reasons in defending a truth permanently; it was not the time of newspapers where reasons of today are valid only until tomorrow.

From dialectics comes what one can call scientific and learned conscience, and everyone who wants to participate in science should have it. Not everything and anything can be defended in a rational way; therein lay the great importance of this training, to discern conscientiously here. Later this gradually degenerated so that in the later Middle Ages, for example, someone could offer to defend any random statement for twenty-four hours against the attacks of all the professors, students, and laymen of Paris.

Trained by dialectics, those who came to the judicial profession were not so much the chairmen of the courts as those who issued the judgments.

When Goethe has his protagonist say in the beginning of *Faust*: "Indeed, I am cleverer than all the monks, doctors, magisters, clerks, and priests,"[†] he thereby indicates the dignities and offices to which one attained at that time through a scientific education. "Doctor" was the one who could use his knowledge independently. Magister was the one allowed to teach at the universities. Clerks were all those who were employed in secular service, whether in a higher or lower position. Priests were all clergymen. The word priest (*Pfaffe*) in those times was not yet a swear word but a title of honor. Thus, in the fourteenth century, Meister Eckhart calls Plato the great Greek priest.

The four higher sciences were geometry, arithmetic, astronomy, and music.

Geometry is the theory of space, of dimension. Arithmetic is higher calculation. Astronomy corresponded approximately to what we understand by it today. Music, however, was not the same as what we call by that name. Music was the science of the harmony of the universe. People believed that the entire universe stood in harmonious relationships with its individual components. People tried to find all these relationships, which were expressed by numbers, because, in fact, colors, tones, and so on are based on certain numbers. In music, the laws of harmony, the rhythmic relationships, were sought everywhere; the harmony of the laws of the world was taught.

I have tried to give you an idea of what the ruling class was doing by means of education. This education gained more and more the upper hand in the Western Empire, which we now call France. It was different in Germany. These tribes had remained unbroken. They had preserved their simple customs and their freedom, for the most part. The dark side of these primitive conditions, however, was that here the clergy was uneducated; therefore, the clergy allowed itself to be used as a means of power in the hands of the dukes and emperors.

The rule of the Western Empire remained with the Carolingians. But the rulers from this house became more and more inferior. At last, the incompetence of these Carolingian rulers became especially evident when warlike pirates, the Normans, troubled the country from the north. These Normans invaded the country from the mouths of rivers, the Elbe and the Weser, plundering the coasts everywhere, especially in France where they occupied the northern regions and penetrated as far as Paris. At that time, Charles III[†] reigned, and he was completely incapable of doing anything against these people. Therefore, it was easy for an unknown duke in Austria, Arnulf of Carinthia,[†] to put an end to the Carolingian rule and to seize power. At first, he enjoyed great prestige since he succeeded in defeating the Normans. But the jealousy among the nobility was so great that Arnulf was compelled to turn to the Church and make a covenant with it. He was required to make a pilgrimage to Italy and in general submit to Church rule in many ways. The consequence is then that we see how the Church uses its power after his death. Instead of a secular prince or count, the archbishop Hatto of Mainz becomes the guardian of his son, Louis the Child. Thus, an archbishop, acting as regent, assumes all the rights of a secular ruler. From then on, we see the foundation laid for the rule of the Church, which is no longer merely exploited by secular rulers but inserts itself more and more into secular rule and exercises secular jurisdiction. In consequence, the struggle between secular and ecclesiastical power dawned, and that important period of history began—the struggle between emperors and popes.

It is wrong when conventional history describes these two powers as completely different from each other. They are only rivals in the struggle for external power. They are equal powers working in the same direction. We are not dealing with a struggle between spiritual and secular power but with a struggle of the secularized Church with secular power. We see two directions of power spreading, and, as a third, we see the "free cities" emerging and spreading all over Europe.

Lecture Seven

BERLIN, DECEMBER 13, 1904

Eight days ago, I developed for you the contrast between the Western and Eastern Empires, between what is now France and what is now Germany and Austria, as this contrast had developed in the eighth, ninth, and tenth centuries.

In the Western Empire, the old Roman culture left its traces, and the Church soon came to power by acquiring large estates for itself. This led to the struggle of the lay nobility with the rising Church. Above all, we are dealing with a different kind of Church, which had been endowed, especially by Charlemagne, with powerful, large estates, making it the ally of secular rulers by bringing it into the top-down form of feudal relations.

The subjects had come into a feudal relationship with the conquerors, and the nobles developed into feudatories of the kings. The kingdom had established itself more and more. The Western kingdom had to deal with the opposition between the feudatories and the Church. It was different in the Eastern kingdom. Here, the old sense of freedom and independence was still alive, so that the tribal dukes[†] did not want to enter into a relationship of dependence. The ninth, tenth, and eleventh centuries are filled with so-called kings who were indeed chosen but were nevertheless only kings in name, and who had continuously to try to make the tribal dukes dependent on them.

History tells a lot about such battles. The Carolingians were followed by the Saxon royal house after Conrad the Frank, and much is told of the deeds of Henry I, Ottos I, II, and III, and Henry II, as well as of the subsequent Frankish kings, Conrads I and II, Henrys III, IV, and V. These kings, chosen in the Eastern Empire, did not have any say in the constitution or the legislation of the tribes, and they had no judicial power at their disposal. It is much more important to know what the Empire actually signified at that time than to form an exact idea of the individual battles.

There were larger duchies. They came into being in the way described above. During the original migration to these regions, individuals who had acquired large landholdings had become more and more powerful. Smaller landowners became dependent on them and had to hand over their possessions as fiefs and then pay taxes.

The tribal dukes had gradually confiscated the small landholdings and, by giving some of the large landholdings to others in fief, had secured for themselves the right to provide them with a certain number of warriors and to pay a certain sum.

Through the absorption of the smaller landholdings by the larger ones, the duchies of Saxony, Franconia, Swabia, Bavaria, and so on had come into being. Gradually, jurisdiction also passed from the local village courts (*Gaugerichte*) to the manorial courts (*Hofgerichte*), which the dukes had imposed on their feudatories and peasants. The Church, according to its regulations, had to have its jurisdiction exercised by stewards (*Vögte*). The king was also nothing but a great landowner. He had vassals and a military entourage that he forced under his control. He had also acquired royal domains, establishing power relationships here and there. The relationship of the duke to the king was also only that of a vassal in that he delivered certain taxes to the court and made certain earnings available to the itinerant court. Jurisdiction was a matter for the duke. Only in the border areas against the Magyars, Wends, and Danes was jurisdiction exercised by royal margraves and palatines. There were no large states with uniform administration and a uniform military. This caused endless wars between the kings and the unruly dukes, who did not want to pay taxes. It got to the point that the Church was gradually called in.

It was in keeping with religious piety that taxes for the king were levied on Church lands. Although he was extremely pious and full of faith in the Church itself, Otto I forced the Church to pay dues. The bishoprics were forced to behave in the same way as the other feudatories. Ecclesiastical property was divided into two types. One part of the land was cultivated by bondsmen for the bishop, upon whom they had become totally dependent. Another area remained in a looser relationship. There the peasants had to cultivate the field in the name of the bishop for the emperor.

More and more, the emperors found themselves compelled by new enemies to draw closer to the Church. Powerful enemies threatened Central Europe. The Normans had ceased their invasions after repeatedly disturbing the peoples. This was after they were defeated by Arnulf of Carinthia in the Battle of Louvain and had acquired Brittany. On the other hand, Finno-Ugric tribes, the Magyars, came from the east, and their invasions caused indescribable terror. All reports tell of the horrible brutality of their conquests. The merit of having fended them off is usually attributed to Henry I and Otto I. To a certain extent, this is correct. The invasions of the Magyars were not something that could resemble later warfare with a formal declaration of war.

When the Magyars invaded, the dukes were particularly unruly, and Henry I had to ask for a truce in order to create at least a somewhat unified army. This unification was brought about only for the duration of the field army's campaign and only by urgent necessity.

Henry I is usually celebrated as the founder of cities. This is a misrepresentation. At that time, the general founding of cities throughout Europe began, and Henry I was only following the general trend when he supported this movement.

We have seen how jurisdiction gradually passed to the landlords, dukes, and kings. More and more undignified conditions arose. A lot of people, who used to be free peasants, had to give up everything they had in order to become subject to the authority of the landowners. They were used as farmers, messengers, craftsmen, and soldiers.

Due to the increased yield of the soil (which became greater and greater through the use of this large labor force) a kind of trade developed. At the same time, a special class of craftsmen was formed. This did not exist before. As already mentioned, the necessary work in the house was done by slaves and women. At most, the blacksmith and goldsmith trades existed. But now, through this kind of transition, a new class of craftsmen and tradesmen was formed. In the places where suitable markets existed, settlements arose, and fixed places were founded everywhere in Europe. To this was added the discontent of the poorly treated people so that the rush to the cities only grew stronger. This trend of the times forced the king to rely on the cities.

A cavalry army was needed against the Magyar cavalry. This cavalry army formed the basis for the knighthood that was created at that time. It is necessary to summarize all this to get a true picture of how everything happened at that time. This is more important than the detailed appreciation of those battles.

In the Battle of Riade in 933 and in the Battle of Lechfeld in 955, the Magyars were defeated and suffered such a terrible defeat that they actually lost the desire for further invasions. They established an empire in the Danube region in what is now Hungary. Since that time, the emperors were forced to rely on the Church, and Christianity was exploited politically. The Magyars were converted to Christianity, especially from the bishopric of Passau. If one wants to understand what arose in souls at that time, one must not reckon with later concepts. In the hearts of the people there lived an intense faith, a religious feeling that intensified to rapture. They listened in all things to the churchmen, by whom they were guided in all matters. The dukes and kings supported this kind of servility. From Charlemagne on, this rule over the soul can be seen. Thus, the clergy became the best and strongest advisors and embedded themselves in the souls and hearts of the people.

In addition to this, a strong influence took place at that time through the Arabs, who brought scientific and certain literary influences, through which a new spiritual trend entered the Middle Ages. A great collection of sagas, fairy tales, legends, feelings, and images was transplanted into the folk soul. This spiritual influence from the Orient to Europe was so intense that we see how the original rough Germanic soul took on a milder morality. Its piety became imbued with an element of great importance—the cult of the Virgin Mary and the women's ministry that developed from it. Whoever does not appreciate this does not know anything about the history of the Middle Ages. He closes his eyes to facts such as how great masses of people were sometimes seized by epidemics of fear. The people were seized by such fear around the year 1000—during the reign of Emperor Otto

III—which was supposed to bring the end of the world. This great event, for which people wanted to prepare themselves by penitential exercises and pilgrimages, excited the whole of Germany. Emperor Otto III himself undertook a pilgrimage to the grave of St. Adalbert of Prussia.† All this resulted from the folk soul of that time. The person who does not understand this does not understand the origin of the later crusades. Here, too, material motives were present, but anyone who does not look at it from this point of view is missing the point.

The secularization of the bishops and abbots could not remain without reaction, without repercussion; therefore, a powerful movement for reform emanated from Cluny. The influence of the Cluniac monks was immense. The fact that it was possible to enforce the peace of God is proof of this. At a time when there was no unified empire anywhere, the efforts of the monks of Cluny succeeded in restricting combat for a few days of the week—from Friday to Monday—so that during this time feuds were not fought. It is necessary to remember that at that time there was no law but a complete rulership by the most powerful. The harsh struggle between the German emperors and the popes did not only arise out of selfish interests but also out of fanaticism on the part of the Church. The pope felt himself to be the representative of Christ, the lord also of the secular territories. He believed that the secular rule of the kingdom of Christ should also be his.

Pope Gregory VII, who forced the German Emperor Henry IV to go to Canossa, was first a monk of Cluny and from there he developed his fanaticism. It became the tendency of the papacy to declare: As there are two rulers in the solar system—the sun and the moon—so also in human life. The pope is the sun and the king the moon, which receives its light only from the Church. This attitude was accepted and is also recognized as just by the great poet Dante, who, in the distribution of power, describes the supremacy of the spiritual over the temporal power as right and just. Now this struggle between emperor and pope had become such a powerful one because in the meantime a certain process of unification had taken place. The various duchies were forged together by external force. The dukes now considered themselves obliged to follow the army and to pay certain tributes to the emperor. All these lands—Italy, Burgundy, Lorraine, Franconia, Saxony, Austria, Hungary, and Poland—were temporarily in fiefdom to the German crown.

In fact, this is how a certain uniformity was achieved in the eleventh century. In the process, the Church becomes more and more powerful. At the death of Henry III, it was not secular nobles who were appointed to the guardianship of the young king, Henry IV, but the archbishops Hanno of Cologne and later Adalbert of Bremen.

The saturation of the folk soul with religious sentiments had led to a blind faith in authority. Now the time had come for Rome. A wise policy was initiated from Rome. The clergy had to be torn out of all worldly interests in order to have only one thing in mind: preaching and sovereignty over the people. For this purpose, it had to be made completely independent. Thus, in the eleventh century, celibacy was imposed on the clergy, and priestly marriage was forbidden, for anyone connected with the world through self-chosen blood ties would fall into dependence and could not serve so unreservedly.

This gave the clergy and the papacy the tendency to an unbending development of will with only one thing in mind: the rule of the Church. It came about that the Church could demand that only the Church should have a say in the filling of bishoprics. In the past, the secular nobles had occupied every bishopric that became vacant. Now, only ecclesiastical interests were to be decisive, and the power of the Church was increased through the fact that the posts were filled only by the Church. This led to the Investiture Controversy, which led Henry IV, who would not put up with this, to go to Canossa.

These trends culminate in the dispute between secular and spiritual power. As Clovis accepted the God of the Christians as his own because He led armies to victory, we see at this point how the Church itself rises to power. This must be understood if we are to comprehend the new conditions brought about by the Crusades.

We have seen in the Franks what emerged from the tribes that were displaced from their homes by the migration of peoples. We saw how Christianity became decisive in all conditions of life, how monasteries and bishoprics became the center of settlements, how the monks were not only the leaders of the people in the spiritual field but taught them how to cultivate various crops, how the monks were the builders of the churches, and so on.

Cities willingly formed around the existing bishoprics. We see everywhere the powerful influence of the Church. We see the influence of the Moors breaking through in science and literature. We will get to know another influence, more important than many others, through the crusades that also came from the Orient. Through these influences, the great inventions and discoveries were instigated. For there, in the Orient and in China, many things were known of which the West knew nothing: papermaking, silk weaving, the use of gunpowder, and so on. The first impulse was given to the great inventions by these migrations.

Powerful impulses exerted their influence on medieval humanity from two sides. Combine this with the founding of cities, and you will feel that a century is dawning which powerfully prepares the next stage of development. If you want to follow it in the right way, it is not enough to take it in only intellectually. Nobody who wants to grasp events only with the intellect and not with feeling truly understands them. No one who is unable to live into the subtleties of the folk souls and grasp what is happening and being prepared in the inner life can really understand the course of history. To those who do not possess this capacity, the words of Faust apply:

> What you call the spirit of the times
> Is really the rulers' own spirit
> In which the times are reflected.[†]

Lecture Eight

BERLIN, DECEMBER 20, 1904

We are in the middle of the Middle Ages and have to consider the period of the eleventh, twelfth, thirteenth, and fourteenth centuries. This period is significant because in this epoch we can study the emergence of great empires. In antiquity, too, we got to know great state structures—Persia, the Roman Empire, and so on—but they are so far in the past that it is difficult for us to make a real, historical assessment. In the Middle Ages, however, we see developing from small origins something that has a common army, court, and constitution. Previously, there was no such thing in Germany. These areas were still divided into separate territories in the thirteenth and fourteenth centuries. It was not until the reign of Henry III that something happened which contributed to the unification of the imperial territories. The emperor succeeded in making the individual hereditary dukes into imperial officials, so to speak. Previously, they had been sovereigns of their domains. Now they had become what are called *ministeriales*, or servants of the emperor. Gradually, the lower feudatories, who had previously been independent but had become vassals, were put on an equal footing with the *ministeriales*. In time, they formed what is called the lesser nobility from which the knighthood was recruited. The knighthood played an important role in the Crusades and later during the reign of Henry IV.

When Pope Gregory VII excommunicated the emperor, the German nobility only partially adhered to the emperor, while others, under the influence of the Pope, elected various counter-kings. All these struggles are not important. What is important is that the knighthood acquired a special significance through these various disputes. Knights and cities were soon wooed by the Pope, then by the king. Continuous feuds and wars prevailed; crudeness increased more and more. During the plundering campaigns, the peasantry suffered heavily. The last free peasants could no longer hold on and were absorbed by the lords and dukes who were then absorbed by the kings. From this unpleasant process, we see emerging what we know as the "Empire."

There was no difference between secular and ecclesiastical nobility, but there was a great difference between the secularized clergy and those in the monasteries. The clergy ruled by the bishops was mostly illiterate, could not read and write, and exploited their feudatories. The bishop was occupied with the administration of his estates and was as illiterate as the knights and peasants. There was nothing of what we can call education today; therefore, it was possible, from Rome, to fortify the political position of the Church more and more.

It was different in the monasteries. Here, much work was done by men and women. Deep scholarship was to be found here; all education of the time emanated only from the monasteries. They did not allow themselves to be dependent on the political power of Rome, which rested on the secular power of the clergy. What came from Rome can be judged in many different ways. A certain struggle was to be waged against the crudeness, against the right of conquest prevalent among the Germanic peoples. Zeal for spiritual goods, the desire to spread the power of medieval thinking over the world was what was wanted from Rome. In any case, a better will emanated from Rome than from the German nobility. In this sense, one must understand what Gregory VII wanted when he demanded celibacy and when he did not want to tolerate secular princely power that assigned itself an influence over the appointments to the bishoprics. It was an opposition against the rampant crudeness in the German lands. Thus, Henry IV's battles with the Saxons were not only almost as bloody as Charlemagne's wars against the Saxons, but they were fought with a special attitude of belief in the cause.

Through all these struggles, prosperity was more and more shattered. Out of the storms of the time, a deeply religious trait arose, which increased to the point of rapture in the year 1000, as I have already told you. Again and again, this religious enthusiasm drove the masses on pilgrimages to the Orient.

Originally, the Christian religion had known no adherence to any dogma. It was the content of ideas that mattered, not the external dressing. You have seen how in the *Heliand*,† the idea of Christ was freely developed, how the poet transposed the life of Christ into the old Saxon world for his compatriots. He took the externalities quite freely, as if the events could just as well have happened here in Germany as in Palestine.

Under the ever more secularized conditions, the external shaping of the faith became an existential question for the Church. It could no longer leave it up to local communities to decide how they wanted to understand Christ. As a side effect of political power, dogmas also became fixed and rigid.

The nobility tried to use the worldly power of the Church in their interest. The bishop's chairs were filled with younger brothers who seemed physically or spiritually unfit for anything else. Gradually, circumstances changed and the old time grew into a new one.

This is how the Crusades came about, which we can only understand psychologically from the mood that dominated the Middle Ages. The existing religious fervor made it easy for the Pope to incite people to the Crusades through his own agents, such as Peter of Amiens and others. In addition, a large number of people had become completely destitute. Thus, it was not only religious motives that were involved. More and more freemen had become bondsmen, and others had had to leave their possessions to become itinerant people who had nothing but the clothes on their backs. Among these itinerant people who came from all classes (including the nobility), there was a large number who had nothing to do and were ready for any undertaking, including a crusade.

A great number of factors were at work: religious fervor, rigid dogma, and material oppression. The strength of these causes can be seen in the fact that when the first crusade took place, there were half a million people who went to the Orient. The first external impulse for this was the bad treatment of the numerous pilgrims by the Saracens. But deeper causes lay at the root of it. There was a rigid dogma to which people submitted. One can know nothing of the Middle Ages if one does not understand how people at that time clung to religion with heart and soul. A sermon could light a fire in the people if the preacher hit on the right words. Many believed they would find help through such action; others sought forgiveness of their sins. From our contemporary perspective, it is hard to get a clear picture of this phenomenon of the Middle Ages. We are dealing here with many intangible causes.

It is not the causes but the effects of the Crusades that were of particular importance for subsequent developments. Soon after they began, one of these effects became evident—namely, a much more intimate exchange between the individual countries. Hitherto, Germany had generally remained quite unknown to the Southern European countries, but now they were brought closer together by a brotherhood of arms. Moorish science, too, only really found its way into Europe along this path. Previously, university chairs had existed only in Spain, Italy, and France. In Germany, they were established only after the Crusades. Only now did the influence of true science come from the East. This had hitherto been completely closed off but had preserved great educational treasures in the writings of the Greek classics. Observed comprehensively, it was only through contact with the East that science came into being.

The vague urge of religious enthusiasm had taken on a definite form and had become what is called medieval science. I would like to characterize this science for you a little.

Above all, two ways of thinking had developed which made themselves felt in the scientific life of the Middle Ages. The Scholastic way of thinking was divided into two currents: realism and nominalism. It is a seemingly abstract subject when I speak of nominalism and realism, but for the Middle Ages (and also for later times), this dispute acquired a profound significance. Theological and secular scientists were divided according to these two camps. Nominalists were believers in names; realists were those who believe that things are independent of what they might be named. Realists, in the medieval sense, were those who believed in the reality of thought, in a real meaning (*Sinn*) of the world. They assumed that the world had a meaning and was not formed by chance. From the point of view of materialism, this may be considered a foolish perspective; however, those who do not consider thought to be an empty fantasy must admit that the thought of a law governing the world, which one seeks and finds in oneself, also has a meaning for the world.

The nominalists were those who did not believe that thoughts are something real, who saw in them only names, coincidences, things of no meaning. All those who believe to see only blind coincidences in that which human thought achieves, like Kant, but also Schopenhauer—who conceive of the world as simply imagination—form an outgrowth of medieval nominalism. These currents divided the army of monks into two camps. In such important questions, it is remarkable how the Church did not exert any coercion and, as far as it concerns scholarship, could calmly allow someone to raise the question of whether the divine Trinity is not also merely a name and therefore nothing real. Nevertheless, you see in this a great freedom of the medieval Church. It was only at the end of this period that persecutions of heretics began, and it is significant that the first heretic judge in Germany, Conrad of Marburg,[†] was slain by the people. It was only then that people began to persecute opinions. This is an important shift. You can see how free ecclesiastical thinking was by studying the great teacher and thinker Albertus Magnus.[†] He was an excellent scholar who immersed himself in the whole of science. He possessed ecclesiastical erudition, Arabic knowledge, scientific and physical thinking, as well as complete mastery of philosophy. He was regarded by the people as a magician. Scholarly wisdom and popular superstition collided harshly and were exploited by a secularized clergy.

In this period, cities are on the rise. In the cities, we see a powerful bourgeoisie emerge. Crafts flourish and craft workers join together in guilds. No longer does the craftsman have to bow under the oppression of a landlord as he once did as a serf. Soon kings and nobles form alliances with the medieval cities. Emperor Frederick Barbarossa[†] fought for years with the northern Italian cities. A strong sense of freedom and immediate personal worth developed among the bourgeoisie. On the one hand, we see a religious attitude in the countryside with increasing outward pressure; on the other hand, we see a free bourgeoisie in the cities, bound, to be sure, to a strictly regulated guild constitution, but precisely because of this, the freedom of the cities flourished at that time. In the countryside, we see a moribund existence, the rule of might makes right, and general crudeness. After the Crusades, chivalry fell into an empty courtly life that led nowhere. The knights occupied themselves with feuds, tournaments, and fights at arms, and their customs took on increasingly crude forms. In particular, the Minne service[†] took on the most ridiculous forms over time. Those knights who could write poetry wrote verses to their ladies, while the others courted them in other ways. A great ignorance was united with this court life. The men were almost all completely illiterate, while the women had to be able to read and write. The women occupied a very peculiar position. On one hand, they were idolized, and, on the other, they were oppressed. A kind of barbarism prevailed, a licentious life, which led to the fact that the right of hospitality led to the dishonor of women.

Meanwhile, in the cities, what would later be called culture was being prepared. Clearly, it had to happen there, because new things develop where they have the possibility to develop freely. Real spiritual progress takes place where economic life is not constricted. Spiritual life does not spring from material progress, but true spiritual progress is found where economic life is not oppressed and constricted.

A rich culture arose in the cities at that time. Almost everything that was given to us in the works of painting, architecture, and inventions comes from this time thanks to city culture. Dante also came from such a rich Italian urban culture. In Germany, too, we find significant intellectual achievements under the influence of this urban culture. It is true that the first important poets were knights, such as Wolfram von Eschenbach, Gottfried von Strassburg, and others, but without the support that the cities provided, these achievements would not have been possible. In this period, when a free air was blowing in the cities, university life was also born. At first, if a German wanted to find higher knowledge, he had to go to Italy or France. Now the first German universities were founded—in Prague in 1348, in Vienna in 1365, in Heidelberg in 1386. Freedom cleared away the medieval darkness.

The secular clergy, like the nobility, was involved in egoistic struggles over interests, and the Church had also adopted this trait. Whoever follows the development will understand that a new spiritual current, German mysticism, could only arise in this way—in rugged opposition to a secularized clergy. Especially along the Rhine, in Cologne, Strasbourg, and southern Germany, this movement spread, and men like Eckhart, Tauler, Suso,[†] and the like had made themselves independent of the Roman clergy. For this independence, they were declared heretics, and their lives were made difficult in every way. Their writings are characterized by an inwardness. They had withdrawn into the human heart to come to terms with themselves. These monks, who had made themselves independent, spoke to the heart of the people in their native language. The German language was ennobled in a way that one does not understand today unless one reads the writings of Meister Eckhart, Tauler, or the author of the *Theologia Deutsch*.[†] Mysticism implanted beauty into the language, and the translations of that time far surpass the later ones in their beautiful use of the language. This development of the German language was abruptly interrupted by Luther's creation of the German Bible in the most pedantic, philistine dialect of the time, from which the present High German has developed. All this happened in opposition to the clergy. Many things that were sought back then have not yet been achieved in many areas even today. I have described many things to you differently than you are used to. It is always asserted that something unheard of happened through Luther's translation of the Bible, but you see how much higher things had been achieved before that. I have sketched for you a tableau for what will occupy us in the following period.

We are approaching the Renaissance period. The consolidation of conditions that took place in that era consisted essentially in the fact that larger and larger areas came under the rule of sovereigns. Also, a large part of the medieval freedom of the cities was absorbed by the constitutions of these large states. Everything has its two sides. Today, people will certainly be repelled by many things, and there is a lot of talk today about the arbitrariness that prevailed in those days. Of course, freedom has its reverse side, and it is not yet freedom if one's own arbitrariness is limited by the arbitrariness of others.

For example, a discussion could be led at the universities in the middle of the Middle Ages against the arbitrariness of the secular rulers, as perhaps only Fichte was able to do later. The documents of the universities of that time preserve for us the words of the free spirits of that time. Today, not only secular rule but also science is nationalized.

Without apportioning light and shadow according to the catchwords of the present, I have described these times to you. I sought to dwell on the points where real progress exists. If we want to be free people, we must have a heart for those who have striven for freedom before us. We must understand that other times also had people who gave something to freedom.

History is the history of humanity's development toward freedom,[†] and to understand it we must study freedom in all its high points.

Lecture Nine

BERLIN, DECEMBER 28, 1904

We have seen how the life of the Middle Ages developed in the cities. We have come to the point where public life takes place mainly in the life of cities. Originally, the reasons for settling in the cities were the oppression of the country people and the spread of commerce.

We have seen how those who had escaped from their oppressors or had devoted themselves to trade settled either in a bishop's see or in some other place of medieval power. At first, the part of the population that inhabited the cities was not in a pleasant position. They had to pay dues to their former lord of the manor and supply weapons, clothes, and so on. Those who had moved to the cities and devoted themselves to trade, as well as those who were royal, episcopal, or other officials, at first formed the free privileged classes. Increasingly, the privileges of the officials and the merchants who formed the patriciate were taken away from those who served the oppressors. On the Rhine in southern Germany, this equality was won in the thirteenth and fourteenth centuries, and kings and emperors had to reckon with it.

In the past, the itinerant kings had held court here and there, but now they settled in the cities. The rulers had to reckon with cities. They found in them grounds for their own development of power; therefore, certain rights were transferred to the cities—legal jurisdiction over their own citizens, the right to mint coins, and so on. In this way, their power grew more and more. A democratic element was now formed in Germany. In the past, the landed nobility, the feudal nobility had given the era its particular character. Now something new arose in its place. More and more feudal privileges were eliminated in the cities. Instead of making general observations, let us turn to specific examples. Cologne had long been an important trading city, the seat of a powerful clerical office. In the spiritual sphere, too, the cities were becoming a power. There, the subordinate class soon acquired equal rights with the patrician class, and a kind of constitution called the "Oath Book" (*Eidbuch*) was created to record what rights individuals had. The guilds, of which there were twenty-two in Cologne, had joined together. Before the fourteenth century, they had also been dependent on the patricians. Now, in 1321, they achieved equal rights.

The city council was not only composed of patricians—the members of the guilds also had equal voting rights. In order to make this council as democratic as possible, the members were always to be elected for only half a year and were not to be eligible for re-election for three years afterwards. With the implementation of this democratic principle, the interest of the individual citizen in the flourishing of the cities also grew. Until the twelfth century, such cities were not much more than dirty villages with thatched houses; however, they grew in a few years in quite a striking way. Every man is now a citizen, and with the participation of individuals, the prestige and beauty of the city grows.

What the cities modeled had a decisive effect on all high politics. What could interest cities like Hamburg, Lübeck, and Cologne politically in like manner to the earlier kings and dukes? When the cities began to practice politics, it was done in an urban way. Widely dispersed areas forged alliances to protect their urban interests. Such powerful alliances of cities were first formed in northern Germany, later the northern Italian cities formed such alliances. The German cities also gained considerable influence abroad. In Bergen and London, they had powerful expatriate guildhalls.

Just as the nobility had to decide to grant the cities the right to such policies, the cities also gradually became the center of a new culture. A material culture, to be sure, but one that led to the settlement of wider areas. New cultural centers were formed in which a lively trade with the northern countries, especially with Russia, flourished. The legendary Vineta[†] was such a trading center. We see how trade policy develops, and powerful trade routes emerge along the Rhine through northern and central Germany with important trading cities such as Magdeburg, Hildesheim, Erfurt, Breslau, and so on. From these alliances of cities emerged what is called the Hanseatic League.† In the course of time, it became necessary to pursue not only trade but also military policy and war. In the background lurked enemies—the knights and dukes—who enviously followed the development of the cities. The cities had to surround themselves with walls and defend themselves against their enemies. They became more and more powerful cultural centers as well as centers of spiritual life. Whatever spiritual life was felt in those days was drawn together in the cities. Art also blossomed in the medieval cities under the influence of the free bourgeoisie. In Venice, Titian† painted the Hall of the Clothiers.

A new form of warfare also emerged. The use of gunpowder, which was already known in the Orient but was only now discovered in Europe, gave rise to a new, democratic form of combat as opposed to the single combat of the armored knights. The use of gunpowder continued to develop. First there were crude blunderbusses and mortars, but soon more highly developed weapons were invented, especially by Kaspar Zöllner† in Vienna.

What developed in the cities in connection with the spirit of church life is of special importance for the progress of culture. We have seen how the highest ecstasy of religious enthusiasm is represented in the Crusades. We have seen how German mysticism blossomed (especially on the Rhine) and how the Brethren of the Common Life† cultivated a deep piety quite independently of Rome. Two different currents of time now confront us: on the one hand, the bourgeoise is concerned with the elevation of material life; and, on the other, we see a spiritual life directed inwardly. In the early Middle Ages, material and spiritual life were closely intertwined. The peasant believed that the prosperity of the fruit of his labor, like his religious feeling, was encouraged and blessed by the Church. Now, when personal efficiency came to the fore, these directions split.

The unique architectural style of the Middle Ages, which is mistakenly called Gothic, came from the south of France, from areas where such pious heretics as the Cathars and Waldensians lived. They strove to deepen their inner life and break with the opulent life of the bishops and the clergy. A peculiar spiritual life spread from there, and German mysticism was strongly influenced by it.

The deep influence this attitude also had on the outer form of these churches is evident from the fact that all these Gothic cathedrals possessed a mystical decoration in the form of wonderful stained-glass windows. This art (which was completely lost in the seventeenth century) was not artistic allegory; rather, the symbols that were painted there really exerted a mystical influence on the crowd when the sun shone through them into the dim, high churches. This type of construction was closely related to the conditions of the medieval cities. The town hall and the guildhall were also built in Gothic style. The city, which was surrounded by walls, was dependent on expanding within these walls, and the Romanesque architectural style was not sufficient for this. This is how the towering Gothic churches came into being, an expression at the same time of the inwardness of the life of the time. The Dances of Death that often decorate them showed the transience of everything earthly.

In caring for the cleanliness and beauty of their city, the citizens find a noble way to keep their name in the memory of their fellow citizens. Especially beautiful fountains are erected everywhere. We see that at that time, something comes into being which gained special importance in the Middle Ages—public baths, which were not missing from any town. In the later Middle Ages, these baths gave rise to moral outrages and for this reason were eradicated by Protestantism. But this civic spirit went even further. It intervened in public life by creating charitable institutions that can still be considered models today. These charitable institutions were also urgently needed because in the fourteenth century, Europe was afflicted by severe epidemics, famines, leprosy, the plague (or, as it was called at that time, "the black death"). But medieval people knew how to counter this. Infirmaries, hospitals, and priests' houses were built everywhere, and even strangers were cared for in the so-called *Elendsherberge* (hostels of misery). At that time, "misery" (*Elend*) meant "strange" (*fremd*) and only later acquired a different meaning.

In addition to these bright sides of medieval life, there were, of course, some dark ones. First and foremost, the harsh treatment of all those who did not belong to a fixed community. They were outcasts, something for which the cities did not pay. All those who did not belong to the guild suffered bad treatment, especially the "traveling people" (*fahrenden Leute*). The name "dishonest people" was created at that time, a terrible name for the traveling people. The "dishonest people" belonged to all kinds of professions—actors, jugglers, shepherds, and so on. They were not allowed to join the guilds, and they could not show themselves anywhere without the risk of being tortured.

The same happened to the Jews. The prejudice against them is not very old. In the early Middle Ages, we find many Jews recognized as scholars. In later times, they met the monetary needs of the nobility. Due to the peculiar conditions of the Middle Ages, they attained the position of money lenders, and this position stood between commerce and usury, earning them hatred. However, the kings' need for money always gave the Jewish people certain rights. This activity earned them the strange name of royal chamberlains.

Another dark side was the judicial system, the criminal law that necessarily developed during the Middle Ages. In earlier times, justice was related to revenge—either damage should be repaired or revenge should be taken. The concept of punishment did not exist; it arose only at this point. Roman legal concepts were becoming established. Judicial power was a valuable prerogative for a city, and the citizens were proud not only of their churches and walls but also of their high court. Often the harshest punishments were imposed for the most trivial reasons.

Thus, the fifteenth and sixteenth centuries of medieval life are under the influence of urban life. Another current went alongside it. What we understand today as international relations was connected with this other current. This is the movement known as that of the heretics or Cathars. You can appreciate the scope of this movement if you consider the fact that in Italy in the thirteenth century, there were more heretics than orthodox believers.

Here also lay the real conflict that led to the Crusades. When the decision to launch them was made at the Church assembly at

Clermont in 1095, it was not only riffraff who went on the Crusades. It was also decent people who set out in disorderly crowds under Peter of Amiens and the knight Walter von Habenichts† for the promised land. It was a papal enterprise, and it was not merely born of enthusiasm. It was a matter of the papal influence being pressed by the heretics. The Pope's ambition was to create a drain for the heretics.

In the first real Crusade,† it was largely heretics who set out. This is also evident from their leader. Gottfried von Bouillon was of a decidedly anti-papal disposition, as can be seen from his life up to this point. For when, at the instigation of Pope Gregory, a counter-king was set up against Emperor Henry IV in the person of Duke Rudolf of Swabia,† Gottfried von Bouillon fought on the side of Emperor Henry and killed Rudolf of Swabia. It is necessary to see what his aim was, although it did not come to fruition. He wished to found an anti-Rome in Jerusalem. That is why he called himself only "Protector of the Holy Sepulcher" and tried to raise the flag of anti-Roman Christianity in Jerusalem with unpretentious modesty. After the Crusades, the Ghibelline party arose from the representatives of such views; opposite them, on the side of the Pope, stood the Guelfs.

We also see the same phenomena when we look at the second Crusade, which Emperor Conrad III undertook at the instigation of Bernard of Clairvaux† in 1147. These crusades had no further significance in themselves. They only showed what spirit was blowing through the world. Barbarossa, who undertook five Roman campaigns against the Pope and the northern Italian cities that sided with the Pope in order to subdue them, had to grant them independence in the Peace of Constance† after he had failed to take their fortress of Alessandria.

The German papal party consisted especially of the princely families who had remained from the old nobility. Henry the Proud and his son Henry the Lion fought for the old ducal power against the imperial power. Usually, by marriage with an emperor's daughter, these reluctant nobles were then bound to imperial power. Through the enfeoffment of the emperor's relatives with the duchies that had been settled, such rearrangements as a balance of power were subsequently affected again and again.

Emperor Frederick Barbarossa undertook the third Crusade, which also did not lead to any real successes but which became important through the Kyffhäuser saga,† which was tied to it. Those who can read legends know that here they are dealing with one of the most important ones. It did not originate from the folk soul, as is usually said, for it was created by an individual and then was spread among the people, as also happens with folk songs, which professors nevertheless claim originate directly from the people and do not come from the heads of individuals. The legend originated from the mind of a man who knew how to use symbols that had a deep meaning, such as the cave in Kyffhäuser, the ravens, and so on. It is one of those legends which can be found all over the world, a proof that there is something similar everywhere.

The Barbarossa saga is a particularly important saga in terms of cultural history. Rome was the advocate within the Church of what resulted from external ornamentation being imposed on the Germanic spirit in connection with Christianity. The emperor was supposed to be hidden in a grotto. Since time immemorial, grottoes were secret places of worship. The Mithras service was generally held in grottoes. In this worship, Mithras was depicted mounted on a bull, the symbol of the lower animal nature, which was overcome by Mithras, the predecessor of Christ. In the Kyffhäuser legend, the emperor, hidden in the rocky grotto, became the advocate of that which turned against Rome and its influence in German spiritual life. How much there is in this legend! A pure Christianity that was longed for by many at that time was to emerge from hiding when the time came.

Under Emperor Frederick II of the Hohenstaufen dynasty,† the Mongol invasion took place, devastating Europe. I do not want to give you a history of the Hohenstaufens here, only to point out what developed from the Crusades: expanded trade relations and a revival of the sciences and arts through contact with Asia. What the crusaders gained in new experiences and goods, they brought back home.

It was also at this time that the two great monastic orders emerged, becoming of particular importance for spiritual life: the Dominicans and the Franciscans. The Dominicans represented the spiritual direction known as realism, while the Franciscans leaned toward nominalism. It was in the Holy Land that the spiritual orders of knights were founded. The Order of St. John was first founded for the care of the sick.

From a similar mood to that of Gottfried von Bouillon arose the second order of knights—the Knights Templar. Its real aims were kept secret, but through intimate agitators, the order had soon become very powerful. An anti-Roman principle prevailed in it. This was also evident in the Dominicans, who were often in complete opposition to Rome; for example, they were in violent opposition to the Pope on the dogma of the Immaculate Conception. The Templars sought to purify Christianity. Referring to John the Baptist, they advocated an ascetic tendency. Their acts of worship were so hostile to the Church because of their opposition to the Roman secularization that it is not appropriate to speak about them publicly today. The order had become very inconvenient to the clergy and princes because of its power. It had to suffer severe persecutions and perished after its last Grand Master, Jacques de Molay, had suffered martyrdom with a number of friars in 1314.

The Order of Teutonic Knights was of similar origin. With the Livonian Brothers of the Sword, which joined it, its special task was to convert the areas of Europe that still remained pagan, especially in the East, from its headquarters in Marienburg. From the reports of contemporaries, one gets a strange picture of the inhabitants of the areas that today form the provinces of East and West Prussia. Albert von Bremen[†] describes the old Prussians as complete heathens. Among this people, of whom it is not exactly certain whether they were of Germanic or Slavic stock, are found the old pagan customs of eating horse flesh and drinking horse blood. The chronicler describes them as a pagan and cruel people. Before coming into contact with the German knights, the Brothers of the Sword had especially striven for worldly power.

One can only construe the development. Although the cities had been formed, a part of the ducal power and that of the robber barons had remained. It was not enthusiasm for Christianity but mere egoism that caused the remnants of the feudal nobility to gather in these two German orders of knights. In these areas, no significant influence of the cities was felt. The other two Christian orders were compounds of those who were not connected with Rome. If one examines the historical sources, one will often find alliances between them and the cities.

Besides these two currents of urban development and deeper religious life, we see that the imperial power had lost all importance. In the years 1254 to 1273, there was no bearer of imperial power in Germany. The imperial dignity was temporarily sold to foreign princes, one of whom, Richard of Cornwall,[†] came to Germany only twice, while the second, Alfonso of Castile,[†] never came at all.

When at last a proper imperial election was resumed, the effort was not to establish any central imperial power or to try again to create an imperial power but to decisively bring order with respect to the robber baronry.

They chose Count Rudolf of Habsburg.[†] If one should ask what he and his successors did for the empire, it would be difficult to say because they were not active in public relations. They were busy establishing their domestic power. Thus, after the death of Duke Heinrich Jasomirgott,[†] Rudolf of Habsburg granted Lower Austria to his son and thus established the power of the House of Habsburg. His successors sought to increase this power by conquests and especially by marriage alliances and no longer cared about anything connected with the public good.

You can see what was really important for further development: the events that gave to the medieval conditions that which finally led to the great discoveries and inventions at the end of the Middle Ages. We see the cities with a powerfully rising but secularized culture. In the Church, we see fracturing, schism, separation. Out of this current, the last act of the medieval drama breaks forth; we see the twilight of the Middle Ages, the dawn of a new age.

Lecture Ten

BERLIN, DECEMBER 29, 1904

We are progressing in our consideration of history ever closer to the times when the great inventions and discoveries took place in the fifteenth century.

The modern era begins. This new era is of special interest for historical consideration; the transition to the great nation-states of Europe takes place in characteristic manner. We have seen how the transition to the post-medieval princely power develops from feudal power. It signifies a reaction on the part of remnants from earlier times and only in a certain way is it a renewal. What remained of the old pretentions of princes and dukes, what was left over, rallies its forces again and determines the map of Europe through private family relations.

The importance of landed property ownership had been replaced by cities. The bourgeoisie flourished and all true culture emanated from the cities. The emperorship had sunk to a shadow power, and, after a long interregnum, Rudolf of Habsburg was elected. However, the emperor had become very unnecessary in the empire by then, and he hardly needed to be seen there. The Habsburg dynasty only endeavored to increase its domestic power by means of this imperial power in those places where it maintained its rights outside the power of the cities. It is a simple process that takes place here; the others—princes and dukes—also gather what remains to them in order to strengthen the power of their houses, thus creating the basis for large political territories.

The Mongol invasion and later the Turkish invasions give rise to this. Only larger princes are able to defend their territories; the smaller ones join the more powerful ones and thus form the basis for future states. The new emperor meant very little. As mentioned, Rudolf of Habsburg was only anxious to establish domestic power. After overcoming Ottokar of Bohemia,† his son was enfeoffed with his lands, and later the power of the House of Habsburg was strengthened by always marrying new territories to it.

The only thing that can interest us in all these purely private undertakings is that they resulted in the uprising of the Swiss Confederates,† who wanted to be free from the claims that Rudolf of Habsburg's successor, Emperor Albrecht I,† was making on them. Through hard battle, they achieved a unique status: to be subject only to imperial power—imperial immediacy. They did not want to have anything to do with princely power.

The effort to increase the power of their own house continued under subsequent emperors. Adolf of Nassau† seized a large part of Thuringia, wresting it from the weaker princes. Albrecht of Austria and his successor Henry of Luxembourg† also sought to enrich themselves in this way, the latter by marrying his son to a Bohemian princess. This is a typical case for the development of the conditions of that time.

This stream continued under a new flourishing of ecclesiastical power, but, at the same time, there was also a flourishing of the stream that did not want to have anything to do with the Church. The teachings of the Waldensians or Cathars had a stirring effect, and there were tremendous struggles against the re-emergence of princely power. The situation of the peasants, which had been elevated by the emergence of the cities, now became more and more oppressive because of the feudal and robber barons, the bishoprics and abbeys, to which they had to submit. The cities had had a time to bloom, and at that time the principle had applied: city air makes you free. However, in the course of time, many cities had become dependent. The Hohenstaufen dynasty in particular had succeeded in bringing many cities into dependence. Now the cities tried to prevent any further influx of the rural population. They ended the practice and sought royal support. As a result, the peasant population became more dependent on their landlords. The mood of the oppressed was stirred up by the Waldensians and heretics, for whom the Church was no longer enough.

The cry for freedom and the Christian heretical mood went hand in hand. Religious sentiment merged with the political movement, and this popular mood found its expression in the peasant wars. Whoever wants to grasp this spiritual heretical mood, independent of external Church and royal power, must realize that especially in the Rhine regions, "the Holy Roman Empire's *Pfaffengasse* [priest alley],"[†] hard battles were waged for decades by the full might of the nobility against the peasants. Popular preachers, especially from the Dominican Order, resisted and even fought against this repression because these preachers did not want to add to the oppression of the people by papal power. They, too, did not agree with the political expansion of power of the papacy and the expansion of the power of the nobility.

The French kings saw in the papacy a support in the struggle with German princely power, so the Pope was brought to Avignon. For about seventy years, the Popes had their seat there. Henry of Luxembourg fought against the Pope to whom the King of France lent his support. Thus, from Avignon, from France, the Pope dominated Christendom, and as the princes increasingly asserted their power over their feudatories, so the Popes strove to extend their authority more and more, by means of secular clergy—the politically and economically powerful abbeys and bishoprics that were dependent on the Pope. Meanwhile, the princes arbitrarily shaped the map of Europe. Emperor Charles IV[†] united Brandenburg, Hungary, and Bohemia under the power of his house. Imperial dignity became a mere title, and the emperors were content to administer their private lands. The imperial title was bartered around among noble families.

If we want to understand the real history, we must keep in mind how the great change from the Middle Ages to the modern era consisted in the fact that the princes used that dissatisfied mood for their private interests. The states that are formed spread their tentacles over a popular movement that had lasted for centuries, and this movement for religious freedom is used first to fight the papacy and to halt its power, and then to allow the states themselves to creep into this position of power.

That movement developed on the basis of the folk soul; it aspired to something quite different from what the Reformation then brought. The secularized clergy had become as much an oppressor as the secular nobility. The urban population, in their egoism, did not feel compelled to side with the oppressed; only when their own freedom was threatened did they endeavor to preserve it. Thus, in the Swabian League of Cities and in the Palatinate region, they did not succeed in asserting themselves after all, and the new power of the nobility emerged here as well.

Already during the reign of Emperor Sigismund,† there was an outburst of a peculiar religious movement in Bohemia. It was a movement that was spread by one man who—one may acknowledge or deny what he represented—nevertheless relied only on his own conviction. His conviction was based on the purest will, on the fire in his own heart. This man was Jan Hus of Husinec,† a preacher and professor at the University of Prague. His conviction was based on something that was spreading throughout Europe—for even before that in England, Wycliffe† had urged the reestablishment of original Christianity—but that received special splendor through the fiery eloquence of this outstanding man. Hus found approval everywhere. Everywhere his words found acceptance because one only had to point out the shameful behavior of the secular clergy, such as the sale of the bishoprics and so on.

They were heartfelt words because they proclaimed something that went through all of Europe as a mood and only emerged where an individual personality could give it expression. Through the popes and the counter-popes, the Church had fallen into disarray. The popes themselves had to do something; therefore, the Council of Constance was convened.† It constituted a turning point in medieval life. A transformation into a pure Church was sought. This project set in motion a lively opposition. Political motives played a part, and Emperor Sigismund himself was keenly interested. The worst abuses of the Church were to be corrected, for the clergy was completely depraved, and incredible abuses had also broken out in the monasteries. In Italy, Savonarola† had begun his powerful agitation against the secularization of the Church. The Council also wanted to settle accounts with this. The head of the Council was Gerson,[†] the Chancellor of the University of Paris, a second Tauler[†] for the Romance-language countries. This fact was significant for the outcome of the Council because with the help of Gerson, it had become possible for the emperor to wrest the leadership from the popes and to put an end to Hussitism. The reason this movement was so dangerous for the ecclesiastical, and especially for the secular rulers, was because it had nothing to do with the development of political power but arose from the deepest folk soul of the people. Hus fell victim not only to Rome but also to the emerging power of the nobility. The Hussites did not wage their war for a republican Christianity only against the Church. It was waged against the encroaching power of the nobility.

In Protestantism, however, the nobility allies itself with religious discontent in order to exploit it for its own purposes. The successors of Hus were condemned to death because, in fact, the power of the nobility had triumphed. Otherwise, the emperors of that time did not have very much power. Emperor Frederick III, for example, was generally called the "useless emperor."[†]

This gives us a picture of the peculiar development of that time. In the increasingly ascendent cities, there exists a flourishing life, whereas where feudal power had asserted itself, there is continuously increasing oppression; at the same time, in the sphere of deeper religious life, influenced by both factors, a strong movement arises, as witnessed in the appearance of a Wycliffe, a Hus. Italy offers us a brilliant picture of urban life in its city republics. In Florence, for example, it was the Medici[†] merchants who had a fundamental effect on the culture of Italy. All these cities were decisive factors in the development of culture.

Thus, you see that the means by which people had previously attained power were no longer sufficient. In the Middle Ages, except for the number of clergymen who worked in the monasteries and in civil service positions, no one had been able to read and write. Now this relationship has become different. Reading and writing are spread by the new streams that now flood over the masses. The great copying houses spread in duplicate what was formerly forbidden to the people, and these copies were bought in the same way as books were later on. They contained writings of the New Testament, book-length popular scientific works, collections of sagas, legends, heroes, and medical texts. All these were disseminated to the people in the fourteenth century.

Schools had been established everywhere, particularly by the Brethren of the Common Life, as already mentioned. Especially along the Rhine, what had formerly been hidden in monasteries was now brought to light. A formal transcription industry arose in Hagenau in Alsace, whose announcements, such as those of Lambert, are similar to today's publishers' catalogs. A sustained manuscript trade also emanated from Cologne, and the Brethren of the Common Life were also called "The Brothers of the Pen."

Here we have the preparatory stage for the art of book publishing. It arose from a deep need; it did not arrive like a shot but was prepared through the fact that it had become a need, for the books produced by hand-copying were too expensive and the poorer classes desired books. It was a means, at that time, of shaking the people up.

The men who led the peasants' cause at that time were only able to spread these pamphlets among the people because the circumstances were favorable to them. Thus, there arose the peasants' alliances, the "Armer Konrad,"[†] the "Bundschuh" movement[†] with its slogan: "We'll never recover from priests and nobles." On all sides, the need for something new was felt, and when Gutenberg invented movable type around 1445, the means were provided to accelerate the cultural life of the time. People were extraordinarily receptive and prepared to expand the scope of knowledge. The secularization of the arts and sciences developed under the influence of this mood, and with it the subsequent era of inventions and discoveries flourished. Formerly, the Church alone was the bearer of the arts and sciences; however, now the cities and the bourgeoisie became the bearers of culture. The former exclusively Church-based culture was transferred to the cities and secularized.

We come to the discoveries, which we can only briefly enumerate, that extended the scope of human history into vast unknown territories. In addition, there was the invasion of Greece by the Turks, one result of which was that the culture that had been preserved there gained influence across Europe. A great number of Greek artists and scholars emigrated to other countries, especially Italy, and found accommodation in the cities. They fertilized the spirit of the Occident. This restructuring is called the Renaissance. Ancient Greece rose again, and only now did people get to know the scriptures on which Christianity was based. The ancient Hebrew Testament was read, thanks to Reuchlin† in particular, and through him and Desiderius Erasmus of Rotterdam,† the movement we know as humanism was set in motion. From the efforts initiated by these influences came the dawn of the new era.

There was another consequence of the spread of Turkish power. The Occident had long been in contact with the Orient. Through the Italian cities' mastery of the seas, with Venice as the center, it had been possible to transport the products of the Orient, especially Indian spices, to Europe. When the invasion of the Turks made the possibility of this connection more difficult for the merchants, the need arose to find another way to India around Africa. From Portugal and other southern countries, ships went out to explore the areas around Africa. Bartolomeu Dias† succeeded in finding the "Cape of Storms," later named the Cape of Good Hope, and Vasco da Gama† found the sea route to India in 1498. This marked the beginning of a new era for European economic life, which culminated in the discovery of America by Columbus† in 1492. That, however, belongs to the history of more recent times.

We have gotten to know the end of the Middle Ages and the factors that led to a new era. At this point, we see the whole of life shaken to its foundations. If you tend to think that the divisions in history are chosen arbitrarily, this division is really significant. A truly seismic shift happened, as we saw with the founding of cities in the middle of the Middle Ages and with the great migrations of peoples before that.

Now, under the aegis of the city culture, in connection with all of these inventions and with the great scientific triumph of Copernicus,† a whole new culture is brought forth. The secularization of culture and a strengthening of the power of the nobility is brought about by this stream. Smaller territories had not been able to resist the devastating advances of the Turks and were forced to join more powerful ones. The expansion of the great states is due to all these factors. We have seen the conditions change with manifold examples. We have seen how the bourgeoisie arises, how it blossoms, and how it is confronted with a dangerous opponent in the power of the nobility.

You know that the present is the result of the past. We will therefore study history in the right way if we learn from the past for the sake of the present and the future. This appreciation comes to us in the saying of an old Celtic bard. The bard says that the most beautiful music for him is when he hears of the great deeds of the past, because they stir and inspire him. As true as it is that human existence is the most important phenomenon and thus the human being himself the worthiest object of study, it is also true that the human being remains a great mystery to himself. When he realizes that he remains a mystery to himself, he will be compelled to study in the right way. For only then will he face himself with the correct appreciation. Then he will know that this is his secret: his individual existence stands in relationship with all existence. This gives him the right basis for all his deeds and actions.

But if he wants to learn something about this secret of his own existence, he must turn to that form of knowledge which tells about his own striving. In world history, we see how feelings and thoughts turn into actions. We should learn world history so that we can inspire our hopes, thoughts, and feelings with it. Let us bring over from the past what we need for the future, what we need for life, for action!

II

LECTURES AT
THE INDEPENDENT COLLEGE IN BERLIN

Platonic Mysticism and *Docta Ignorantia*

Lecture One

BERLIN, OCTOBER 29, 1904

AT THE BEGINNING of what we call Christian mysticism, during the time of the Gnostics,† mysticism was called *mathesis*.† It was a knowledge of the world on a large scale, built on the pattern of mathematics. The mystic does not merely seek to know the external world according to inwardly acquired laws, but rather seeks to know all life; he engages in the study of the laws of all life. Starting from the very simplest, he ascends to the ideal. The basis of mystical thought, the fundamental concepts of mysticism, the content of what is called mysticism, is little understood, and not only because it is judged merely by its external designation. Reading descriptions of mysticism is like reading a description in which the angles and corners of a house are discussed, as if a mathematician were trying to describe the actual mathematics of angles and corners. The words of mysticism, however, pertain to the interconnectedness of life.

We will now look at a picture of the mystical way of thinking up to Meister Eckhart in the thirteenth and fourteenth centuries, whose sermons inspired all later mystics. We have to go back to a name that is often misunderstood, that of Dionysius the Areopagite. In the Acts of the Apostles, we are told of a Dionysius who is said to have been a disciple of the Apostle Paul. In the sixth century, some writings appeared that are extremely stimulating for those who need a religion of the soul. They were translated from Greek into Latin, and thus they became known to occidental spiritual life. This happened at the court of Charles the Bald through the efforts of the theologian Scotus Eriugena.†

In scholarly writings today, the works of Dionysius are attributed to pseudo-Dionysius. The writings of Dionysius cannot be found any further back than the sixth century. But since they were handed down by oral tradition, we can assume with certainty that the texts date to the earliest times of the occidental world. However, they were only written down in the sixth century.

The mystic thinks differently than the rationalist and materialist. The mystic says: I look out into space and see a world of laws according to which the stars move. I grasp these laws and re-create them. Therefore, the spirit has a power of re-creation. Thought is not merely something imaginary for the mystic. The thought that lives in the human being is only a re-creating thought in which one relives what creates outside in the world. The spirit, which creates outside in the world, is the same spirit which thinks its laws in me. Outside in the world, he sees thoughts speaking. The creative powers of the universe have imprinted the laws on the orbits of the stars. This spirit celebrates its recognition of itself, its rebirth, in the human spirit. The mystic says to himself: In the universe outside, thinking works creatively. To the degree that a person possesses understanding, his understanding is objective thought outside. In the human being, cosmic thought becomes subjective thought. There is a connection that at the same time separates the human being in his inner experience from the thought outside and causes this thought to flow into him from outside.

If we look at a crystal, we see the thought of a cube or some other thought realized in the crystal. If I want to understand this thought, I have to reconstruct the thought, to relive it. That which lives in the outer world comes into relation to me through sensation from inside, by way of the eye, sensation which relives the thought.

We have to distinguish, first, the creating thought in the universe; second, the physicality or corporeality of the human being as the connecting link; and third, the subsequent thought in the human being. The physical body opens the gateway for creative thought to flow in from outside and thereby shine forth again within. The physical body forms the mediation between both thoughts—the creating and the re-creating. That which is initially creative thought operating in nature, one calls the spirit. That which senses the thought, we call body. That which relives the thought, we call the soul. The spirit is the creator of the thought. The body is the receiver of the thought. The soul is the one who experiences the thought.

The mystic understands the creating spirit outside under three concepts. This is clearly explained by Aristotle.† He presents quite a strange concept of the creator of the world. He says that this world creator cannot be found directly; however, he is contained in everything. If the divine spirit were present today somewhere in some form, and if we were to form a picture of the creator afterwards, we would still have only an imperfect picture of him. We must not make a specific, finite concept of the world spirit. Only in the future will we know what the world actually impels and sets in motion. The world is grasped in a continuous process of perfection. The one who creates in the world is the actual mover, the primal mover, the unmoved mover. It is to him that we must look up and in him know the primal power that lives in all. The primal spirit of Aristotle moves everything in the world, but in no being does he exhaust himself entirely; he is the creative, formative spirit that moves the outer world.

Everything is already actualized in the world. We raise our gaze to the stars of a solar system, and there we find a great perfection. Thinking in the sense of the principle of evolution, we must understand that this world system was not always there but that it has been formed. Wherever we look out into the universe, we must say that it has formed up to a certain degree of perfection. To different degrees of perfection, all that has been accomplished is present through the efforts of an unmoved mover. In everything you can distinguish between what is already present—the realized—and the distant, divine goal. But why does a world system, an Earth, move toward this distant goal? It must have in itself a striving toward the unmoved mover. In mysticism, you need a designation for this striving in the individual world system. One asked oneself: How has the human being striven for this unmoved mover? The answer: he directed his mind to it. The expression of this inclination has always been given in the content of his religious creeds, which even today contain guidance on how to reach the unmoved mover.

In India, the expression of striving was called *Veda* or "Word."

Among the Greeks, it was called *Logos*, Word. It is the striving of man toward the unmoved mover, who draws us to itself. That which has been realized was called the Spirit, the Holy Spirit, in the earliest days of Christian mysticism. That which strives toward it is the Word. In Gnosticism and in Augustine,† the Holy Spirit is the thought that shapes the universe. That which strives in all things to reach the form of the Spirit is called *Logos* or Word. The third is the unmoved mover itself, what the Christian mysticism of the first centuries calls the Father. This is the threefold aspect under which thought presents itself in the external world. The earliest Christian mysticism said: God presents himself in three masks (mask—persona, from *personare*, to sound through), that is, in three masks or three persons of the divine spirit. Under these three masks, the spirit shows itself in the universe.

What lives as spirit in the inner human being is the soul. This soul cannot create a thought for itself. It must first have the sensation of an object. Then it can spiritually re-create the object in itself. Only then do we get the idea in the soul; then the consciousness of the idea comes to us. What lives in the soul can be represented under two aspects: the aspect of sensation, which acts as the great stimulator, the great fertilizer; then comes that which lights up in the soul as inner picture; that is the resting element in the soul, which receives its content from outside. The resting soul, which is fertilized by the impressions from the world, is the Mother. The sum of the sensations throughout the universe is the soul masculine, the Father. That which allows itself to be fertilized is the soul feminine, the mother soul, the eternal feminine. That through which man becomes conscious of himself, the mystic calls the Son. The aspects of the soul are: Father, Mother, and Son. They correspond to the three aspects in the cosmos: Father, Son, and Holy Spirit, the aspects of the World Spirit.

By letting his soul be fertilized by sensation, the human being gives birth once more to the whole universe out of his soul as son. This universe born out of the soul as mother, the mystic calls the Christ. One who approaches the ideal of becoming more and more conscious of the universe approaches what the mystic calls the Christ in Man. Meister Eckhart† says that in the soul Christ is born. Likewise, Tauler† says: Christ is the universe reborn in every human being. This trinity was present in ancient Egyptian mythology as Osiris, Isis, and Horus.

Thirdly, the mystic considers the bodily self. The mystic distinguishes, as his own experience, the three persons of the universal spiritual life as Father, Mother, and Son. This is the sense in which Meister Eckhart must be read. The activity of knowing is for Meister Eckhart a resurrection. He says that God has created in him an eye with which He can look at Himself.[†] When the human being feels himself as an organ of the Godhead, which thereby looks at itself, then he has become a mystic; a higher knowledge has then arisen for him.

Lecture Two

BERLIN, NOVEMBER 5, 1904

We have seen that the mysticism of the Middle Ages is based on the idea of the threefoldness of human nature and of the whole universe. We have seen how the mystic pictured the spirit as well as the physical and soul nature. It is in the nature of the mystical way of thinking that the mystic experiences in the spirit what is outside in nature. He re-creates from himself what is outside in nature. In all knowledge, in all inner experience, he seeks a reawakening of the universe from the human soul. In the laws that rule the universe, he sees the great world-thoughts, world-ideas. He stands completely on the standpoint of the Platonic worldview.

Plato[†] was the great mystic of antiquity, and all those who practiced mysticism in the Middle Ages were rooted in Platonism. If the mystic therefore sees in nature the creating thought, the cosmic thought, then each thing that surrounds the mystic becomes an expression of the spiritual. He distinguishes, first, the great laws of the world, the creative thoughts; second, formless matter; and third, the force that matter becomes through the spirit's activity in it. So, first, law or world-thought; second, matter; and third, force. The force arises from the fact that the world-thought expresses itself in the matter. Nothing could be perceived with the senses if the force did not press itself on the senses and exert an effect on the senses. In the outer physical world, there are therefore three members. In the soul, the external arises again inwardly.

We distinguish in the sense of the mystic: first, the Father principle, the sum of all perceptions and sensations; second, the soul Mother, that which receives the sensation in the soul; and third, the Son, consciousness itself, in which the sensation comes to life. This is the connection of sensation, inner picturing, and thought.

In the soul itself, the mystic experiences the spirit in its inwardness directly as spirit, in three members: first, the unmoved mover of Aristotle—the Father Spirit; second, the longing for the unmoved mover that lived in the soul—the Word, or *Logos*; third, the resurrection in the spiritual world—the Spirit.

The soul can sink down into itself, can look spiritually, through inspiration or intuition. The mystic says: When I look out into nature, its force acts on me, and I feel the force that acts on me—which I call energetics, the life of force. By immersing itself in the external world, the soul must be animated by sensation, according to Aristotle. He says: If I want to see the unmoved mover, I must be free from all external sensation. This immersion within the soul he calls catharsis, purification. After catharsis, the soul unites with the spirit when it becomes intuitive, when it does not unite with the sensation from the external world.

Henosis[†]—union—is the immersion into the spirit, the union with the divine primal spirit. This can happen only when the soul is purified from external sensation. This purified soul, free from external sensation, is called by the mystic the virgin soul. It is not impregnated by external sensation. Just as the soul is otherwise fertilized by the outer world through sensation, so is it fertilized inwardly through the idea. If the soul experiences the idea in itself, if it lets itself be virginally fertilized by the spirit, then this conception is for the mystic the immaculate, virginal conception: the *conceptio immaculata*. The idea will produce in the soul not only the Son who reproduces the external world but the Son who is the Spirit itself. The resurrection of the second principle of the Spirit, the Word or *Logos*, in the virgin soul—this the mystic calls the resurrection of the Christ principle. Thus, the soul can be impregnated by sensation and can allow the Christ, who is buried in the external world, to be resurrected within it; or the soul can be impregnated by the idea, and then it gives birth within itself to the spiritual Christ, the Word or *Logos*.

For Meister Eckhart, only one who experiences in himself the Christ, the *Logos*, is a real participant in the Christ principle in the higher sense. It is of no use for a person to know himself united with his God if he regards the God as an external reality. Rather, he must let the Christ principle come to life in his soul. With his teaching, Meister Eckhart has made hearts glow again and again by showing people how one can become drunk if one experiences this within oneself. The deepest birth of the spirit must be born from one's own soul. The mystics have all understood this.

Eckhart says that what matters is not the image that has become present but that which is always present to man. God and I are one in recognition. God became man so that I might become God. He further speaks of how in each individual human being the higher, inner human being, who leads up to the spirit, comes to life. Two people live in each one—the worldly and the spiritual human being. The inner, spiritual human being goes its own way. The outer human being can lead a life for himself, but the inner life takes its own course by letting itself be fertilized inwardly by the *Logos*. Again and again, Eckhart presented this through his powerful sermons. The little spark in the soul is the essential thing. The spark is an eternal Oneness.

When the human being experiences the resurrection of the small spark, he feels God Himself in his soul. There is an artistic expression among the mystics: The soul has let itself into its foundation. This is connected to the image of the door with the hinge. As the hinge on which the door turns remains unmoved, so also the inner human being remains unmoved. Inside, he leads his own life. The inner experience of God is what comes about when the soul lets itself into its foundation. The mystic calls the awareness of the divine life in himself self-abandonment [*Gelassenheit*] (Angelus Silesius).[†] The mystic experiences God within himself. Through this, God is present in the person as in a dwelling. The mystic feels himself as a mediator between God and the world, and he carries out the commands of the Godhead that have been implanted into his soul. He has the idea that God needs man. This idea runs like a leitmotif through the whole mysticism of the Middle Ages. This is what makes mysticism so solemn.

Eckhart compares the world to a building and the people to building stones. Man, as a building stone, should not withdraw from the world. The mystic feels united with the primordial divine life. This is what it means to be enlightened (in mysticism it is called the self-knowledge of man). It shows that, just as the mathematician generates numbers, the human being can generate the highest from himself. Self-knowledge becomes direct enthusiasm, because self-knowledge means devotion to the Godhead.

In Johannes Tauler, this mood of the mystic comes to expression in his whole life. His life was an exposition of the divine life. He says: As long as I only discuss and present the highest divine wisdom, I have not achieved the right thing. I myself must completely disappear and must let God speak from me. He says, God looks at His own laws, through which He created the world, through me. My self is the very life of self : I must allow God to experience Himself in me.

The mysticism of Eckhart is a mystical knowledge; in Tauler, we find mystical life. From that time on, a special artistic expression is used to describe mystics: The one who experiences God in himself is called "the friend of God."

An unknown personality appeared during Tauler's sermon. He is called "The Friend of God from the Oberland." We never meet him in any other way than that he appears, as it were, as a mirror of the other personalities who are influenced by him. Johannes Tauler states in his *Meisterbuch*[†] that he communicated knowledge of God to people, but he could not yet let life overflow. Then the Friend of God came and gave Johannes Tauler his enlightenment. The original source itself came alive in him. For a long time, he gave up all preaching and withdrew with the unknown Friend of God from the Oberland in order to bring himself into the state of mind in which this spiritual life arose, thus making himself into the channel of divine wisdom, which overflowed through him into others. His speech gained fire. He made the greatest impression;[†] people were transformed by his words, finding the spark within themselves kindled. The dying away for everything that lives in the outside world is the awakening of the new human being. That is what Johannes Tauler could now bring about through the power of his words. Goethe says: "For as long as you do not have this, this dying and becoming, you are only a dull guest on the dark earth."[†] The experience of the *conceptio immaculata* is the dying and becoming, in the lower sense and in the higher sense. Those who listened to Tauler experienced the *unio mystica*. As the human being experiences all external beauties, which come from outside, through perception, so the mystic experiences the beauty of the spiritual world through Christ, whom he experiences. It is an experience that makes him drunk: this is the true music of the spheres. Just as the human being feels the sensual harmony in the world of sensation, so the mystic feels in the soul the coherence of the great laws of the world, the working, the creating of the *Logos*, of God Himself, the music of the spheres. Through the human soul, the eternal God expresses himself in his *Logos*. John of Ruusbroec,[†] the Belgian mystic, emphasizes this thought in a particularly intense way. The mystic understands in mysticism the lighting up of the divine source in his own soul. The mystic feels in himself, in self-knowledge, the divinity. Through this, Tauler found such flaming words for it.

Lecture Three

BERLIN, NOVEMBER 12, 1904

Today we come to a high point of medieval mysticism, to the mystic who was at the same time one of the most important scholars of his time: Nicolaus Chrypffs or Krebs, von Kues on the Mosel, also called Cusanus.† We will call him Nicholas of Cusa. He was one of the most interesting personalities of his time. He lived from 1401 to 1464. During his era, he stood at the height of the various sciences. He was a mathematician, physicist, judicial theorist, and originally a lawyer. He was also one of the leading men of his age. Indeed, he was extraordinarily ahead of his time. About a hundred years later, Nicolaus Copernicus† reoriented the world's understanding of astronomy. But Nicholas of Cusa had already clearly stated that the earth moves around the sun. Even more significant seems to be that Nicholas of Cusa was not only a deep, leading thinker, but a clear thinker. He is a thinker who had absorbed scholasticism† completely. That which is expressed through scholasticism is very little studied today. Its tremendous clarity and sharpness of conceptualization is the essential thing about it. Never has there been such a careful attention to conceptual contours, never such a strict delimitation of the concepts related to spiritual life. Whoever wants to train himself in clear thinking, whoever works with firm, conceptual outlines, must immerse himself in one of the scholastic works. Nicholas of Cusa went through this training.

He also possessed everything related to the social knowledge of his time. He had a comprehensive range of interests. In 1432, at the Council of Basel,† he took an important position. Thereafter he made extensive journeys through Germany and the Netherlands, dedicated especially to the reform of education. He worked on behalf of the Brethren of the Common Life.† They were dedicated to a comprehensive education of the soul and a clear education of the intellect. Nicholas of Cusa undertook his journeys in the service of this movement. Scientifically trained, clear and sharp thinking—he stands there independently, as a personality of imposing character. If he had wanted to, he could have achieved many things in the scientific field. As a preacher, he knew how to reach his audience in the depth of their souls through his sermons. What made his preaching so significant was the stream that emerged from medieval mysticism, the stream that we find in Eckhart, in Tauler, in Suso, and in another form in Giordano Bruno and Paracelsus.†

The depth of his mind, the fire of his soul, was paired with a completely transparent, sharp conceptual ability. Everything that the mind can comprehend, that reason can survey, gave Nicholas of Cusa only the substructure for what he had to say to the world. He was sent by the Pope to Constantinople to bring about a union between the Greek and Roman Churches. On his way home, he had an epiphany in which he felt that there was something else besides the knowledge of the mind. From then on, he attributed the highest value only to that which is higher than knowledge. He wrote the work *De docta ignorantia*† out of this mood. The title, *Of learned ignorance*, should mean: something that goes beyond the mere sensory and intellectual knowledge, a seeing, a being enlightened. If one wants to understand this completely, one has to use some concepts that were only introduced in the nineteenth century.

The nineteenth century has developed a peculiar physiology of the senses—for example, in the famous laws of sensory energies of the physiologist Johannes Müller.† He says that we can see a color, take in light, because our eye is built in a certain way. If we did not have the eye, the world shining in light and colors would be lightless, without the perception of colors. The same can be said about the arrangement of our ear. How the external world penetrates us depends on the arrangement of our senses. How we perceive the world depends on the specific energies of our senses. Helmholtz† has described how he thinks of the relationship. He says: How can I know how the light itself, the sound itself is formed? Our sense impressions are only signifiers of the outer world. Nicholas of Cusa describes "knowledge" in the same way, namely, as the impressions processed by the mind.

We now ask: Do our senses not have an intimate relationship with what we see, hear, and so on? We must imagine that the eye itself is built by the light, that the senses are not only there for the outside world but come from the outside world. The eye has been formed by the light. Who then are those who build on our senses? If the human being were not limited by the boundaries of his ordinary consciousness, he would know this.

That power which forms the senses must be in each person. In embryonic life, light must be active, and sound must be active. In embryonic life, they must work in the individual himself and form the organs. Light opens the eye from within, and sound opens the ear. We perceive the external qualities only through the senses. These external qualities have also formed the senses. They are the builders of our own organs. We ourselves are light from the world light; we are sound from the world sound.

The mystic lives into what lives and weaves around him and in him. He feels the creating light that works outside and creates inside. He is himself shining and resounding in a shining and resounding world. When he lives in the creative light, lives in the creative sound, then he has mystical life. Then something comes over him that is different from the light from outside and the sound from outside. Whoever has experienced this once, feels it as truth. The Gnostics, the Egyptian mystics, and the mystics of the Middle Ages all speak of the creating light. They call it the "Light of Eons." It is a light which from the mystic awakens the objects around him to living life. This is the *pleroma*[†] of the Gnostics. Thus, the mystic feels blessed in the world-light. He feels blissfully interwoven with this Light of Eons. There, he is not separated from the essence of things; there, he is partaker of the immediate creative power. This is what the mystic calls his bliss in the creative light. The Vedanta wisdom calls the world-wisdom *chit*, but the bliss where the mystic is immersed in the things, where the soul merges completely with the things, is called *ānanda*.[†] *Chit* is the wisdom of the world and *ānanda* is the wisdom that merges directly with the Light of Eons, that feels one with the All-Light shining through the world. Nicholas of Cusa calls this mood *docta ignorantia*.

Just as one can have the experience of merging with the Light of Eons, with the *pleroma*, so one can also merge with the cosmic world-thought. Then one feels the world-thoughts resounding in one's own inner being. When man becomes aware of the thought that brings the lawfulness to existence in things and feels this welling up in him as his own lawfulness, then the things resound in their own essence in his soul. Then, he becomes intimate with the things, as friends become intimate.

This perception of the whole world is what the Pythagoreans called the harmony of the spheres. This is the resounding of the essence of things in the individual human soul. There he feels united with the power of God. That is the hearing of the harmony of the spheres, of the creating universal law. That is being interwoven with the being of things. That is where the things themselves speak, and the things speak from him through the language of his soul. Then he has achieved what Nicholas of Cusa says no words are capable of expressing.

The existing is the seen. This does not express sublime existence, which is the predicate of the things when the mystic unites himself in the deepest way with the things. This sublime existence is the *sat* of the Indians.

The Pythagorean school distinguishes three stages: First, the external perception (*chit*); second, the *pleroma* (*ānanda*); and third, the harmony of the spheres (*sat*).

These are the three stages of cognition in Nicholas of Cusa: first, knowledge; second, supra-knowledge or beatification; and third, deification. This is how he names them in his *De docta ignorantia*. That he knows these conditions gives his writings such a melodiousness, such a softness, that one can say they are sweet with ripeness. Moreover, his writings are wonderfully clear, transparent, and full of powerful ideas.

He was truly a leading spirit. All those who follow him then stand on the foundation he created (among them, Giordano Bruno). Nicholas of Cusa drew his wisdom from the Pythagorean school. He understood what was meant by the *pleroma*, the Light of Eons, and the harmony of the spheres. Ruysbroek and Suso, too, in their refined and spiritual manner are the precursors of Nicholas of Cusa.

The *Theologia Deutsch*[†] is like an overture to what Nicholas of Cusa wrote. A reprint of it was procured by Franz Pfeiffer, made from a manuscript from 1497. Deep, warm-hearted tones of a historically unknown personality are contained in this writing. If someone wants to understand the *sat* of Vedanta philosophy, he must pour out his will completely—just like how with *ānanda* he must pour himself out into the world. In becoming divine (*sat*), the selfless will must be present; his will must have become impersonal. The one who wrote the *Theologia Deutsch* made sure that his name did not come down to posterity. He calls himself only "the Frankfurter." Man must surrender his will to the divine and let it become a messenger of the divine, and that which man wills of himself, the author of this writing calls a mutual offering.

Before Nicholas of Cusa, mysticism strove to ascend from mere knowledge to an initiation into the *pleroma*, the creating world-light. In the learned not-knowing, this then came out in a learned and perceptive way. Knowledge and understanding were awakened to immediate, new life. The not-knowing of Nicholas of Cusa is at the same time a supra-knowledge. He distinguishes three stages: knowledge, bliss, deification—*chit*, *ānanda*, *sat*. He is at the same time the greatest scholar and one of the most profound human beings.

Schiller and Our Age

Preface by Rudolf Steiner
to the 1st Printed Edition (1905)

A Few Words to the Reader

THE FOLLOWING is a reproduction of the lectures I gave on Schiller at the Berlin *Freie Hochschule* (Independent College) from January to March. The reprint is only based on notes that two listeners took during the lectures. I myself was not in a position to look through the notes. I only complied with an urgent wish when I gave my consent to the printing. Actually, I am not of the opinion that lectures should be printed. What is spoken is to be styled on being heard and not on being read. Spoken treatises or spoken books are an absurdity. And likewise books that spring from rewritten lectures. Those who have a sense of style will agree with me. Exceptions to this rule may be made in individual cases. Such an exception is present here. It seems to me to confirm the rule.

Berlin, April 1905
Dr. Rudolf Steiner

Lecture One

Schiller's Life and Character

BERLIN, JANUARY 21, 1905

May 9, 1905, will mark one hundred years since Schiller's death. The German literary world will undoubtedly celebrate the memory of this event in a festive way.

Three generations separate us from Schiller's death. It seems necessary to look at what Schiller means to us today. In 1859, the most recent major Schiller celebration took place in a completely different way than it could be done today. Times have changed immeasurably since then: other images, questions, and thoughts occupy the minds of our contemporaries. When the Schiller celebration took place in 1859, it was something that deeply touched the hearts of the German people. At that time, there were still personalities who themselves lived completely in the ideas that were brought forth by Schiller's poetic power. It is certainly possible that this time around there will be additional exuberant festivities; however, there can no longer be such sympathy from the depths of the soul. The question forces itself upon us: What has happened since then and how can Schiller still mean something to us?

The great images of the Schiller-Goethe period have faded away. At that time, those views were still embodied in personalities that the older among us got to know in our youth. These leading spirits, who were completely rooted in the traditions of that time, are today among the deceased. The youngest among us no longer know them. In the person of my own teacher, Schröer,[†] who enthusiastically presented the Goethe period to us, I had the privilege of getting to know a person who was completely rooted in the traditions of that time. With the passing of Herman Grimm,[†] the last of those whose souls were completely connected with that time has died.

Today, all that has become history. Other questions occupy us now. Political questions and social questions have become so burning that we no longer understand that intimate contemplation of art. The contemporaries of Schiller and Goethe seem strange to us. We have lost the intimate, soulful contemplation of art. This is not meant to be a reproach; our time has become hardened.

Let us look at three leading spirits of today—how differently they speak about what drives the times. First, Ibsen:[†] We see him describing in a comprehensive way the cultural problems of the present. He found the most haunting tones for the heart of the present, for a civilization going into chaos. Then, Zola:[†] How should today's art relate to the life that flares up in social struggles? That is the question he raises. This life seems to us so solid, so impenetrable, and so determined by powers quite different from those of our imagination and soul. Finally, Tolstoy:[†] He started from art and only from it did he become a preacher and social reformer. Today, a purely aesthetic culture seems impossible, as Schröer characterized it for the Schiller-Goethe period. At that time, what we can call the aesthetic conscience had become the decisive question of life. Beauty, taste, and artistic sensibility were taken for such serious and important questions as politics and freedom are today. Art was regarded as something that should intervene in the wheels of culture. Today it is different: Tolstoy, who had achieved the highest in the field of art, abandoned art and looked for other means to speak to the feelings of his contemporaries.

Schiller can therefore not be appreciated in our time in the way he was in the eighteenth century. What has remained, however, is the most penetrating depth of his worldview. We see numerous questions put into a completely new light by Schiller's view of the world. Let us try to look at them from this point of view. This will be the task of these lectures.

In treating of the questions of today and of culture—in the realm of science as well as in artistic striving—confusion and lack of clarity prevail in many cases. Every young writer believes himself called to establish a new worldview. Literature is filled with books about questions that have long since been solved. Problems are raised which, as they confront us, seem immature, because those who try to solve them have not really dealt with the questions. Often, the questions are not asked properly at all. The problem lies in the way the questions are posed.

We see Schiller's personality growing out of two currents. On the one hand, there is the rise of materialism and, on the other hand, the longing for the assertion of personality. What we call the Enlightenment is rooted in these two currents. Ancient traditions were shaken in the eighteenth century. Before that, in the sixteenth and seventeenth centuries, the deepest questions of the human spirit were still solved out of tradition. The relationship of man to the world, to the primordial source of the world, was not shaken.

Now it became different. To solve the basic truths about human spiritual life in the way in which they had been solved for centuries had become impossible. In France, stimulated by English sensualism,† a rationalistic, materialistic worldview arose. People began to derive the soul from material conditions, from the material; they tried to explain everything spiritual from the physical. The encyclopedists let the spirit emerge from matter. Vortices of atomic movements moved around what one saw in the world. "Man is a machine," is approximately how La Mettrie† formulated his materialistic creed. Already Goethe, when he became acquainted with the writings of these French materialists—Holbach's *Systeme de la nature* [The system of nature]†—complained about his uneasiness concerning the presumption to want to explain the whole world with a few pat concepts.†

In addition, there was another current, the one that started from Rousseau.† Rousseau's writings made the greatest impression on the most important people of that time. It is said of Kant† that he, who was a great pedant, took his daily walk with such punctuality that the inhabitants of Königsberg could set their watches by it. Once, however, to the greatest astonishment of the citizens, the philosopher stayed home for a few days because he had been reading Rousseau's writings. He had read Rousseau's writings and was so fascinated by them that he forgot to take his usual walk.

The basis of all culture was put in doubt by Rousseau. He had raised the question as to whether humanity had elevated itself through culture and had answered in the negative. In his opinion, people had been happier in the state of nature than now, when they let the personality in themselves degenerate. In the times when man, grounded in old traditions, still thought he knew something of the interrelationships of the world, he was not so much dependent on personality. Now, when individual personality had cut the chains of connection between itself and the world, the question arose: How should this personality again stand firmly in the world? People now believed they were able to know nothing about the original reason for the world or the soul. But if nothing was fixed in the world, the urge for better conditions had to become powerful in all hearts. The revolutionary striving of the eighteenth century started from here. It was connected with the materialistic current. A good Christian of the seventeenth century could not have spoken of freedom, equality, and brotherhood in this way. This striving for freedom must be considered the most original current of that time.

Schiller was young at the time when the thoughts of freedom were maturing. Rousseau's ideals, as I said, made a tremendous impression on the most outstanding German men, such as Kant, Herder, Wieland, and so on. The young Schiller was also seized by this current. We find him already at the *Karlsschule*† busy reading Rousseau, Voltaire, and others. At that time, the past had come to a dead end, the higher classes had lost all moral support, and external tyranny ruled even at school. In Schiller's case, we find a peculiar depth of disposition that already emerged in the boy as an inclination to religion; therefore, he originally intended to choose theological studies. His whole mind urged him to the deepest questions of existence. It was a form of that striving for freedom which took on this particular character in Germany: piety united with an infinite longing for emancipation. The drive for freedom of personality (not only in religion) is also what speaks from Klopstock's *Messiah*.† It was precisely in his religious sensibilities that the German wanted to be free. The *Messiah* made a tremendous impression on Schiller.

Schiller chose to study medicine. The way in which he took up medicine is connected with the questions that occupied him above all. Through serious study of nature, he sought to gain insight into the questions before him. The instruction in the *Karlsschule* affected him in quite a comprehensive way. The damages, which are often inherent in today's grammar school lessons, did not exist in the *Karlsschule*. Physics and natural sciences were treated in depth, and philosophy was the center of study. Serious questions of metaphysics and logic were discussed. Schiller entered his medical studies with a philosophical spirit. The way he grasped it is important and significant for his life. One does not fully understand Schiller unless one reads his two dissertations, which he wrote after completing his studies. They deal with the questions, "What is the connection between matter and spirit?" and "On the connection between the animal and spiritual nature of man." Little of the first dissertation has survived. In the second, Schiller poses the question: How are we to interpret the workings of matter in the human body?

For Schiller, there is already something spiritual in the material body. There are people who see in the body only something low, something animal. But it is not a deep, substantial worldview to degrade and detest the physical in such a way. It was not the worldview of the young Schiller. For Schiller, the body is the temple of the spirit, built by wisdom, and not for nothing does it have an influence on the spiritual. What is the importance of the body for the spiritual? Schiller, to whom the physical was also sacred, sought to resolve this question. He describes, for example, how the soul expresses itself in affect, in gesture, and he tries to explain, in a fine, spiritually vibrant way, the lasting aspect of the soul's movement through expressions. He says at the end of his treatise:

> Matter decays (at death) into its final elements, which now wander in other forms and conditions, through the realms of nature, to serve other purposes. The soul continues to exercise its thinking power in other areas and to look at the universe from other sides. It can be said, of course, that the soul has not exhausted this sphere in the least, that it could have left it in a more perfect form, but is one aware that this sphere is lost for it? We may now put aside a book we do not understand, but perhaps in a few years we will understand it better.

Thus, Schiller tries to clarify the relationship of the eternal aspect of the spirit within physical nature but without underestimating the physical. This question now remained Schiller's basic and core question for the whole of his life: "How is man born out of the physical, and how does his soul, the freedom of his personality, relate to the world? How shall the soul find its center, since the old traditions are gone?"

After he had exhausted his whole urge for emancipation in the roaring of his early dramas and thus won the heart of the people, he delved into history and philosophy, and we touch the deepest questions of cultural history when we look at Schiller's dramas. Every person at that time had an element of Marquis Posa[†] in him. This gave Schiller's problem a new face. Deep questions were raised about the human soul, about the meaning of life. Schiller saw how little had been achieved on the external plane. In Germany, people now tried to solve the problem of freedom in an artistic way, and this resulted in the meaning of the "aesthetic conscience." Schiller, too, had now posed the question in this sense. It was clear to him that the artist had to bring the highest elements to the people. He dealt with this problem in later years. In his letters *On the Aesthetic Education of Man*,[†] he says: Man acts unfree in the world of the senses out of necessity. In the world of reason, he is subject to the necessity of logic; therefore, man is limited by reality and the ideal of reason. But there is another, middle state between reason and the world of sense—the aesthetic. The one who has artistic feeling enjoys the spirit in the sensual; he sees the spirit interwoven into nature. Nature is for him a beautiful image of the spiritual. The sensual is then only the imprint of the spirit. In the work of art, the sensual is ennobled by the spirit. The spirit is brought down from the realm of necessity. In beauty, man lives as in freedom. Art is thus the mediator between the sensual and the rational in the realm of freedom.

Goethe also felt this way as he stood in front of works of art in Italy. In the beautiful, the urge for freedom—for these men—found its satisfaction; here, it is absolved of iron necessity. Not in the laws of the state or other forms of compulsion but in aesthetic enjoyment did Shiller see an education toward harmony. As a human being, he feels free through art. Schiller would like to transform the whole world into a work of art.

We see here the difference of that time from ours. Today, art stands in the corner, while at that time, Schiller wanted to give life an immediate impression through art. Tolstoy today must condemn art; Ibsen in his art becomes the critic of social life. At that time, Schiller wanted to intervene in life itself through his art. During his activity as a Mannheim theater consultant, he wrote his treatise on "Theater Considered as a Moral Institution"[†] in order to give a cultural impulse directly through art.

Lecture Two

Schiller's Work and Its Transformations

BERLIN, JANUARY 28, 1905

We have seen how Schiller grew out of the ideas of the eighteenth century, how the ideals of the Age of Enlightenment took root in his soul. They had already taken on their particular form when he left the *Karlsschule* and wrote those treatises mentioned earlier. If we want to characterize these views succinctly, we can say that it was about the emancipation of the personality. This liberation from ancient traditions goes even further. When the medieval person, before the Age of Enlightenment, thought about his relationship to himself, to nature, to the universe, to God, he found himself placed in this universe. He worshipped the same God outside who lived in his own soul, and the same world powers he found in nature were active in his own soul. There was a certain unity seen in the laws of the universe and in man's nature. You need only recall such minds as Giordano Bruno. This monistic conviction of the connection of nature with the human being speaks from his writings. Thus, there was no separation between what are called moral demands and the objective laws in nature.

This contrast came only later, when nature was excluded from divine influence. What arose in materialism did not know any connection between nature and moral feeling—that which one forms in oneself as a moral demand. From this emerged what was called Rousseauism. It is a revolutionary sentiment in the deepest sense, a protest against the whole development up to now. It teaches that when we consider man's call for freedom, his demand for morality, we find a deep discord. He asks: Can there exist a difference between the objective world and human nature, that people must long to be free, free of the whole of culture?

These spiritual storms were lived out in the attitude of the young Schiller. In his three youthful dramas, this yearning takes on a new form. In *The Robbers*, in *Fiesco,* and in *Intrigue and Love*, we see quite vividly portrayed, with tremendous pathos, the demand that man must do something to bring about this harmony. The figure of Karl Moor is portrayed as a man who carries within himself the conflict between the objective order and human demands and who feels called upon to bring about this harmony between nature and himself. He is tragic because he believes that he can help restore order through lawlessness and arbitrariness. In *Fiesco*, the longing for freedom fails because of ambition. The ideal of freedom perishes through this disharmony in the soul of the ambitious Fiesco, who cannot find his way into the order of the moral ideal. In *Intrigue and Love*, the demands of human nature in the aspiring bourgeoisie are set against the demands of the world as expressed by the ruling classes. The connection between the moral ideals and the universal world-ideas was lost. This discord resounds grandly with all the youthful immaturity of Schiller's first dramas.

Natures such as Schiller's are more difficult compared to straightforward, simple, naive natures, just as natural development shows that lower creatures need shorter preparatory stages than highly developed animals. Great natures have the characteristic that they have to go through the most difficult transformations because their innermost genius must be brought out of deep sources. Those who have much in them, who come into the world with an expectation of genius, will find their way through with difficulty and will have to work their way through manifold initial stages, as the embryonic development of higher animal species shows us as an analogy.

What Schiller lacked was knowledge of the world and of human nature. The first dramas show Schiller with all his resulting shortcomings, but also with all his merits, as they are hardly ever found later. This judgment is conveyed from a certain height: one must know what one owes to Schiller's greatness. But it could not remain so for long. Schiller had to get beyond this small horizon, and now we see how, in the fourth of his dramas, *Don Carlos*, he works his way toward another point of view. We can look at *Don Carlos* from a double perspective: first from the perspective of Carlos and second from the perspective of Marquis Posa. Schiller himself tells us how he first became interested in the youthful, fiery Carlos and then moved on to the cosmopolitan Posa. This represents a deep change in Schiller's own personality.

Schiller had been called to Dresden by his friend Körner to work quietly there. There he became acquainted with a worldview that was to exert a profound influence on his own personality—Kantianism. Schiller's nature was such that this preoccupation with Kant became necessary for him, and we will learn to understand his point of view even more deeply through this, if we deal with what affected him at that time.

We have two very definite currents in German intellectual life at that time. One current expresses itself most thoroughly in Herder's *Ideas for the History of the Philosophy of Mankind.*† The second is Kantian philosophy. In Herder, we have the longing to place man within the whole of nature and to understand him from there. It is this striving for unity that makes Herder appear to us as a modern spirit. What today rebels against the so-called *Kathederphilosophie*,† the still-prevailing Kantianism with its dualism, is already present in Herder's metacriticism. Herder encompasses a wealth of great ideas. Everywhere there is a striving for unity between nature and man. From the lowest elements of nature all the way up to the human thoughts, lives one law. What presents itself in man as a moral law exists within a crystal as the law of its formation. One fundamental force of development runs through all existing things so that what in a plant grows to blossoming also develops the human being to his humanity. It is the same worldview that also emerges in Goethe, which he expressed in his *Faust* with the words: "How everything weaves itself into the whole! / One works and lives in the other . . ."† and which he depicts in his *Hymn to Nature.*†

Goethe is completely suffused with this striving for unity as it is expressed in Giordano Bruno, the Pythagorean. He places himself completely in this current:

> What kind of a God, would only push from the outside,
> Would let the universe run on his finger in a circle,

It befits him to move the world in the inside,
To nurture nature in Himself, Himself in nature.
So that what lives and weaves and is in Him,
Never misses His power, never misses His spirit.[†]

This is the monistic current, to which Schiller was still a stranger at that time. For him there is still the twoness, the dualism.

In his *Critique of Pure Reason* and in his *Critique of Practical Reason*, Kant set a decisive limit to the human cognitive faculty. The human capacity for understanding goes only as far as reason reaches. It can only deal with the surface of things; it is not capable of reaching the essence of things. What the thing-in-itself is remains hidden behind the appearances. The human being is incapable of speaking about that at all, but something lives in his vision that cannot possibly be only appearance. This is moral law. On the one hand, there is the world of appearances. On the other hand, moral law—the categorical imperative, the "Thou shalt," in which no fault can be found. Moral law is sublimely above knowledge and is not to be understood from its manifestation. Thus, in Kant's philosophy, not only the duality we saw earlier confronts us but the whole world of human spiritual life separates into two halves. One half is then supposed to be sublime above all criticism, and that is the moral law. This moral law is not actually knowledge at all but practical faith, which is subject to no laws of cognition but only moral postulates. Thus, Kantianism appears as the harshest exposition of dualism.

Before Kant, there was a science that pertained to external appearances, and then there was a science of reason, which could penetrate to God, soul, and immortality by inborn activity. This is how Wolff's philosophy[†] presents itself. Kant, who studied the English sensualists[†] Hume and Locke, came into doubt on this point. He said to himself: Where does that get you if you try to examine the highest concepts, like God, freedom, and immortality, if you repeatedly try to test them for their reasonableness? He explains in the introduction to his *Critique of Pure Reason*: "I had to abolish knowledge in order to make room for faith." Because one should believe, and so that one can believe, he has overthrown knowledge from its throne. He wanted to start from undoubted foundations and therefore says: knowledge cannot penetrate at all to these things, but the "Thou shalt" speaks so strongly that the harmony which man is powerless to find must be brought about by God. This leads to Kant's postulating a God. We are enclosed between barriers as physical beings but must be free as moral beings. This yields an unbridgeable dualism with no balance between man and nature.

Schiller, who at that time held to the opposition between nature and man, describes in *Don Carlos* the growth of a man over and above all nature to reach ideals. He does not pose the question of what is possible but only the question of "thou shalt." In Carlos, Schiller does not give us a critique of court life. This takes a back seat to practical moral postulates. "Become a human being in such a way that the laws of your actions may become general laws of mankind,"[†] Kant had demanded. In the Marquis Posa, the cosmopolitan idealist, Schiller makes the demand for the independence of the ideal from everything that grows out of nature.

When *Don Carlos* was finished, Schiller stood in the greatest possible opposition to the worldview of Goethe and Herder; therefore, no rapprochement with them could take place during the beginning of his life in Weimar. Now, however, Schiller has become the reformer of Kantianism. He now strives for monism but finds unity only in the aesthetic field, in the problem of beauty. He shows us how the human being fulfills his potential only where he elevates nature to himself and takes up the moral element from above into his nature. The categorical imperative does not force him under a yoke, but he voluntarily serves what is contained in the "Thou shalt." Thus, Schiller achieves his eminence by growing beyond Kant. He turns against Kant, who does not want to make man a free being but a slave bent under the yoke of duty. It became clear to him that something completely different lives in the human being than this bending under a "Thou shalt." In monumental sentences, he expresses how he approaches what Goethe's and Herder's view already is: "Gladly I serve my friends, but alas I do it with inclination, and thus I am frequently pained by my lack of virtue."[†]

Kant had devalued what one does out of inclination, what one does voluntarily, and praised as something higher what one does out of duty. Kant turns to pathetic apostrophes when he discusses strict duty, which is not supposed to contain anything entangling. Schiller rescues the human being from his own weakness by making the moral law the law of his own nature. Through the study of history, through sincere inclination and devotion to human life, he arrived at the lost harmony and thus at Goethe's understanding.

Schiller describes Goethe's approach magnificently in the memorable letter of August 23, 1794:

> For a long time now, although from quite a distance, I have watched the course of your mind, and have noticed with ever renewed admiration the path you have marked out for yourself. You seek the necessity of nature, but you seek it by the most difficult way, which every weaker spirit will seek to avoid. You take the whole of nature together in order to shed light on the individual pieces; in the unity of its modes of appearance, you seek the explanatory ground for the individual phenomenon.[†]

With this, Schiller had reached the height to which he had to develop. Starting from the duality, he had now come to the unity between man and nature. Thus, he came to the kind of creativity that belonged to him in the last period beginning in the middle of the 1790s, and to a friendship with Goethe. It was a historic friendship because it did not seek happiness for the two of them alone but was fruitful for the world, for humanity. In what we have in Goethe and Schiller, we have not only Goethe and Schiller, but we have a third: Goethe *plus* Schiller. Whoever follows the course of spiritual life will see in it a being which could only arise from the fact that in selfless friendship and mutual devotion, something developed which stood as a new being above the individual personality. This mood will give us the right transition to Goethe and what he was to mean for Schiller.

Lecture Three
Schiller and Goethe

BERLIN, FEBRUARY 4, 1905

Today we come to one of the most important chapters in German intellectual history—the relationship between Goethe and Schiller. The behavior of the two is unique in the world. They came from two entirely different backgrounds: Goethe from Herder and everything connected with the unity of spirit and nature, and Schiller from Kantian philosophy, from dualism. Moreover, Goethe's and Schiller's natures were fundamentally different. Take Goethe's *Faust,* how he seeks to penetrate nature, how he feels unsatisfied in comprehending the spiritual in abstractions and strives to draw it directly from nature. For Schiller, at first, nature was something lowly, and the world of ideals was something special to him, something springing from the spirit and in contradiction with mere physical reality. Both had extraordinarily deep natures and thus could find each other only with difficulty. Therefore, we see that these two great geniuses could not understand each other at all in their first personal meeting.

When Schiller came to Weimar, he felt repelled rather than attracted by what he heard from Goethe, and even a personal meeting could not change this. In 1788, Schiller wrote a derogatory review of *Egmont,*[†] this fruit of mature artistic study. He could not understand how Goethe had portrayed Egmont not as a heroic enthusiast (as would have been Schiller's approach at the time) but, in his opinion, as a kind of weakling who let himself be determined by the given circumstances. Schiller could not understand *Iphigenia*[†] at that time either.

Schiller and Goethe agreed on one point. In an essay on Bürger's poems, Schiller had said that the lack of idealism in Bürger did not satisfy him. Goethe agreed with this essay so much that he said he would like to have written the essay himself, but it still becomes apparent how different the course of the two spirits is in Schiller's essay *On Grace and Dignity*.† In this essay, Schiller's entire striving for freedom confronts us. He cannot find grace in necessity. A work of nature cannot appear as graceful. Only in the work of art which is a symbol, a symbol of freedom, can we speak of "grace." As "dignity" we can speak only of the higher spiritual. In all this, Schiller's old tendency to grasp the concept of the ideal as something opposed to the natural remains apparent.

Even the professorship in Jena, which Goethe obtained for Schiller, is not to be understood as a favor to a friend. This event was of far-reaching importance for Schiller. By studying historical figures, he was able to take a deep look into the spirit's course of development. It also gave him the opportunity to establish a household and to marry Charlotte von Lengefeld. It was the study of history that allowed Schiller to mature, as his inaugural topic, "What does universal history mean and to what end does one study it?" meaningfully expresses. In this way, Schiller became more and more involved in reality.

After the year 1790, following a visit to Christian Gottfried Körner,† who acted as a mediator between the two, Goethe probably took a completely different view of Schiller, but their friendship would not be based on the points of common sympathy in their everyday natures. It was not from personal interests that this alliance was to arise. Given the differences in their personalities, their friendship would never have become of such global significance.

It was after a meeting of the Society for Natural Scientific Research in 1794—probably in July—when Goethe and Schiller were on their way home and got into a conversation about the lecture they had just heard. Schiller said that everything seemed so fragmented to him, like nothing but details, whereupon Goethe said that he could probably imagine a different way of looking at nature. He told him about his views on the connection of all living beings, how the whole plant kingdom should be regarded as in continuous development. With a few characteristic strokes, Goethe sketched out the archetypal plant as he conceived it on a sheet of paper. "But the archetypal plant is not reality; it is an idea," Schiller objected. "Well, if that is an idea," said Goethe, "I see my ideas with my own eyes." In this disagreement, both forms of thinking reveal themselves. Goethe saw the spirit in nature. That which the spirit grasps intuitively was for him as real as the sense-perceptible; nature for him embraces the spirit. The true greatness in man now showed itself in Schiller's attempt to fathom what Goethe's spirit was rooted in. He wanted to find the right point of view. In recognition, free of jealousy, of that which met him in this way, Schiller established the deep friendship that was now to unite the two. One of the most beautiful human documents is the letter of August 23, 1794, in which Schiller writes to Goethe after he has immersed himself in Goethe's work.

> For a long time now, although from quite a distance, I have watched the course of your mind, and have noticed with ever renewed admiration the path you have marked out for yourself. You seek the necessity of nature, but you seek it by the most difficult way, which every weaker spirit will seek to avoid. You take the whole of nature together in order to shed light on the individual pieces; in the unity of its modes of appearance, you seek the explanatory ground for the individual phenomenon.[†]

This is how Schiller, having recognized his greatness, appreciated Goethe. There is no deeper psychological description of Goethe. It remained like this until Schiller's death. This friendship was unquestionable, although envy and resentment tried to separate the two by the lowest means. Now they worked together in such a way that the advice of one always had a fertilizing effect on the other. Schiller, in a greatness that has not yet been surpassed by other philosophers of aesthetics today, asks himself, "How does this or that concept fit in with the spirit of Goethe?" He finds an account of the different kinds of artistic creation, which he sets down in his treatise *On Naïve and Sentimental Poetry*.[†] The poet creates in a naïve mode when he still stands in connection with nature and is himself still natural in nature. This is how the Greeks created. The sentimental artist, on the other hand, is one who longs to return to nature after having been torn out of it. This is the essence of modern art.

There is something great in the way art was conceived by these two friends. An ancient teaching, which lives on in Eastern wisdom, of the transient nature of all appearance, of the veil of *maya*, is expressed here. Only he lives in reality who rises above illusion into the region of the spirit. The highest reality contains nothing external. Everything urged the two toward an inward way of working. True, Goethe had his Faust say, "In the beginning was the deed." But in Germany at that time, the conditions were not yet so far advanced as to create, as in France, the opportunity for external actions,[†] and only the longing for freedom existed. These spirits sought their deeds in the realm of the beautiful, in artistic creation. A reflection of the higher reality, of nature within nature, was to be introduced into life through the manifestation of the beautiful.

Goethe's *Wilhelm Meister*[†] stands under this sign. In *Wilhelm Meister*, the aim is to lead beyond the illusory in everyday life to the perfection of the personality. Thus, *Wilhelm Meister* becomes the most beautiful *Bildungsroman*[†] to which Schiller's words could apply as a motto: "Only through the dawn of beauty do you press on into the land of knowledge."[†] The spirit from which we act is the highest. It was not possible at that time to show that the spiritual world of the spirit is born from within. In *Wilhelm Meister*, the liberation of the world through artistic beauty was first portrayed.

The continuing collaboration and the advice of Schiller helped to bring out the personal moments in *Wilhelm Meister*. We see here, on the one hand, that which is to be regarded as the deeper cause of man, what a newer spiritual science calls the *causal body*,[†] and on the other hand, the external influences. Nothing develops that is not already present in a germinal form, but it is influenced by external factors. This interaction can be seen in Schiller's creative activity. His ballads, his *Wallenstein*,[†] would not have been possible if Goethe's influence had not had a fertilizing effect. It was a kind of modesty with which the two met each other, in which lies a tremendous greatness. They only became a whole through the complementarity of their two natures, through which tremendously great things could come about.

The deep and strong friendship made it so that everything philistine rebelled against them. The two were stalked by envy and jealousy because the small has never been able to understand the great. Today, one can hardly believe the attacks that were unleashed on these great figures by small minds. The *Annalen für Philosophie* [Annals of philosophy], for example, spoke of them in a dismissive way. A certain Manso† called them "the sloppy cooks of Weimar and Jena. . . ." They had to defend themselves against all these attacks, and what they produced in the *Xenien*† in 1796 is a beautiful monument to their friendship. In these passages, they pulled off an epic retort to all those who had offended either them or good taste, and it is not always possible to distinguish what came from Goethe and what from Schiller. Their friendship makes them appear as one person. By the example of Schiller and Goethe, we can perceive how greatness knows how to resist everyday life, and how friendship, which rests in the spiritual realm, truly bears and raises itself up.

And they both sought truth: Schiller first in the human heart, Goethe in all of nature.

Lecture Four

Schiller's Worldview and His *Wallenstein*

BERLIN, FEBRUARY 11, 1905

One cannot speak of Schiller's worldview in the same sense as of the philosophical worldviews of others because it is in a continuous flow, in constant ascent. Small personalities have an easy time arriving at a worldview. Great personalities have significant difficulty in developing one. This is because a small personality is not able to see through the great riddles. For greater personalities, a new riddle presents itself with every experience in life. These modify their views on an ongoing basis, and their worldview must be formed anew. Goethe went through this until the end of his life, and Schiller also went through the process on an ongoing basis. Schiller, of all people, said that he basically knew only a small circle of his own becoming but his mind was constantly working on a deepening, a harmonization of this stock of his concepts and life experiences. Characteristic of this is how Schiller conducted conversations. In this he was an antithesis of Herder, and a certain light falls on Schiller through this juxtaposition.

When Herder was in the company of people who were interested, he elaborated his views, and rarely was an objection made. He stood so firmly, so clearly, that he did not want to take a question further in dialectical conversation. It was quite different with Schiller. With him, every conversation came alive. He took up every objection, every related topic was discussed, and thereby he brought the conversation along all possible side paths. Everything was illuminated from all sides. It is in conversation—in the life he embraced in personal discussions—that we find most beautifully expressed how his views were in eternal flux. We have here the same striving for truth that Lessing expressed in the words: "If God stood before me, in one hand the full truth, in the other the striving for truth, I would ask him: Lord, give me the pursuit of truth, for the full truth is there for God alone."[†]

Thus, we see how Schiller, through all the periods of his life, was engaged in a continuous striving for a higher worldview. We see how, when he went to Jena to become a professor, he was compelled to bring his ideas to life and we see how he struggled to grasp the great forces at work in the world and to make them fruitful in lively lectures.

Schiller's shorter essays on the philosophy of history show us how he wrestled with these ideas. Besides the already mentioned lecture *What does universal history mean and to what end does one study it?*, he tried to characterize the importance of such a lawgiver as Moses. Then he treats of the time of the Crusades, and there is perhaps nothing more beautiful and interesting than the way in which Schiller describes the property and feudal relations of the Middle Ages. The great struggle for the independence of the Netherlands[†] is described in such a way that one can learn from it how the development of history inwardly proceeds. Then, there is the history of the Thirty Years' War,[†] in which he is captivated above all by the figure of Wallenstein.[†] Wallenstein shows him the man with the law of will in himself, firm in his person but afflicted with petty ambition, wavering in his goals and full of unclear concepts, brooding over the interpretation of the stars. Later, Schiller tries to unravel this figure poetically. But before that, he seeks clarification through the philosophical study of Kant's works. Not unprepared, Schiller also approached Kantianism as a philosopher. There was something in him at that time that could only come out through leaning on Kant.

One must grasp this point in Schiller's being deeply to be able to understand properly his great personality. There is a series of letters between Julius and Rafael in Schiller's *Philosophical Letters*.[†] The philosophy Schiller develops there is something innate to him. The worldview he has formed out of his deep personality is represented by the one who is called Julius, while in Rafael we must think of a man, like his friend Körner,[†] who has arrived at a certain completeness, even if not in such a deep way. For in life, the lesser often appears as cleverer, superior to the one who struggles and strives for higher things. The striving one, who still lives unsatisfied in disharmonies, sketches his worldview in the "Theosophy of Julius"† in the following way: "Everything in the world originates from a spiritual primordial cause. Man, too, has emerged from this primordial cause; he is a confluence of all the forces of the world. He acts like an excerpt, like a union of all that is spread out in nature. All existence apart from him is only a hieroglyph of a force that is similar to him. In the image of the butterfly, which rises from the caterpillar newly rejuvenated into the air, we have an image of human immortality. Only by being able to rise to the ideal implanted in us could we attain satisfaction."

Schiller calls this worldview the "Theosophy of Julius." The world is a thought of God. Everything lives only in the infinite love of God. Everything in me and outside of me is only a hieroglyph of the supreme being. Goethe in his prose hymn to nature had expressed it as: Man is placed unasked and unwarned into the cycle of life by nature so that she herself speaks and acts in him. In a certain way, Schiller comes to a similar standpoint in this "Theosophy of Julius." But he feels unsatisfied at first: Only a God could look at the world from such a point of view, he thinks. Can the human soul, which is so small and limited, really live with such a picture of the world?

From Kantianism, Schiller initially gained a new worldview that lasted until the mid-1790s. The world riddle has become a human riddle for him. It is the problem of freedom that initially occupies him. The question comes before his mind: How can man attain completeness?

Schiller's worldview is most pure and beautiful in the Aesthetic Letters.† On the one hand, man is subject to his lower nature, to his drives. Nature is necessity in the form of perceptible objects that assail him. On the other hand, there is spiritual necessity in man's thinking, and there is logic to which he must submit. He is a slave to the necessity of nature and at the same time a slave to the necessity of reason. Kant answers this contradiction with a demotion of natural necessity in relation to spiritual necessity. Schiller grasped in its profundity the gap between the necessity of nature and the necessity of reason. He saw in this a problem that spreads over all human relations. The laws that govern people are partly derived from the necessity of nature (from the dynamic forces that work in people) and partly from the moral order that they carry within themselves. Disharmony and oppression must follow from this. Thus, we have the dynamic state and the moral state, and both act as an iron necessity.

Only he can call himself free who has made the iron laws of reason and logic so much his own that he follows them without compulsion. He is free who has purified his moral feeling to such an extent that he cannot help wanting what is pure, because his inclinations have organized themselves upward toward the spiritual life. Only one who has brought down the laws of reason into the drives and inclinations of the soul and raised up the human passions to the knowledge of the moral order will so master these dynamic laws that harmony will ensue between his drives and his reason. Schiller calls the mood in which such a person finds himself, when he has thus purified his instincts, the aesthetic mood. He calls the state in which such people work the aesthetic society. Man must realize what appears to him as his highest dignity.

In the "Theosophy of Julius," Schiller had set up an ideal worldview. An education to the ideal is what Schiller demands from the individual and from human society. Development is what Schiller presents to his readers.

This is expressed in the poem "The Walk."[†] The harmony of the world does not appear to him as something achieved but as a goal of development. The eternal harmony of nature seems beautiful to him, but it seems like something that one should also strive for in oneself. It must become man's ideal to bring about a state in which people live in such harmony as is exemplified in nature. What Schiller had earlier striven for as the content of knowledge now became for him a moral-aesthetic ideal. Now, under the influence of Goethe, he became a poet again. In this way, he believed he could best show how the human spirit is in the process of development, how the various forces in him work together, and how he strives from the depths to the heights.

In *Wallenstein*, he poetically presented the fundamental problem he was working through in a very significant way. It became difficult for him to depict human nature, and this was more difficult for him than for lesser artists. Schiller did not create his figures out of abstract ideas and then seek the flesh to go with his skeleton of ideas, as has often been claimed. It was not like that with his figures, and it was especially not like that with Wallenstein. Schiller started from an inner musical mood, as he called it, not from ideas. Like it is with melodies, the stream of the forces involved in individual development poured into his interior, dissolving into harmony or sinking into disharmony. Then he searched for the characters, the individual moods. Before his eyes stood the contrasting soul forces of Wallenstein, which drove him by necessity to a great catastrophe. Unfortunately, this mood cannot be reproduced by any other means than by thoughts. There is a self-made personality who falls in tragic fashion. But it is tragic in the true sense of tragedy only when the personality fails of itself. Schiller intuitively grasped what Hebbel demands as a necessary prerequisite of the tragic, "that it had to end this way,"[†] that nothing can be tragic which could have been done in another way. He grasped this idea, although he did not yet express it!

But Schiller is under the influence of another tragic idea that cannot be resolved and that is expressed above all in the person of Wallenstein himself. It is the awareness that something higher plays into human life which cannot be solved within this framework. Only at the end of the world, when man will have reached perfection, will his gaze be able to survey his destiny in this way. Until then, there will always have to be errors, something insoluble for which Wallenstein seeks a solution in the stars, something imponderable in his own heart. Wallenstein believes he reads his destiny in the stars but must now see how Octavio deceives him, contrary to the oracle of the stars. But man's freedom remains supreme, and an inner necessity makes him seek the solution in the stars. He is faced with a new riddle: the stars have lied to him. But no, the stars cannot lie. One who violates the most sacred laws of feeling and of the heart disrupts the harmony of the stars. There can be no order in nature that contradicts the laws of the human spirit. Whoever looks at the character of Wallenstein in this way will see Schiller's own person looking through the person of Wallenstein in deep meaning.

Schiller wanted to look the contradictions of the world in the eye and show how one lives with these contradictions. There must be a truth in the world, he says to himself, and he has searched for it as he already has in the letter of Julius. The contradiction lies in the individual appearances. Schiller here comes to the realization of what the ancient Indians and other wise sages recognized as illusion. He wanted to live in truth and he regarded art as a gate through which man must pass in order to reach the dawn of beauty and freedom. In the poem "The Artists," he urges artists to place themselves in the cosmic plan and participate in the realization of the ideal. He calls to them: "The dignity of mankind is given into your hands. Preserve it!"[†]

Lecture Five
Schiller, Greek Drama, and Nietzsche

BERLIN, FEBRUARY 18, 1905

The time in which Schiller wrote *Wallenstein* was a time of transition for him, a time of purification in which he tried to rise from his earlier worldview to grasp what he called the purely artistic. We have seen how Schiller tried to see in the beautiful, the artistic, something that is able to elevate human soul forces and bring them into harmony so that it is artistic creation that gives man freedom. As he wrote to Goethe regarding *Wilhelm Meister*, the artist was the only true human being, and the philosopher only a caricature next to him. This was a radical turn that reflected what Schiller had felt at the time.

In *Fiesco*, *Intrigue and Love*, and *Don Carlos*, the characters are to be understood in such a way that some are sympathetic to him, others antipathetic. He wanted to discard this moral judgment, this moral evaluation, at the height of his artistry. Now he wanted to treat the criminal with the same love and care as the hero. The work of art should no longer be linked to something he himself felt as sympathy or antipathy.

When the reproach was raised against *Wilhelm Meister* that several characters offended against moral sensibility, he wrote to Goethe something to the effect, "If someone were able to show that the immorality stems from the author and not from the characters, then he could reproach you."[†] To him, *Wilhelm Meister* is a lesson in aesthetics.

Schiller, who had recognized the autonomy of the human personality, tries to rise to the pinnacle of genuine artistry. Therefore, a new kind of relationship to his creations arises. We see it already in *Wallenstein*. No longer was Schiller to have a personal investment, no longer did he want to judge and evaluate morally. He only wanted to act as an artist.

This view is reminiscent of a conversation Schiller had with Goethe in which they discussed architecture.[†] In this conversation, Goethe made a deeply significant point, which at first might sound somewhat paradoxical. Goethe demanded of a beautiful building that it make a harmonious impression not only on the eye but also on the person who would be led through it blindfolded. When all sense-perception has been erased, it is possible to enter into it with the spirit.

What was demanded here was not expediency but idealism of the spirit. At first glance, this demand seems paradoxical: it was created out of Goethe's and Schiller's high view of art. A circle of artists formed around them who saw things similarly. For example, Wilhelm von Humboldt,[†] a fine connoisseur of art, whose aesthetic treatises were significant for the intellectual milieu, joined the group. Schiller was thereby led on a collision course with his earlier artistic views and with Kantianism, which basically wanted to allow the supersensible to apply only in regard to morality. But no artist can see it in this way. In returning to the artistic, Kant no longer suffices for Schiller. Schiller's conception of tragic conflict was the one that Hebbel later formulated, saying that only that which is unchangeable is tragic.[†] This is how Schiller felt. This is how he had tried to elaborate it in *Wallenstein* and how he wanted to portray the tragic. In Shakespeare's *Richard III*, he saw fate breaking in with such immutability. But he had already taken a liking to Greek drama. In Shakespeare's drama, the person of the hero stands in the center, and the necessity of development arises from the character of the hero.

It is completely different in Greek drama. There, everything is already predetermined, everything is ready. Man is placed in a higher spiritual order. At the same time, because he is a being of the senses, he is crushed by it. Not character, not personality, but superhuman destiny is the determining factor. Thus, the Erinyes[†] of Greek tragedy were not originally goddesses of vengeance but actually signified something of a twilight, something that cannot be completely dissolved but that suffuses human fate. On his return to artistic creative activity, Schiller came to this conception of the tragic. Whoever wants to feel the tragic in such a way must eliminate the personal and detach it from the merely human. Only in this way will one understand *Wallenstein* correctly. Having outgrown the personality, something super-personal hovers over Wallenstein. That the human being belongs to a higher order, to a higher spiritual world, signifies for Schiller the meaning of the stars that guide human destiny. There in the stars, Wallenstein is supposed to read his fate.

Carlyle† points to this super-personality when, in Wallenstein's camp, he finds in the character of the individual personages a parallelism that plays out beyond them to the personalities of the leaders. In this way, the Irish dragoon, trusting to the play of fortune in war, points to his chief, Buttler; the first cavalryman, representing the nobler side of the life of war, points to Max Piccolomini; the trumpeter, in his unconditional devotion, points to Terczky; while the constable, pedantically quoting the sayings of his commander, appears as a caricature of Wallenstein.

We see here a great regularity that goes beyond the merely personal. The whole composition of the work proves the point of view that Schiller thought he had achieved. First, we have the camp, where Wallenstein does not appear at all. Second, we have the Piccolomini scene, where Wallenstein does not actually intervene at all. He learns what has happened through Max Piccolomini, and from his wife he hears what is going on at the Viennese court. He allows his generals to join forces and sign the famous document. The action takes place around him. The thought of betrayal is only casually grasped by him and then takes possession of his soul. Third, Wallenstein's death occurs. Now Wallenstein's own thoughts push him into events. His thoughts have taken on an objective life, and they have pushed him into a supra-personal fate. A monumental language characterizes this situation. It is placed in an iron necessity. The personal, which has nothing special to do with the overall direction, is pushed to the side. There are also shocking tones, as in the conversation with Max Piccolomini:

> *Wallenstein (has fixed his gaze on him silently and now approaches him):*
>
> Max, remain with me.

> Go you not from me, Max! Hark! I will tell thee—
> How when at Prague, our winter quarters, thou
> Wert brought into my tent a tender boy,
> Not yet accustomed to the German winters;
> Thy hand was frozen to the heavy colors;
> Thou wouldst not let them go.
> At that time did I take thee in my arms,
> And with my mantle did I cover thee;
> I was thy nurse, no woman could have been
> A kinder to thee; I was not ashamed
> To do for thee all little offices,
> However strange to me; I tended thee
> Till life returned; and when thine eyes first opened,
> I had thee in my arms. Since then, when have
> Altered my feelings toward thee? Many thousands
> Have I made rich, presented them with lands;
> Rewarded them with dignities and honors;
> Thee have I loved: my heart, my self, I gave
> To thee; They all were aliens: thou wert
> Our child and inmate. — Max! Thou canst not leave me;
> It cannot be; I may not, will not think
> That Max can leave me.[†]

This does not actually interfere with the plot. The great thing in this drama by Schiller is that he keeps high tragedy and the personal elements apart, as in the above example. He does this to show how Wallenstein cannot help but take action after he has let his thoughts play freely around him. He shows us here how freedom becomes a kind of north star of necessity. In this whole direction of thought lie concepts of the present that only need to be kindled in order to become fruitful.

The next drama, *Mary Stuart,* is conceived in the same way. Basically, everything has already happened at the beginning, and nothing takes place except what has long been prepared. Only the character, the inner life, unfolds before us, and this inner life again acts as a necessity.

In the later dramas, Schiller attempted to flesh out the aspects pertaining to fate more and more. In *The Maid of Orleans,* something supra-personal is expressed in the visions where she is confronted by her *daemon*,† who calls her to her mission and opposes her when she is unfaithful to its commandments until she reconciles with it through repentance.

In *The Bride of Messina*, he practically attempts to bring Greek tragedy back into modern life. He expresses the supra-personal here by introducing a choir. What did Schiller want with a choir? He looked back to the origin of tragedy, which arose from religion. In the original drama, they reenacted Dionysus, the suffering god, being redeemed by humanity. Recent investigations have led to this truth. When the Greek mystery dramas were secularized, the first beginnings of dramatic art emerged. Thus, in Aeschylus we still encounter an echo of that from which art had emerged, of the mystery cults in which the world-drama of the world-redemption was depicted. Édouard Schuré† depicted these Eleusinian mysteries in his *Sanctuaires d'Orient*, a preliminary sort of religious-artistic solution of the world riddle. The world-embracing actions of this original drama do not find a suitable instrument in language. Language is the expression of personal relations. When drama switched to the word, it dealt with more personal relationships, as in the plays of Sophocles and Euripides. The archetypal drama had arrived at the representation of the personal. The ancient dramas had used a supra-personal language, something similar to music. It started from the chorus that accompanied the mimed action. Thus, the later spoken drama developed from musical drama. Friedrich Nietzsche developed this idea further in his writing *The Birth of Tragedy from the Spirit of Music*.† To him, the word-based drama is a kind of decadence. Hence his admiration for Wagner, who wanted to create a new religious art, born out of the mythical world. Richard Wagner was not enthusiastic about the personal but rather the supra-personal. He therefore takes as the basis of his dramas not historical but mythical actions, and where it is necessary to represent the supra-personal, he does not use ordinary language but instead uses the elevated language of music.

Schiller intuitively anticipated what was later discovered and elaborated about Greek tragedy. He wanted to introduce a musical element in order, as he mentions in his preface, to raise art through the mood to a special height. Thus, what took place in radical form in the Wagnerian and Nietzschean circles is already present in Schiller. Only it is not treated by Wagner in such a detached manner as it is by Schiller.

Already in Schiller lives the great thought to lead humanity back to the source from which the spiritual has sprung, to lead art back to the native source from which religion, art, and science have sprung. To him, beauty could be the dawn of truth. Even today, we will find in Schiller what points to our best hopes for the present and the future. Thus, Schiller precedes us as a prophet for a better future.

Lecture Six

Schiller's Late Dramas

BERLIN, FEBRUARY 25, 1905

We have seen how Schiller always tried anew to solve the problem of the dramatic form in each of his later dramas. Schiller's dramas were extraordinary successes acclaimed by the leading figures of his age (though there was no lack of hostility). There is something uplifting in seeing how Schiller tries to climb to a higher stage with each new drama after each great success.

All of his later dramas—*William Tell, The Bride of Messina, The Maid of Orleans,* and *Demetrius*—are attempts to approach the problem of the dramatic and tragic in a new form. He would never have been satisfied with the belief that he had exhausted psychology. In *Mary Stuart,* we have seen him deal with the problem of fate, creating a perfect situation in which only the characters unfold. In *The Maid of Orleans,* he descended even deeper into the human soul. He knew how to plumb the depths of human psychology, establishing the problem in the way Hebbel had presented it when he said that the tragic must refer to something that is in a certain way irrational.[†] Thus, we have in *The Maid of Orleans* the interplay of dark soul forces: she is a kind of somnambulist and is under the influence of what one can call a *daemonic*[†] force. It is this that drives her forward. She is depicted standing high above the human level. Only because she is a virginal maid does she have the right to maraud like an avenging angel through the ranks of the enemy in the service of her homeland.

In *The Bride of Messina,* Schiller tries to take the drama to a higher level by achieving a sort of primordial drama. He reached back to the original dramatic form that preceded Aeschylus. That was not only art but an integrating element of the truth encompassing religion, science, and art. He reaches back to that Dionysus drama which brought the suffering, dying, resurrecting god onto the stage as the representative of all humanity. The plot did not have the character of what is called poetry today. The drama of the world was to be presented, the truth in a beautiful, artistic form. It was supposed to bring upliftment and religious edification to the people. For the spectator, the mystery drama contained at the same time what later developed separately as religion, art, and philosophy. This train of thought, which Friedrich Nietzsche elaborates in his book *The Birth of Tragedy from the Spirit of Music*, in which he positions the original drama as the higher form—this basic idea already lived in Schiller. Schiller's idea of raising the beautiful to higher spheres by reintroducing the musical element was taken up again by Wagner on a grand scale and found monumental expression in the musical drama of Wagner's operas. Wagner resorted to myth and chose music to express the important aspects not in everyday language but in elevated language. The direction that art took in Wagner's circle was present as intention in Schiller. In his short introduction to the *Bride of Messina,* he finds an expression for it as vivid as it is concise. Freedom of the mind in the lively play of all its powers is what true art is supposed to provide. From this, we recognize what lived in Schiller. We have seen how Schiller's spirit ascended to Goethe. He himself called Goethe's spirit the intuitive and his own the symbolizing. This is a significant statement.

Schiller always thought of people as representatives of a type and he thought of them in a kind of symphony. With him, we see dramas growing out of a musical mood. His symphony of human characters, of acting and suffering characters, results from this. This meant that he had to make the individual traits into symbols of profound human experience. In this way, Schiller became the poet of idealism. He brought down the ideals through experience in order to form them as characters. The problem of the human I was central to him, the question: How does man function within his environment?

In *The Bride of Messina*, he wanted to create Greek tragedy in a new form. There must be something in the human soul which causes him not to carry out his decisions in a rational way; otherwise, he would act more wisely. Something dark must live in him, something similar to the *daemon* of Socrates.† This must have an effect on him from the spiritual world. Schiller lets this something that cannot be grasped with the intellect play into the tragedy. In the way he does this, Schiller shows himself to be a completely modern character. In his work, the action starts from two dreams: The Prince of Messina dreams of a flame that consumes two laurel trees. This dream is interpreted by an Arabian astrologer as meaning that the daughter born to him will bring disaster to his sons, and he gives orders to kill her. At the same time, however, the princess has dreamed of a child with whom the eagle and the lion nestle peacefully. The dream is also interpreted to her. A Christian monk promises her that the daughter will unite the two quarreling brothers in love. She saves the child. Thus, the dark indeterminate element is placed at the outset of the plot. It seems very tidy that the first dream is interpreted by an Arab and the second by a Christian, but Schiller decides for neither. If one removes everything that is mystical or dreamlike, only the fight of the brothers remains, and this rational plot still remains dramatic. What is spiritual and especially artistic is that each element is something whole. Even without the mystical, the plot is a whole. In this direction, Schiller has put something into this drama with subtlety and art that goes beyond human consciousness. Thus, he had come to an even higher answer to his question.

He works on the same human psychology in *Wilhelm Tell.* I do not want to analyze the drama, only to show what Schiller was to the nineteenth century and what he still is to us. It is not for nothing that Schiller singles out Tell from the rest of the structure of the drama:

> Yet, whatsoever you do, spare me from council!
> I was not born to ponder and select;
> But when your course of action is resolved,
> Then call on Tell; you shall not find him fail.†

He does not act like the others under the impression of the idea of freedom, but he acts out of purely personal feeling, the aggrieved fatherly feeling. Schiller lets two lines run together: something that concerns Tell alone and that which the Swiss people feel.

Schiller wanted to show how not everything happens so

straightforwardly in human beings. We can find the same thing in Hebbel's *Judith*,† where the plight of the fatherland coincides with the offended feeling of womanhood. The poet needs something that grows directly out of human passions. Schiller does not want the merely moral, nor does he want the merely sensual. He wants that the moral should descend and become a personal passion. Man becomes free only by being able to carry out his personal interests in such a way that they coincide with general interest. Schiller worked bit by bit on the development of his psychology, and we see his idealism in a perpetual clarification. This is the magic that lives in Schiller's dramas. He did not write his profound, aesthetic writings in vain. He did not immerse himself in these problems in vain.

In everything that has been written about aesthetics in the nineteenth century by Vischer, Hartmann, Fechner,† and so on, as important and accurate as much of it is, the beautiful is shifted out of the human being. Schiller, however, has always studied what goes on in the human soul and has concerned himself with how beauty affects the human soul. That is why what he says touches us so intimately, finds in us a home. That is why Schiller's prose writings can always be read with delight. It would be a worthy celebration of Schiller if these writings were widely distributed and read because they could contribute greatly to the deepening of the human spirit in regard to its artistic and moral dimensions. A pedagogical bounty could be harvested from Schiller's Aesthetic Letters,† and a new impulse would come into our entire educational system.

Whoever wants to understand Schiller's dramas must draw the refined instructive lessons from his aesthetic writings. Those who study the unfortunately unfinished *Demetrius* will see how Schiller wanted to plumb ever deeper depths of the human heart. *Demetrius* could have been a shocking and powerful drama, equal in every regard to the best of Shakespeare. Many attempts have been made to complete *Demetrius*, but no one has been equal to the magnitude of the task. The thoroughly tragic conflict, with the richest plot (the Polish Parliament scene for example) is—and this is the significant thing—entirely transferred to the human I. We cannot say that our sentiments, our feeling and sensing, is our I. We are what we are because the thinking and feeling of our environment penetrates to us. The character of Demetrius has grown up in such a way that he does not know what his I is. There is found in him, in a meaningful deed for which he is to be executed, a jewel. It seems that he is entitled to the Tsar's throne. Everything comes together, and he cannot believe otherwise than that he is the real heir to the Russian throne. Thus, he is driven into a certain configuration of his I. Threads spun from the outside drive him on. The movement is victorious, and Demetrius develops into a Tsar-character. Now that the I is in harmony with the world around him, he learns that he was in error: he is not the true heir to the throne. He is no longer the character he thought himself to be. He faces his mother: she adores him, but the voice of nature is so strong in her that she cannot recognize him as a son. He, however, has become what he imagined himself to be. He can no longer discard this way of being, but the external prerequisites of this self fall away from him. This is an infinitely tragic conflict. We can believe it. Everything is placed at the peak of the personality, a personality drawn with infinite art, which we believe "does not want to rule over slaves."[†]

The exterior, too, was composed with all the art of which only Schiller was capable. In Sapieha, the opponent of Demetrius, the character of Demetrius is foreshadowed. Here, too, the symmetry is aimed at what is achieved in *Wallenstein*. The drama was not completed because death intervened. Schiller's death acquires something tragic. All the hopes that were placed in Schiller were expressed in the letters and statements of his contemporaries. Deeply shaken by the loss of one from whom so much was still expected, the tragedy resounds in the letters of the best minds of that age, such as Wilhelm von Humboldt:

> He was snatched from the world in the most perfect maturity of his spiritual power and could still have accomplished infinite things. His goal was set in such a way that he could never reach an endpoint, and the ever-progressing activity of his spirit would not have allowed him to worry about a standstill; for a very long time to come, he could have relished the joy, the delight—indeed, as he so inimitably describes it in a letter on the occasion of the plan for an idyll—the bliss of poetic creation.[†]

This is the tone that first elevates Schiller's death to tragedy, for in the ordinary course of events, death does not have that irrational quality. Out of this mood, Goethe found the words for his dead friend in the "Epilogue to Schiller's Bell":[†]

> And behind him in immaterial radiance
> Lay what tames us all, the communal.

We can see this great idealistic trait flowing away in the nineteenth century. People became aware that Schiller's spirit was uplifting so that henceforth he could be a comfort and a paragon for his people in all their struggles.

The continuing effect of Schiller's idealism in German spiritual life was expressed by Karl Gutzkow[†] in his speech at the Schiller celebration in the Harmonie in Dresden on November 10, 1859, in the apt words:

> That is the secret of our love for Schiller: The elevation of our hearts! The courage to act! The faithful assistance which the nation always finds in its favorite! What reminds us of Schiller awakens courage and joyfulness. As lovely, as rich, as deeply intimate as Goethe seems to us, that in his creations which reminds us of German manner and custom is like ivy that nestles mournfully dreaming of the past. But with Schiller everything is future, flag waving, or laurel. That is why we celebrate the centenary commemoration of his name as soundingly and resoundingly as the beating of an iron shield. Hail the poet of action, a treasure of the German fatherland.

Lecture Seven

Schiller's Effect on the Nineteenth Century

BERLIN, MARCH 4, 1905

Today I would like to talk about the kind of effect Schiller had on the nineteenth century in order to then move on to the significance of Schiller for the present and to what Schiller can be for the future. In the final lecture, I will give an overall picture of Schiller. Whoever wants to describe Schiller's relationship to the nineteenth century cannot possibly get caught up in details; therefore, we do not want to dwell on individual incidents in particular if they do not have special symptomatic significance. It is a matter of showing how the details relate to the entire cultural life of the nineteenth century and Schiller's place within it.

In general, it is difficult to say how great Schiller's influence is on individual periods because the channels cannot be traced in detail. Schiller's influence can be compared in part to the influence exerted by Herder[†] at the beginning of the century, of whom Goethe said to Eckermann: "Who still reads Herder's philosophical works? But everywhere one encounters ideas that he sowed." This is a more intense effect than that associated with the name. This is also the case with Schiller. His work cannot be separated from the effect of the great classical period. One thing, however, can be emphasized: Schiller's effect and recognition—which was evinced by the national festival on November 10, 1859—proceeded by no means easily and without contradiction. Schiller did not get his way so easily. Much had to happen in order to let Schiller's spirit flow into the youth in an imponderable way. Thus, the "Song of the Bell"[†] initially aroused the most vehement opposition in the circles of the Romantics. Caroline von Schlegel, the wife of August Wilhelm von Schlegel,[†] called it a philistine bourgeois poem.

Not only in what confronts us in the *Xenien*† but in general in the circles of those who were called the Romantics, we find lively opposition to Schiller. The Romantics saw in Goethe's *Wilhelm Meister* their ideal and had Goethe, the faithful friend, shouting after Schiller the words, "And behind him in immaterial radiance / Lay what tames us all, the communal," at Schiller's expense. Schiller's ability to elevate the moral and ethical to such heights was something quite unappealing to them. Harsh words flowed from the Romantics against Schiller, the bourgeois ethicist. Those today who have grown up in the era of Schiller veneration will find it difficult to understand words such as those Friedrich von Schlegel† wrote about him in reviews of Schiller and Goethe. He calls Schiller's imagination "shattered." There is nothing there of that which drew all hearts to Schiller. About the end of the 1820s, the correspondence of Goethe and Schiller appeared with that monument which Goethe set to his friend and to friendship. One can learn infinitely much from it, and its importance for the German view of art is immeasurable. There, too, the Romantics were thoroughly hostile. They had biting ridicule for it. The difficulty with which Schiller's fame eventually gained ground is shown by the braggadocio of the personalities who opposed Schiller most vehemently.

A. W. Schlegel, the commendable translator of Shakespeare, wrote a sonnet to himself in which he expresses how he perceived his own relationship to the German people. He speaks of his poetic significance with a self-confidence that seems strange to us today. It concludes:

> What the mouth of the future will call him
> Is unknown, but this generation knew him
> by the name August Wilhelm Schlegel.†

The man does not merely represent an individual phenomenon; he represents the Romantic theory. He can be understood only if one understands what the Romantic school wanted. The Romantics wanted a new art, a summary of everything artistic. Their theory had actually grown out of what Schiller had presented in his aesthetic essays, but it was a caricatured conception. Schiller's words, "Man is only fully man there where he plays,"† became a kind of motto for them. Thus, the

Romantic irony was born, which made everything a game of genius. The view prevailed that it is simply a person's arbitrary decision to be a genius. If Schiller called art a game, it was because he wanted to give the game all seriousness. In the overcoming of the material element through the form lies the artistic secret of the master, says Schiller,† while the Romantics neglected the form and demanded of the material itself that it should have an artistic effect. It was a direction (I do not want to criticize but to characterize it) that was fundamentally opposed to Schiller. The correspondence of Goethe and Schiller was therefore, as I said, received by them as something that disturbed them. They found the rules of art discussed in it to be simplistic. A. W. von Schlegel wrote mischievous epigrams under the impression of this correspondence. The Romantics regarded each other with the greatest admiration. All this shows how Schiller's life's work aroused the fiercest opposition. On the other hand, Schiller's personality was so formidable that recognition and admiration were also paid to him from these circles. Ludwig Tieck† wrote about Schiller's *Wallenstein* with understanding and admiration.

We see that Schiller was gradually gaining more and more influence, embedding himself in the hearts of the nation. Theodor Körner† is the most important but not the only phenomenon who lives completely in the spirit of Schiller—Körner, who also dies a hero's death, completely filled with the ideals that Schiller implanted in him. He seemed consecrated thereto by the personal friendship that connected his family with Schiller. It was a warm friendship that linked Körner's father and Schiller. Schiller was Theodor Körner's godfather, and Schiller bought the lyre that accompanied Theodor Körner everywhere. Schiller slowly but surely crept into the hearts of the youth.

Whoever follows the literary development among the struggling Romantics encounters the influence of Schiller himself in the phrases he coined. Through Schiller, what can be called German education in the first half of the nineteenth century developed. It is formed entirely as if by imponderable means through what Schiller implanted in the collective mind. What emanated from Herder and the other classical authors flowed into the nation through the images and didactic phrases of Schiller. Even though some individuals at the height of aesthetic education resisted, Schiller became more and more established. This is how his influence grows ever greater. As the centenary of Schiller's birth approaches, it is the best who celebrate him, the best of the nation. In a book about Schiller, the speeches that were held at that time are collected. Important luminaries gave those speeches: Jakob Grimm, Theodore Vischer (the great philosopher of aesthetics), Karl Gutzkow, Ernst Curtius, Moriz Carriere, and many others.† The seed sown by Schiller had sprouted.

Yet it must be said that the language spoken at that time, in 1859, was quite alien to what was just then emerging as something new. The emphasis on the Ideal in 1859 is strangely consistent with something else that came to light in that year. There are four important phenomena in particular that I want to point out here: Charles Darwin's *On the Origin of Species* appeared in 1859, and then Fechner's *Vorschule der Ästhetik* [Elements of aesthetics].† Fechner gained a great influence over a contemporary cultural current. He started from Hegel, who himself had defended Schiller against the Romantics. Vischer, who came from the Goethe-Schiller period and who advocated an idealistic aesthetics, finds himself in contradiction to what he had previously known; he sees this direction superseded by Fechner. This is an aesthetics from below, whereas an aesthetics from above used to be advocated.

From below, from small symptoms, one now wanted to recognize the essence of the beautiful. The third work, which dealt with spatial relations, stands in a certain contrast to Schiller's approach. In one of his epigrams to astronomers, Schiller had addressed himself thus:

> Do not prattle so much to me about nebulae and suns.
> Is nature only great because it gives you things to count?
> Your object is the most sublime thing in space, of course,
> But, friends, the sublime does not dwell in space.†

This third work was the "spectral analysis" discovered by Kirchhoff and Bunsen.† Through it, the sun could be recognized in its components, and an analysis of the most distant nebulae could be undertaken.

The fourth work was Karl Marx's *Critique of Political Economy*.† It was a strange contrast between what was spoken during the celebration of Schiller and what those times actually produced.

Schiller, and the German classical authors in general, took on a peculiar standpoint regarding world culture. One cannot think of Raphael or Michelangelo without the connection with their age, out of which they were born, out of which they created. Likewise, Homer's art exists in intimate connection with what lived in all of his contemporaries. Homer needed only to give form to that which permeated his contemporaries as feeling and thinking. It was quite different with the German classical authors. Homer, of whom did he write? He spoke to Greeks of Greeks. Likewise, Dante, Michelangelo, and even Shakespeare were completely placed in their time. It was different with the German classical authors.

Lessing was enthusiastic about Winckelmann,[†] and from Winckelmann's expositions he formed his views of art. Lessing also went back to Aristotle. Schiller and Goethe studied Aristotle with the same devotion as Lessing. This explains where such a detached ideal of beauty came from, an art so detached from the life of the times, especially in the later years of the poets' lives. The youthful dramas of Schiller—*The Robbers*, *Intrigue and Love*—are still connected with his own life. Goethe developed himself especially in Italy. There, art had become to him an end in itself, abstractly detached from real life. Goethe and Schiller had become indifferent to the immediate material world. We see that Schiller now seeks his subject matter everywhere in the world. He has lifted himself out of his immediate surroundings and has placed himself on his own feet. Nothing characterizes Schiller's influence more than the fact that he was followed by Romanticism, which assimilated everything foreign. Translations from all areas of world literature are a major achievement of the Romantic school.

Thus, Schiller's position on art forms something that has a decisive effect on his relationship to the nineteenth century.

Lecture Eight

What Can the Present Time Learn from Schiller?

BERLIN, MARCH 5, 1905

One cannot overlook the fact that the public's relationship to Schiller in the second half of the nineteenth century had to become quite different from what it was in the first half. This was already conditioned by the phenomena I have indicated to you. Schiller stood by truth in such a way that he could say: "Only through the dawn of beauty do you press on into the land of knowledge."[†] For him, the truth was the beautiful. A work of art should be a creation of the Idea, which one thought of as flowing through the universe. His was an idealistic worldview, a fine, subtle one that can be grasped only by those who are able to soar to subtle, spiritual heights. The foundation for Schiller's understanding requires something that makes significant demands.

Therefore, in the second half of the century, there was something less intense in the veneration of Schiller. A cooler relationship was caused by the emerging natural sciences. Now one saw the true only in that which is sense-perceptible. Schiller never did that. Schiller's ideals were always truths, but they were truths on a spiritual basis. What people felt then is no longer a tangible reality today. It was the greatness and breadth of the intellectual horizon out of which Schiller grew: the world of Goethe, Lessing, Herder, and Winckelmann. When outer reality pressed in with its coarser demands, there was no longer a proper connection between the beautiful and the true. On the basis of scientific knowledge, Ludwig Büchner[†] was able to construct a purely materialistic worldview. Schiller, however, is not for a materialistic age, and his words become empty phrases if one refers to his views in such an age. It then came about that Schiller receded somewhat into the background. Goethe could still be something for the second half of the nineteenth century because in him the artistic can be separated from the worldview. Even in Herman Grimm's work, everything resounds in a panegyric on Goethe, the artist. For those who study Goethe in detail, it is unquestionably impossible to separate him from his worldview. After all, with Goethe, a purely aesthetic view is possible, while with Schiller, such a point of view is not possible. Today, art is regarded as something that deals with the realm of imagination. This is already a rejection of their worldview.

A gulf has formed between the spirit of the time in which Schiller lived and that of our own time, in which it is possible for a new Schiller biographer, Otto Brahm,[†] who emerged from the Scherer school,[†] to begin his book with the words: "In my youth, I was a Schiller hater." He only gradually worked his way through scholarship, through insight, to a reverence for Schiller. Schiller has found learned biographers, but the feeling of the time has already become alien to Schiller's actual aims. It cannot understand how one can reconcile what today is called knowledge with what Schiller represents. As already said, the artists of an earlier time, such as Raphael and Michelangelo, grew out of the life of their epoch. It was no longer like that after Goethe's death. We see how an artist like Peter Cornelius[†] creates entirely out of thought. He no longer stood in any connection with the spiritual substance of his time. He always felt alienated, especially in Berlin. Drawn to Catholicism, in which he believed his artistic ideal was founded, he was indifferent to the life of his time.

Thus, the gap between life and art becomes wider and wider. How alien Schiller therefore stands in the life of the nineteenth century. Jakob Minor[†] may have written thick volumes about Schiller's youth, but everything points to how alien to our time Schiller's views have become. What is recognized as true today has grown out of the scientific worldview. In the same way, aesthetics has moved from an idealistic toward a realistic direction. This change was so strong that Vischer[†] could not agree to a second edition of his *Aesthetics*, which was written in an idealistic sense. His later writing had gone astray from what he had represented in his earlier book. The sensibilities of the first half of the century had become so alien for leading minds that such a man criticized himself in this way.

After this development, we will understand how Schiller stands in our present time. It was possible for a man like Emil du Bois-Reymond,[†] who was completely rooted in Schiller's diction, to say in a speech about Goethe's *Faust* that *Faust* was actually a failed work, that by right Faust had to marry Gretchen, make important inventions, and thus lead a useful existence, and so on. Everything that makes *Faust* a tragedy, the entire significance of the character arc, was no longer understood by an important man of the nineteenth century.

This direction had become decisive. No one dares to contradict it; no one dares to emphasize the importance of the ideal. Even art calls itself realistic. An idealistic interpretation finds little favor with the public. Honest are those who confess that Schiller is not sympathetic to them. That the beautiful is a manifestation of the true is no longer valid. The true is called what can be seen with eyes and felt with hands. The everyday is called the true. It was not so for Schiller. For him, the true lay in the great, ideal laws. For him, art was the reproduction of the spiritual hidden in the real, not a reproduction of the everyday. The truth that Schiller sought is recognized today neither by science nor by art because no one today understands what Schiller meant by the true. Hence, we have this contrast. Today, one understands by the true that which Schiller called the sensual-necessary. In the harmony between the spiritual and the sensual-necessary, Schiller seeks the ideal of freedom. What is called artistic today can never be called artistic in Schiller's sense. Another gulf lies between today's views and Schiller's views. Our time no longer has the deep intense urge to penetrate the inner core of the world. This deep earnestness lingers like a fragrance over Schiller's views, this deep earnestness that is no longer present anywhere.

Our time tries to juxtapose great minds of such fundamentally different natures as Tolstoy and Nietzsche in a completely superficial way. Materialism has become a worldview. It has become a gospel, an integrating aspect of our age. The great masses stand on a purely materialistic basis and they do not want to accept any other worldview. True for them is only what natural science allows one to call real.

What this leads to can be seen in the following small episode. It was the last time that an idealistically colored, albeit pessimistic worldview had an effect on the world: Eduard von Hartmann's *Philosophy of the Unconscious.*†

The work was attacked on numerous occasions. A sharp criticism was published under the title, *The Unconscious from the Standpoint of the Theory of Evolution and Darwinism.* The book did not bear the name of the author. It was called by some natural scientists the best refutation of Eduard von Hartmann's work. In the second edition, the author named himself: Eduard von Hartmann. He had wanted to show how easy it is to climb down to the materialistic standpoint when one has climbed to a higher one. Those who stand on a higher standpoint can understand a lower one, and those on a lower one cannot understand the higher one. It is so that he who stands on the idealistic standpoint is quite ready to recognize in a certain way the materialistic one. The one who stands on the standpoint of Schiller can judge Büchner and can judge modern art in its materialistic view. It does not work vice versa. The materialist cannot comprehend the idealist.

Schiller was a believer in the ideal. A profound saying of his goes: "What religion do I profess? None of all the ones you attribute to me. – And why none? – Out of religion."†

The great thing about him is that his aesthetic confession was at the same time his religious one and that his artistic creation was his cultus. That his ideal lived in him in this way is an aspect of his greatness; therefore, we do not ask, "Can Schiller be something to us today?" On the contrary, he must become something to us again, for we have forgotten how to understand that which goes beyond the purely material. Only then will we understand again an art that seeks to reveal the secrets of existence.

We will also learn to understand a new ideal of freedom through him. Today, we hear a lot of talk about freedom, because people want to be free from the fetters of government and economy. Schiller understood freedom differently. How does man become free in himself? How does he become free from his base desires, free from the constraints of logic and reason? Schiller, who wrote about government and life in society, arrives at a new goal, at an indication of future ideals. If in our time one wants to demand in the right way that the individual develop freely, one must understand harmony in the sense of Schiller. Let us measure what is demanded today by what Schiller demanded. We will to focus on two phenomena: Max Stirner† and Schiller. What can seem more dissimilar, more opposite, than Stirner's *The Ego and Its Own*† and Schiller's Aesthetic Letters?† At the time when Schiller's influence was receding into the background, Stirner's influence was growing. Stirner, who had remained neglected for a long time, was rediscovered in the 1890s. His work formed the basis of what is floating around as individualism.† This sentiment of our time has something justified, but in the form in which it appears now, it must appear as something unbridled. In Schiller's Aesthetic Letters, the demand for the liberation of the human personality is upheld almost more radically. In a less philistine way than Stirner, Schiller had put forward this ideal. The ideal of the cooperation of people who have become inwardly free appears as a warning for other people. Commandments, compulsory regulations, do not exist where people live like this. Today people seem to believe that everything must be in disorder if people are not constrained by police regulations. Yet one must be clear: countless things in the history of the world happen without laws. Every day one can observe how, quite by themselves, in the busiest streets, people avoid each other without any regulation. Ninety-eight percent of our life goes on without laws. One day, it will be possible to get along completely without laws, without coercion. For this, however, man must first become inwardly free.

It is an ideal of immeasurable greatness that Schiller sets before us. Art should lead man to freedom. Art, grown out of the cultural substance, should become the great educator of the world. Artists should not deliver photographs of the outer world. They should be messengers of a higher spiritual reality. Then the artists will create again as before, out of the ideal. Schiller wanted to lead through art to a new understanding of reality and he was deeply earnest about this.

If our time wants to understand Schiller correctly, it must summarize what it has gained in knowledge into a higher idealism that lifts it up to spiritual reality. Then those will come who can again speak from the depths of their hearts out of Schiller's spirit.

It is of little use to open theaters in Schiller's honor if the people sitting inside have no understanding of Schiller. Only when we raise ourselves to understand Schiller in this way will there be people who can speak about Schiller as Herman Grimm spoke about Goethe, from the depths of their hearts.

Lecture Nine

Schiller and Idealism (Aesthetics and Morals)

BERLIN, MARCH 25, 1905

Today, in the final lecture, I would like to deal with a special question, which is to follow the lecture on Schiller's effect on the present. The question of German aesthetics can interest us here because Schiller is closely connected with the foundation of aesthetic science. Aesthetics is the science of beauty.

We have seen how Schiller, in different periods of his life, places himself in the beautiful. Schiller saw in the beautiful something that has a very special cultural value. The extent to which something quite special was then developed is evinced by the aesthetic science of today, which is only about one hundred and fifty years old. Of course, Aristotle already wrote about poetics, but throughout the centuries the views about it remained the same. We know that even Lessing often referred back to Aristotle. Only in the eighteenth century, out of Wolffian philosophy,[†] emerged Baumgarten,[†] who wrote a book on the beautiful, *Ästhetica*, in 1750. He distinguishes the beautiful from the true in that, as he says, the true contains a clear idea, while the beautiful embodies unclear, confused ideas. This was not long before Schiller that such thoughts could arise. Now, we have in Kant himself, in the *Critique of Judgment*,[†] a kind of aesthetics; but with him, it was all theory. He never attained a living concept of what beauty is, and he never got further than three miles from his birthplace. Königsberg never saw a significant work of art; thus, he wrote only from the standpoint of abstract philosophy. It was Schiller who first grasped this problem vividly in his Aesthetic Letters.[†]

How did the problem stand at that time? Goethe looked with wistfulness at Greece, and Winckelmann, too, looked longingly back to the time when man reproduced the divine in his works of art. Schiller also suffered from this longing in his second period. This longing is expressed in the poem "The Gods of Greece."[†] What is it other than a religious trait that underlies Greek drama? It is based on the mystery of the god who becomes man, suffers as man, dies, and resurrects. People grasped as a purification of the human being what thus coursed through the soul. A breath of this still wafts through Aristotle's *Poetics*. As Lessing put it, the tragedy should consist of striving for purification from these passions through the performance of actions that arouse fear and pity.[†] It was difficult to understand what was meant by this. Lessing himself thought a great deal about it. In the nineteenth century, a rich literature arose on the subject. Whole libraries have been written concerning the word *catharsis*. It was not understood because people did not know what it came from.

In the drama of Aeschylus,[†] one still recognizes something of the drama of the gods. In the center of the action stands Dionysus as the great dramatic figure, and the chorus surrounding him accompanies the action. This is how Édouard Schuré[†] revived the mystery drama. The dramatic cult action had the very specific task of leading man to a higher level of existence. It was said that man is afflicted with passions. Through the lower life he belongs to them, but he can rise above them if the higher that lives in him is purified. He can rise above them through the contemplation of a divine model. This kind of presentation should lead people to ennoble themselves more easily than through teachings. For, as Schopenhauer says, "Preaching morality is easy; establishing morality is difficult."[†] It was only in a later epoch that Socrates expressed his view that virtue is teachable. But virtue is something that lives in man and is natural to him, like eating and drinking. He can be led to it when the divine is awakened in him through the example of the suffering god. This purification by divine example is called *catharsis*. Thus, fear and pity [or compassion] should be evoked. The ordinary compassion attached to the personal element should be elevated to the great impersonal compassion when one sees God suffering for humanity.

Subsequently, dramatic action was humanized, and in the Middle Ages, we see how morality emancipates itself and appears independently. Later, that which has bodily life in the mystery is formed in a one-sided way in Christianity. The Greek saw with his own eyes the god who rose from humiliation. In the mysteries, virtue was not merely preached but was made visible to the human being.

To make people understand this again, to reunite these two things with each other, was something that lived quite intensely in Schiller. The vein of his poetry was the longing to reconcile these two: sensuality and morality. Strict morality was conceived by Kant in such a way that duty led away from everything that appeared as inclination. Schiller, on the other hand, demanded that duty become inclination. Schiller wanted passion to be purified in such a way that passion itself appeared as duty. That is why he so revered Goethe, seeing in him a perfect union of sensuality and morality. In the beautiful, he sought this union of the sensual and the moral. Because Schiller had a particularly German quality, the aesthetic conscience, he wanted art to be there to elevate man to a higher existence. In the German classical era, there was a strong feeling that the beautiful was not there to fill idle hours but that it was the bridge between the divine and the sensual. And Schiller struggled to find freedom here. Inclination is no longer suppressed. He says that the person who must be virtuous against his inclinations still stands at a lower level. Instead, his inclinations must be developed in such a way that he acts virtuously by himself. Earlier, in his 1784 essay "Theater Considered as a Moral Institution,"[†] he preached something similar to the harsh Kantian morality.

The secret of the master lies in the overcoming of matter by form.[†] What is the material of poetry in general? In what conception lies the right standpoint for the contemplation of the beautiful? As long as I am interested in a particular face, I have not acquired the true artistic view, and there is still a clinging to the material. "Consider *what*, but more, consider *how*!"[†] As long as the poet still shows that he hates the villain in the manner of personal interest, he is still attached to the material, not to the form. He has not yet arrived at the aesthetic view. Only then has he advanced to this view when the villain is presented in such a way that the natural order executes the judgment, not the poet himself. Then world karma takes place, and then world history becomes world judgment. The poet switches himself off and looks objectively at world history. Thereby, what Aristotle has said—that poets are truer than history—occurs. In history, one cannot always survey the whole event. A section lies before us so that we often receive the impression of injustice. In its completeness, therefore, the work of art is truer than history.

Thus, a pure and noble conception of art was created. Purification, catharsis itself, is above sympathy and antipathy. With pure, almost divine feeling, the viewer should stand before the work of art and see before him an objective image of the world, create for himself a microcosm. The dramatist shows us within a narrow framework how guilt and atonement are interlinked and depicts in detail what truth is, giving this truth, however, a universal stamp. Goethe gives expression to this by calling the beautiful a manifestation of the laws of nature, which could never be expressed without the beautiful.

Goethe and Schiller wanted to find a realism, but it had to be an idealistic realism. Today, people believe they can find realism by accurately depicting nature. Schiller and Goethe would have said this is not the whole truth. Sensual nature represents only a part of what is perceptible. The spiritual is missing in it. It can only be accepted as truth if the whole tableau of nature is brought into a work at once, but sense-perceptible nature is always only a portion of the real. Because they strove for truth, they did not accept the superficial truth of nature.

Schiller and Goethe strove to awaken idealism in their time. In ages prior to theirs, this idealism was present. In Dante, we find represented not the external reality as it surrounds us but that which takes place in the human soul. Later ages wanted to see the spiritual externalized. In *Der Groß-Cophta* [The Grand Kofta],[†] Goethe showed how the one who materializes the spirit is exposed to aberrations. Schiller also dealt with the materialization of the spiritual. At that time, many similar things were also sought after in this direction. Much of what appears today as spiritualism occupied wide circles at that time. Thus, the deep work *The Ghost-Seer*,[†] an examination of these currents, came into being. Even before the point in his biography when he had gained through Kantianism and his own artistic development his higher perspectives, Schiller described the dangers to which the one who seeks the spiritual in the outer world instead of in himself is exposed. This is how the *The Ghost-Seer* comes into being.

A prince, alienated from his faith and lacking the power to awaken the spiritual in his own soul, is thrown into a violent excitement by a strange prophecy proclaimed to him by a mysterious stranger, a prophecy that soon comes true. In this mood, he falls into the hands of jugglers, who, by skillful exploitation of certain circumstances, put him in the state of mind that makes him susceptible to a ghostly apparition. The conjuration proceeds, but suddenly, a stranger intervenes and unmasks the conjuror; but now, in place of the apparition of the deceiver, the stranger himself lets an apparition arise, one who makes an important announcement to the prince. The prince is tossed about by doubts that the stranger is the same person who made the prophecy to him; however, soon the doubter suspects that the two are in cahoots, since the first conjurer is arrested and soon disappears. New, inexplicable incidents lead him to strive for the solution of all that is mysterious. In doing so, he becomes completely dependent on a secret society; however, he loses all moral foundations. The novel was not completed, but the struggle of a spirit seeker is depicted here in a shattering way. We see how the longing for the spiritual leads to downfall when one seeks the spiritual in the external world. One who is attached to the sense world cannot penetrate to the spirit, especially not when he demands to see the spiritual appear as sense-perceptible. The spiritual should reveal itself in the human soul.

This is the true secret of the spiritual. That is why the artist sees it first as beauty. The beautiful then, conquered and permeated by the spirit, becomes real in the work of art, and the beautiful is the worthy material of the spiritual. At first, for Schiller, the beautiful was the only thing through which the spiritual could reveal itself. He looked back with wistfulness to the time of the Greeks when there was the possibility of another awakening of the spiritual. Man had elevated himself to God by bringing God below, by letting God become man and elevating himself through him. Now man was to raise himself again to the divine by mastering the material world. In this way, Schiller strove in his dramas to ever higher things, until the physical fell away from him more and more, until "behind him in immaterial radiance, lay what tames us all, the communal," as Goethe recollected of him.† This had become full truth with him. Goethe did not use the word "communal" in a contemptuous, lowly sense here; what is meant here is the generally human, the ordinary aspect of the human being, above which Schiller had risen. Thus Schiller, as a true spirit-seer, has raised himself to the view of the spiritual.

He should stand before us as an example. Only this should be the purpose of these lectures, as far as this was possible in so few hours, to follow this struggling soul of Schiller, how it rises to ever higher spiritual perception, seeking to grasp the spiritual in order to imprint it on the physical. In this struggle, one recognizes Schiller, in that Goethe's words are truly fulfilled in him personally:

> Only he earns freedom, as with life itself,
> Who must conquer it daily.†

Thus, Schiller has risen to become the master of the aesthetic, spirit-filled form.

APPENDIX

DISCUSSIONS AND LECTURES BY RUDOLF STEINER IN THE "GIORDANO BRUNO ASSOCIATION FOR A UNIFIED WORLDVIEW" IN 1902

Reports by members of The Giordano Bruno Association in the magazine *Der Freidenker.*

". . . A second reason was the Giordano Bruno Association. In it, such personalities were to come together who were sympathetic to a spiritual-monistic worldview. It was important to emphasize that there were not two world principles, substance and spirit, but that the spirit as a unifying principle formed all being."

—Rudolf Steiner, *Autobiography*

The Unity of the World

BERLIN, MARCH 1902

Discussion in "The Giordano Bruno Association for a Unified World-view" with an Opinion by Rudolf Steiner

The purpose of the Bruno Association is to promote a unified worldview. It does not regard this as a final achievement but as a task whose solution it seeks to participate in by researching, teaching, organizing, and stimulating discussion. In doing so, it is especially important to bring the different points of view into understanding and where possible to a certain balance. It also strives for unification insofar as it would like to harmoniously unite natural science, philosophy, art, and devotion. The Association considers one of the means to this end to be, in addition to larger public lectures, the discussion of questions of worldviews in a smaller circle, as well as the publication of such Association discussions.

The first attempt to negotiate a unified worldview took place in March 1902. The topic for discussion was: "What does a unified worldview mean in terms of its concepts and values?" The new secretary of the Association, Dr. Hermann Friedmann, had taken over the introductory lecture, but was unable to give it for the time being because of illness. Mr. Wolfgang Kirchbach[†] had kindly stepped in for him to improvise his own views. After the Association Chairman, Dr. Bruno Wille, had pointed out the purpose of the discussion evenings, Fräulein Maria Holgers spoke the moving poem by Hölderlin, "To Nature."

Wolfgang Kirchbach then took the floor: The Chairman has just emphasized that the task of establishing and pursuing a monistic worldview is as difficult as it is attractive and important. Therefore, right today, during our first discussion, I will try to present to you the whole difficulty of the problem we are facing. This hint at the difficulty of our task, however, shall only be a purely academic one.

What I have to talk about is formulated in the question: What does a unified worldview mean to us, or rather to me, according to its concepts and values? I want to present to you shortly the problem as it touches me. For those to whom it should still be unknown, I emphasize that the phrase "unified worldview" is here only a translation of the word "monistic," which expresses the processing of all conceptual and other knowledge into a worldview of the unity-being, of the existence of the world in a unity. The phrase "unified worldview" would probably describe the meaning more appropriately.

When we establish a unified worldview, we cannot deny the question of the value of such a worldview, of the areas in which it is of value and into which it falls. To look for the unity of all phenomena in the field of the "cosmos," as nature in its regularity is popularly called, would be one side of a unified research and thinking. However, natural science as it is at the moment does not give the one who has penetrated deeper into it any right at present to speak objectively of a unity in the cosmos. Quantitatively, we are popularly accustomed to think of this world-entirety in terms of matter and, in connection with matter, the concept of force. The dualism attached to this conceptual connection has led to attempts to resolve it into a unity. Force was said to be a function, an expression of matter and had thus gained a certain unity by imagining matter as something essentially unified. Actual natural science has formed the concept of matter in a completely different way. With the help of its analytical methods, it has extracted more and more elements from the surrounding cosmos and has thus found by empirical work, in place of a monistic matter, about seventy different elements—that is, types of matter. Thus, the term *matter* has only the value of a linguistic abstraction like the term *animal*. No real individual being corresponds to it, but the unity of these seventy elements is for the time being only a hypothesis.

Since Robert Mayer's discovery[†] of the unity of force and the transformability of energy, we find the same thing in regard to the concept of force. You are confronted with the immense riddle that mechanical force, and perhaps the same force that puts the globe and the sun in permanent relation and causes the rotation of the celestial bodies, that perhaps the same force, transformed and transmuted, represents those phenomena which, for example, a thunderstorm exhibits. But the fact remains that this phenomenon of electricity expresses itself differently than, for example, the force that drives a stone to the center of the earth. Science has not yet shown that one must assume a unity of nature in the sense that the different forms of energy are one. The different phenomena have not yet been bridged, and here, too, we are only faced with hypotheses.

The same applies to a whole series of other phenomena. One does not know, for example, where one should distinguish the higher life-concept of the organic from the concept of the inorganic. The whole field of natural science is in a lively dispute about this.

Since, from this perspective, we have to connect the worldview to the material given to us by natural science, we must admit that objectively, the unity of the universe is not yet proven as a fact. What about the other question that must be dealt with in our overall question of a unified worldview? It is the question: How does our own thinking, which is based on unity, relate to its object, the world? Here we are faced with an apparent dualism. We see that there is something outside, and here is something which takes this outside into itself. There we have at first a duality. But we now ask: To what extent can and may we assume that the functions of our brain, the propositional forms, and the categories of our mind form a unity with the world? The fact that you refer all the functions of your mind to a unity could at most be deduced from the fact that you locate them together in your body. First of all, the activity that you perform when you investigate the cause that makes a stone fall to the earth is quite different than when you ask: Is it possible under the conditions now given that this fall occurs? It is possible that the conceptions supplied by the different intellectual activities could come into conflict and therefore no unity would exist within you. Another question would be how the unified picture of the world, which you carry in yourself, agrees with objective reality. To what extent do the laws, which hold sway in my spirit, also work in the outer world? We will have to think dualistically at first. To resolve this dualism into a monism is, however, a supreme urge in thinking itself, but epistemology faces a great problem here. Since Kant, tackling this problem is a duty for everyone who wrestles with questions of worldviews.

Thus, in building up a unified worldview, we must carry out two operations: On the one hand, we have to trace the infinite multiplicity of the world empirically down to its smallest differentiations, and, on the other hand, we always have to form our thinking in an epistemological sense into a monism, into the summary of that multiplicity as a unity.

In working with the material in this direction, we would soon encounter difficulties of no small significance for the field of ethics. The question would soon arise before us: How far can we judge the moral life in man himself and the processes in the cosmos from the point of view of uniform moral laws? For we cannot let any process of this world affect us without at the same time processing it ethically. The joy in contemplating the cosmos, the contemplation of its harmony in its infinite multiplicity, is at the same time a moral examination. So, the question would be: Can we arrive at a monism in ethical thinking itself and connect it with the rest of the monistic view? With it, another question arises at the same time: Could not our moral feeling find satisfaction also by another consideration? Why, for example, does the Church-thinking Christian consider his doctrine, which knows only one God, to be something infinitely higher than paganism, which has several deities? And how has the Christian nevertheless come to a dualism, even to the assumption of an even greater multiplicity in the supernatural world?

If scientific considerations were to result in proof of dualism, then we would have to declare ourselves satisfied with it. To establish a monism only in order to be monistic would be worthless. But we have in the spirit a *monon*, an essence of the things themselves, according to which we can measure the value of all our views—the true, the truth. There is for every single science, for every cognition, only one permanent judgment—namely, that its statements are true (that is, that they agree with objective processes). For a worldview, only this judgment can be true. Only if a monistic explanation proved to be true in all objective circumstances as well as in our subjective activity, in all manifestations of the diversity of life, would it be valuable. I could not consider anything else as a criterion of the value of this worldview. This *monon* of truth can never become untrue. Up to now, this *monon* is the only recognizable eternal unity in which the objective phenomena (in their multiplicity and transitoriness) cooperate with the spirit.

After these words of Kirchbach, Dr. Rudolf Steiner rose to make the following remarks: I would like to keep strictly to the question: What does a unified worldview mean according to its concepts and values? In this I stand in direct contrast to the previous speaker. If I pose the question, Are we entitled from the standpoint of our modern natural and spiritual science to regard the world as a unity? then I must say that we are. We are at any rate placed in the necessity to search for it. In view of the diversity into which the specialization of science has undoubtedly led us, I ask: In what do we have to look for unity? To say from the outset that this or that must be proved as unity seems to me an exaggerated demand of an extreme epistemology. For me, the striving for a unified worldview is already justified in that it is simply an ineradicable need of the human spirit that has existed in all ages, more clearly perhaps in pre-Christian times when it was not yet suppressed by the dogmas and views of the Church. It is above all the duty of an Association that wants to take up the spirit of Giordano Bruno to fight against the Church's dogmas and views.

However, I find that the results of the natural sciences also meet this need. Chemistry has found seventy elements and will perhaps still increase this variety, but, at the same time, it has also found something quite special. Between these elements it has found, for example, with respect to atomic weight, certain relations according to which a table of these elements can be built up, which is at the same time a classification of these elements according to their acoustic, optical, and other physical properties. One has inferred missing elements from a space in this table, predicted their properties to some extent, and actually discovered them afterwards. However different the elements are phenomenally, they represent nevertheless a larger unity that we can grasp by means of calculation.

However, the chemist is forced to look for the unity somewhere other than in the crude concept of an essential unity of matter, namely, in a system of lawful relations. Professor Ostwald[†] spoke about this direction at a congress of natural scientists. Recently, a journal[†] has been founded for the further development of the outdated materialism in this new natural-philosophical sense. Thus, we are faced with a new worldview which we cannot yet complete but to which a perspective has been opened up, namely, a perspective toward unity.

This is also the case with the uniformity of force. On the basis of the phenomena, we will never be able to trace electricity back to pure gravity. But in the mathematical formulae according to which we calculate and convert both, we have something real, something fundamental. And this opens an approach to the unity of force.

Without wanting to place myself exactly on the standpoint of Goethe's theory of metamorphosis, where he initially sought a principle of unity in the field of organic life, I nevertheless think that it also represents a significant step toward a unified worldview. In addition, there is the biogenetic basic law, according to which every being in its embryonic course of formation once again passes through the forms of the species from which it descends.[†] Since it has been possible to produce organic substances in the laboratory, we have been offered a clear path to unity.[†]

If one does not want to demand the unity precisely in phenomenality, this perspective shows us where we must look for the *monon*. And more and more clearly is revealed what all great philosophers had no doubt about: That what we experience in the external world presents itself as synonymous with what we experience in the spirit. If we progress from the external to the internal experience, we will bring about a unified view of the world. For a seeker of unity, the last decades of science are quite comforting because elements are streaming to him from all fields, opening up to him a unified worldview.

Its value consists in the fact that it satisfies a spiritual need which belongs as necessarily as air and light to the happiness of a spirit that forms this need in itself.

Mr. Kirchbach responded in the following sense: On the question, How do we arrive at a unified worldview and how do we envision it? Dr.

Steiner has given many suggestions with which I quite agree. But one can argue on individual points. For example, Goethe's teaching on the metamorphosis of plants, mentioned by the previous speaker, is an example of how even such a great mind could believe that it had found a unity of purpose on a point that later turned out to be questionable. Goethe believed that in the chlorophyll leaf the same morphological principle as in the stem held sway and he saw the principle of the leaves recurring in the shape of the petals and in the pistil so that to him all parts of the plant were only modifications of one and the same morphological principle of design. On the other hand, it is a fact that in the rose the stem leaf has only one central canal while the petal has three, so there is a fundamental difference in the morphological structure of the rose just as there is an underlying chemical one.

The newer cell theory also looks for the unity in a completely different area than in this apparent morphology. Here the cell is the principle of formation and brings forth the total structure by the sum of all factors to which it is subjected. Perhaps it will go similarly with some of the terms of Darwinism.

I have used the example to show how difficult the search for unity is even in the natural field because we must first learn to group the phenomena correctly according to mere perception before we may conclude their essential unity by mathematical or other logical mediation.

Dr. Bruno Wille:† You have just heard two representatives of world-views which, I believe, apart from individual points of difference, are nevertheless in agreement in their basic features. First of all, certain difficulties have been pointed out that seem to stand in the way of the formation of a unified worldview. However, we experience nature at first as a multiplicity, as an immense quantity of different sensations. Only when we compare this multiplicity in the unity-seeking spirit and partly bridge the differences, partly dissolving them, can we come closer to a unified worldview.

To seek such unity is indeed, as Dr. Steiner says, a general human need; first of all, it is a logical need. Our cognitive apparatus, which wants to understand the world, has the tendency to think all multiplicity together into unity. We see a certain commonality in the trees of our local forests, and, in spite of all their diversity, we unite them (for example, the term *pine* represents a unity). We arrange the pines again with the birches, oaks, and aspens, with the blueberries, ferns, and mosses to an even higher unity with the term *plant*. If we compare a plant with ourselves, here again a unity is present, because we are dealing with organic living beings. Thus, our thinking is constantly on the search for superordinate unities and connections.

Here, of course, the significant question of epistemology arises: Does the world correspond to our thinking independently of us? Is the unity of nature more than a mere subjective, intellectual experience? The answer is most intricate. Today, I content myself with a simple *yes*, while I still remark: I look for monism also in the fact that I, in contrast to Kant, conceive subject and object, mind and nature, as an inseparable unity and like the medieval *realists* see in the concept a real (not merely nominal) identity.

For our moral striving, too, the doubt about what is morally true, right, and wholesome can only be removed if we can derive the individual moral ideas from a supreme unity. If there were two or more world principles which stood in absolute opposition, contradictory principles for our moral life could also be derived from them. In general, we would fall into hopeless contradictions in all areas of our life; therefore, our whole idealism points us to monism, to the search for the eternal unity.

Of course, natural science does not yet give a clear answer as to where we should look for unity in the manifold world. The magnificently developed natural science of the last century was, as Dr. Steiner very rightly emphasized, so fruitful for the cause of the unified worldview that the monistic philosopher must not refrain from drawing the full benefit from these fruits. However, the natural scientist should not look contemptuously at the millennia-old work of philosophy but rather take the doubts raised by the philosophical side seriously and try to answer them. I am pleased that Dr. Steiner has acknowledged that the old materialism has become untenable. This insight is a fruit of philosophical criticism. Philosophy and natural science belong together as ways of looking at things which complement each other.

To supplement the scientific facts, in which Dr. Steiner rightly sees important moments of monism, I would like to point out the following aspects of my unified worldview. I would like to emphasize first of all that we find a comprehensive law of nature in all world processes and phenomena for which we have never been able to find an exception: the law of causality. It is a fact that every process follows necessarily from another, which we can call the cause of the following. What I mean is: the process of cause and effect signifies in this regard nothing other than what we call development. The emergence of the effect from the system of its conditions can be understood as the further development of the cause. The law of causality thus pervades all world processes for which we can in turn determine special rules—the special laws of nature. According to such *eternal, iron, grand laws*, the world firmly presents itself to us as unity, in contrast to the dualistic worldview which admits miracles (i.e., exceptions from the laws of nature), which it cannot make plausible without *higher guidance* (i.e., without confession of human ignorance).

Another unity of the world I find in the fact that everything I know of the universe is an experience, either an experience for me or an experience for other beings, as well as a self-experience. This idea-experience regards only the idea as the real element of the world, and it is to be used to approach the idealistic view. If one understands by it not only the idea-experience, then I think we can all agree on this statement: Nobody would be able to prove that there is an existence that is not experienced.

In this principle of my worldview, I have won the balance of important opposites that become dubious to every one-sided materialistic or mechanistic monism. Thus, I have overcome the opposition of matter and spirit. By understanding everything physical as an experience (of course, not as a mere phenomenon for our senses), I see it as an experience in which the eternal One experiences itself. In general, my monism denies all absolute opposites. Death means for me another side of life. I can imagine the emergence of the organic from the inorganic only if there is no absolute opposition between the two kingdoms of nature. In the moral life, I consider evil only as an immature form, a lower stage, of the good; therefore, I do not accept an absolute evil but only a relative evil. Error is only an immature truth, a certain stage of development on the way to knowledge.

As you see, I also seek a unified worldview in the way that I strive for a subjective unity, a unity between my various spiritual aspirations, my manifold experiences, and my forces of personality. I have overcome the opposition between head and heart, between mind and intellect, between true religiosity and scientific knowledge, as well as the opinion that art is only an illusion, a sweet deception, which stands in the way of cool insight. Already at the foundation of our Association, I emphasized that in the cultivation of a unified worldview, man should be guided to shape the divisive hostilities in his inner life into harmony—into a reconciliation. Of course, he should not shape it into a reconciliation of folly but into the clear unity of his highest spiritual activities.

Wolfgang Kirchbach: To conclude this discussion, I would ask you to consider the conversation that has taken place between the three gentlemen as the preface to the discussions that will follow. In the forthcoming conversations, we will perhaps refrain from continuing them in this general way. Lines have been described along which an internal consensus can be traced. We want to select specific questions in the next discussions. All speakers agree that a unified worldview is an indispensable need. Thus, our main task would be to determine how far these efforts have come and to limit the question to certain points. I do not want to give any further details about this yet, and so I would like to conclude the session with a question as follows. For today, to whet your appetite, let us ponder: How will this continue?

Truth and Science

BERLIN, MAY 7, 1902

Introductory lecture by Rudolf Steiner:
"Before what forum can a unified worldview be decided? – An attempt to answer the question of 'truth and science,'" followed by a discussion.

Dr. Rudolf Steiner, as speaker: I have been stimulated by our question "Before what forum must a uniform worldview be decided?" by the earlier discussions of our Association, which wants to cultivate a monistic worldview, and also by my personal participation in the controversy regarding Haeckel's *The Riddle of the Universe.*[†] Here in the Association, the following questions have been often considered: What is the essence of a unified worldview? What is its value? Do we actually have the right to speak of a specifically monistic one?

Once, it was emphasized that we have no right to speak of a unity in material relation according to the present standpoint of science. On another occasion, Dr. Penzig explained that in striving for a unified worldview encompassing the whole of nature and the spiritual world, one cannot help but falsify the picture given objectively by individual science (i.e., do violence to the facts). I had already noted at that time that often the greatest progress has started from such alleged falsifications. Thus the Copernican world system was for its time a "falsification" of the available facts,[†] and the Lamarck-Darwinian evolutionary theory is as well. As Tycho Brahe[†] gave the only possible worldview for his time, so it is easy for the fact fanatic who does not want to go beyond the objectively offered facts with his thinking to prove the "falsifications" which the Lamarck-Haeckel theory of development is supposed to contain according to the present state of science. Nevertheless, I believe, like Copernicus, that Haeckel will be proved right. At that time, I stood up for the much-disputed book *The Riddle of the Universe* with firm determination because I admired the consistency and extreme boldness with which a mind designs and "falsifies" a world picture from a one-sided point of view. Although my own fundamental philosophical views are opposed to him in what in those views he fights against, I am in agreement with what he gives as a positive contribution. At the same time, however, because of my earlier writings, I was called a main opponent of Haeckel. This experience seems to me symptomatic for our time, insofar as in the mind of another, an author's conceptual world can take on a completely different appearance. With our concepts, according to their other position in spiritual life, we bring into the field ideas that say something different than what we want to express.

In these discussions about Haeckel and in the discussions of the Association, a question was revived for me, one that I have often asked myself: How does truth relate to science? Does science contain truth? Does it contain any moments that could lead to the construction of a unified worldview? Do we have the right to want to build a unified worldview out of science or any worldview at all?

This question has already occupied people for centuries. Some of those people were closer to a solution than people in the modern age, which has obstructed the path to a solution with its so-called epistemic theories. In some forum today, something can be settled regarding truth and science. With this question, we must clarify our answer in regard to the truth-content of science.

After the whole development of the nineteenth century, common opinion about the idea of the truth is that it must correspond to the objectively present reality. We are in an age of intensive fact-fanaticism which does not allow us to go any step beyond the recording of data. If truth is only a conceptual repetition of what exists outside of us, then, according to the feeling of those who strive for a worldview today, it is also nothing other than a counter-image of facts existing outside of us, a counter-image of the reality finished outside of us in the world. If it were possible to take a photograph of the world in any corner from the most favorable perspective, then the ideal worldview would be reached. But to build up such a worldview would indeed be superfluous, a mere luxury of the human spirit, if it, like science, should be nothing other than a mere repetition, a kind of photographic counter-image of what is going on in the world, of what is complete. That the individual still forms an individual counter-image alongside science would be viewed as completely unnecessary, infinitely indifferent for the whole world context. If nature has provided and formed everything for us up to the final point, then what the human spirit dreams and creates does not belong to reality. For this point of view, which in a grotesque way emerges in today's science and in Haeckel's *The Riddle of the Universe*, man is nothing but a mere speck of dust in the cosmos who differs only quantitatively from a worm. If he creates a picture of the world for himself, he lives a life of luxury. He does something which does not add in the least to the development of the world. Rather, this view demands that he must never add from his own spirit anything that is not found in the rest of nature but must only register, compare, and logically connect with what already exists outside of him.

We ask: Does this process of merely logically confronting objective nature, never adding anything beyond the present state of conditions, agree with the course of the entities of nature? Is there not perhaps something in nature's direction of development that forces us to add something to reality? The answer is given by nature itself. It is especially given to the evolutionary theorist.

Allow me to explain this in a concise way by asking you to imagine nature in a stage of development where there are only monkeys and no human beings. The monkeys would have investigated the phenomena of the world and they would have found what stands below them in evolution, up to monkeys themselves. If they had taken an empirical point of view, they would have been satisfied with the realization: the world concludes with monkeys. They would perhaps have founded a monkey ethics on the basis of the general monkey feeling; however, they would then remain at that standpoint so that nothing new would be added to the world. But from our point of view, and with our subsequent knowledge, we know that in the principle of development there is something which led beyond the monkey species. Something which, because it was a productive principle, because it pointed beyond that which existed as a closed reality, led to the formation of the human being. This principle of development was not limited to the factual. It exists as a real imagination, as a real intuition in nature. It has led beyond the individual stages and raised nature above the immediate present.

Man, too, as a product of development, as a being in nature, is there to live through evolution, not merely to look back and form a picture of evolution and regard himself as the end of the line. A worldview that seeks to summarize the content of his whole thinking and activity will therefore have to be not merely theoretical-observing but also practical-postulating. The human being should therefore not only repeat nature in some way but see whether there are not forces in him that lead beyond what is immediately given. He should make the evolution spiritually and ideally alive in himself. He should look for the forces that drive the species forwards, that bring forth progress, and not merely examine his mental forces to see whether they correspond with reality. The question "Can we penetrate to the thing in itself, see into the essence of the world?" is a mischief, an obstacle for man. But if he places himself in the evolution, intervening in nature in order to lead it a little further, he comes to a feeling of his sublime task and his position within the world.

There are indeed the beginnings of the formation of this super-scientific point of view, which accepts science but rises above what science offers as a law of logical thought. Maeterlinck,[†] for example, came out with similar views in one of his more recent books, in which he describes the wedding of the bee. One asks: Can we speak of truth in the sense of scientific truth, of agreement with the present reality, which is always in the material trivialities, if it is to be the content of a worldview? Or does it lead as a worldview-truth in a similar way beyond the purely objective truth, as the poetic truth leads, according to the view of those who understand it in the Goethean sense, beyond the immediate naturalistic truth?

Such approaches are to be found in the present age in several places, to the delight of those who see the truth in the lively activity of life and to the horror of the fact-fanatics like Tycho Brahe or the opponents of Haeckel. But it does not belong before their forum. The truth that seeks to fructify will always be a search, will always have to "falsify" the concepts of the fact-fanatics. It stands infinitely above this, in that it forms something intuitive, something spiritual in man. It adds something new to nature that would not exist without the human spirit. What man cherishes in his dreams and creates in his spirit is of more significance than a mere luxury. It contains the cosmic truth in life as something that man has generated anew. Thus, on the substructure of science, he rises to productive work which springs freely from his soul as original intuition. Associated with the highest stage of development, he has a task that no other being in the world has and he adds something that, without him, would be eternally nonexistent.

However much these views may be an abomination to the plain naturalist, I consider it a correct insight that man has a right to be productive in his worldview. This feeling was alive at various times before fact-fanaticism and epistemological theories put blinders on us, in times that were convinced *a priori* of the cosmic character of this addition.

Let me conclude with the words of Angelus Silesius, which express the realization of the unique significance of the human spirit in the world: "Without me, God could not create a single little worm; if I became nothing, it, too, would have to crumble into nothingness."[†]
Schäfer, former spokesman of the free religious and the humanistic community in Berlin, objects to the expression "falsification" for the error of Copernicus. If Copernicus assumed a circular motion instead of an elliptical one, this was a defective view which, like many similar ones, has been clarified by human progress. It will always be man's lot to be forced to get stuck in the imperfections of his views, which will only be solved later.

The speaker would have seen the subject of Heber summarized: "In which forum, in which court of justice can a judgement about a worldview, about truth and untruth, and thus about its right and wrong, be made?"

In this forum there are only individual personalities and their sovereignty. From this understanding then flows the sense of responsibility.

Dr. Stern: A basis that is of importance for our discussion is: Is a worldview, that is, a general philosophical view of the true nature of the world and of everything that exists, at all possible? This question has been answered very differently. While, on the one hand, it is considered unobjectionable to acquire a dogmatic worldview after having experiences, another opinion, to which I profess myself, is critical positivism, which, starting from scientific knowledge, does not stop at the individual fact, but nevertheless does not consider it possible to gain a picture of the ultimate facts, a true picture of the cosmos.

To justify the dogmatic method, reference is made to the metaphysical drive which undoubtedly exists in man. It already exists in the child who breaks the toy in order to get to the core of how it works.

In the formation of metaphysical systems for the satisfaction of this instinct, two psychological mistakes crept in: Greek philosophy picked out unilaterally one of the different parts of the universe and made it the subject, the true essence of nature. Thus, Thales discusses water. In more recent times, one has fallen into the trap of taking various psychological faculties of the human nature individually into consideration and, fantastically magnified, to impute them to nature as an entity. Thus, Hegel makes Reason the world principle, and Schopenhauer puts blind Will at the center. Lotze assumes a comprehensive consciousness that mediates all interaction. Thus, philosophy has happily arrived again where it started out, in hylozoism.[†]

I consider it impossible at all to find a general, true, and correct worldview. On the one hand, I see the subjective nature of the human mind, which sees everything and anything through a subjective lens and, according to Kant, can never recognize the thing-in-itself. On the other hand, I see the objective reason that all our research covers only such a small part of the universe and that it is impossible at all for such a large part of events ever to enter the circle of our experience so that we can draw generally valid conclusions about the world as a whole from it.

Benedikt Lachmann: Dr. Steiner seems to me to set up an opposition between man and nature. The essence of man as of every other form of existence can be resolved into a play of forces, of movement and resistance, which fight with each other to no purpose. It cannot be a question for man to rise above these forces, but he must seek to come to terms with them as well as possible.

Wolfgang Kirchbach: Dr. Steiner has said that it is a danger, even a necessity of the human spirit to arrive at a falsification if it is not content to give a simple image, a copy of reality. In contrast to this, Francis Bacon believed that he could build a correct worldview on the *perceptionibus sensuum* alone. He rejected the Copernican system because it contradicted his conception of the *perceptiones.*[†]

For the determination of truth depends on man's general knowledge and his powers and abilities, which are given to him for the judgement of reality. Among them also belongs the mathematical judgment which corrects perceptions. One can speak of a falsification probably only in the sense that the human being renounces one or the other ability unilaterally. After all, there have also been minds that thought in full possession of all their mental faculties in a certain maturity that we call *reason*. When Mr. Schäfer says that the forum of a worldview is the sovereignty of my personality, he surely meant that this forum is the total possession of the spiritual powers of my personality, and we can agree on the name reason.

The rational concept of truth demands conformity of judgment with reality for every form of thinking, in science as well as in the development of a worldview. It demands observation, perception, correction of perception, the finding of a concept, and its expression. It then expresses the greatest sum of the known facts according to the respective state of knowledge and expresses the greatest conformity of our judgments with reality.

This way alone makes research and imagination productive. It protects itself from error that is refuted by reality and is otherwise contentless and unproductive. Alone, it is possible to add something productively to nature. Even if the poet gives us a picture of the world, we think it better that he creates realistic figures and gives a social or other general law to observe in his work. His work is also only the image of reality, but only the discovery of the real inner symbol is an eminently productive activity, as is the case in science with regard to the discovery of the summarizing, fruitful overarching concept from the sum of opposing and limiting data. It requires, however, a productive imagination, but this is equally a regulator of reason and a limitation of the imagination by reality.

This method has added something to the world by creating new organs. By methodical, reasoned consideration, Kant has added in the moral field to what we commonly call nature—that is, the world of sensation and pleasurable feelings— a completely new moment that far exceeds empirical nature: the categorical imperative.

Dr. Steiner: I must confess that the arguments have not at all touched on what I have spoken today. I have not spoken of an opposition between man and nature. Rather, I have placed myself on the most consistent standpoint of the theory of development. I regard all stages of naturalness, from the lowest to the highest emotions of the spirit, as uniform, which only appear in different forms. But an amoeba, after all, is not a human being, and it is not a question of blurring all distinctions. When I say that in nature everything is only force, resistance, movement, it reminds one too much of the sentence: In the night all cats are gray. It is not possible to deal with the whole world in the twinkling of an eye. Only when I have distinguished things can I search for a unifying, connecting principle. In the sense of the unifying principle of development I have spoken of the human task as one lying within nature, given by the facts of evolution.

I completely agree that we must adhere to reality if we want to be productive and correct our imagination on the basis of it. I only stated that the attempt to give a worldview that is only an imitation of reality, as Büchner[†] seeks to do, does not meet these requirements, and he, too, is forced to do violence to the facts. One must look here not at the will but at the result. One behaves as if one wanted to give a picture of what is really there but cannot. My principle is therefore not theoretical but practical, going beyond reality in the sense of the principle of development, as I see it, where creatures go beyond their own kind. This position of the problem has not been touched at all in the discussion.

I have not used the word falsification in the sense of the imperfection of a conception that will be clarified only later. I meant that researchers are always forced, for the sake of their systems, into intentionally incorrect representations when they are looking for a comprehensive unity. I have asked whether what we are entitled to call reality in the highest sense coincides at all with what natural scientists imagine under the term *reality*. When Haeckel illustrates three stages of embryonic development with the same cliché, he is forced into a falsification in order to provide proof according to the scientific method. I say that with irony because such falsifications nevertheless remain correct, as does Haeckel in relation to his opponents, who hang on the purely factual element of the natural-scientific method. He remains correct because he sees in an intuitive way beyond the single facts, not because what he sees is some fantasy.

But when Dr. Stern rejects on principle the possibility of a world-view, a total view, and in so doing invokes the diversity of philosophical systems in support of his view, this is a *fable convenue* based on incomplete conceptions of the individual systems. The most significant attempts at truth that have been made, from Vedanta philosophy through Greek to German, are approximations to truth in varying degrees.

The forum before which the justification of one or the other point of view is decided can only be the forum of the human being, his sovereign personality, in this I agree with Dr. Schäfer. This sentence seems to me a truly real one, which has flowed not from theoretical musings but from the experience of people who have worked practically. But true as it is that the personality is the ultimate forum, it is equally true that the personality must then always feel the responsibility of this position and the duty to develop steadily, to form the depths of its personality. The child cannot be as forum in the same way as he who stands at the height of knowledge. Therefore, the question arises: Where in us human beings lies that which is to be developed, that which is productive? What corresponds in us to that which drives nature forward, which made the apes leave their species and become man?

If I consider the human being as a product of development, I can, however, regard him as the highest existing form. But I also have the obligation to always call the highest human being within myself into existence and have in no moment of my life the right to recognize myself as a form in full and final instance. But I can, as one standing in the stream of development, devote myself to the expectation that in every moment of my existence a higher point of knowledge than the one I now possess can open up to me. The further development of the personality must be based on science, but it must also go beyond it, as art and poetry do, and, as art and poetry do not consist of blind fantasy if one controls one's personality by the principle of development, even if they go far beyond objective nature, agreement will arise in the most diverse people, as the agreement of philosophical systems of all times shows.

In this sovereign meaning of the human personality lies the solution of the question, To what extent does science contain truth? Can it alone lead to truth?

The world, especially for science, is built dualistically in many respects. Development is only possible because nature has prepared the future in it dualistically. As an apparent and for science at first unresolvable contradiction, nature confronts man as force, matter, and so on.

Here now the meaning of the human personality enters. Only the life activity of the human being can be unifying, monistic. It consists in the dissolution of these apparent opposites into a higher view, productively generated from the human being, in the life of development, in the unification of opposites, in living and doing.

Therefore, the question of the validity of a worldview is to be decided before the forum of life, not before the forum of knowledge.

Monism and Theosophy

BERLIN, OCTOBER 8, 1902

Rudolf Steiner's lecture at the Giordano Bruno Association[†]

Dr. Steiner first emphasizes that a person who is savvy in the ordinary sense would not speak publicly about such a subject in the context of contemporary German spiritual life because hardly any other would be more suited to compromise itself. He then continues:

Theosophy is a name often used by people who want to explore their destiny in spiritualistic circles. And in spite of the fact that it reeks of chicanery, I speak about the subject in its connection with German spiritual life in full consciousness. I much prefer to be in my chemical laboratory than in spiritualistic circles, and I know that you can get your hands just as dirty in either place. But I have washed my hands, and I hope that I will succeed in bringing the word "theosophy" as a serious worldview before you. It must be clearly stated that only on the basis of modern natural science can a serious worldview be sought. I will never deviate from the thought that only in science is salvation. However, natural science still fills hearts and minds with its materialistic worldview, and even if individual enthusiasts claim that we are long past the age of Büchner and so on, if we cannot construct an ideal worldview on the basis of natural science, then the materialism of the 1850s will continue to conquer the world. Practically all natural scientists of the present are materialists, even if they reject the label.

Natural science has shown us how beings gradually developed and perfected themselves until the human being appeared. But here, according to Haeckel in the 22nd part of his *Organic Ancestry*, it stopped.[†] David Friedrich Strauss[†] has praised natural science because it has redeemed us from miracles, in the sense meant by Linnaeus when he said in the eighteenth century, "As many kinds of animals and plants were originally created side by side by the Creator, so many miracles are there."[†] Natural science has dissolved these miracles by the magic word *evolution*. This magic word has transformed spatial juxtaposition into a temporal succession that has become clear. But the miracle that the human being is to himself, science has not been able to dissolve so far. We must attempt to apply the method of natural science to the juxtaposition that we see before us in the Hottentot and in the genius. We must discover, as it were, the spiritual primordial cell that connects both. The method of natural science necessary for this will again be a different one, as natural science always has to model its methods according to its purposes. The geologist has to do more than just collect minerals in order to learn to understand the history of the earth. Haeckel did not discover his basic biogenetic law[†] just because he treated animal bodies in the laboratory with chemical reagents. Just as little will a chemical examination of the brain give a soul-investigator information about the life of the soul. In spite of the tremendous progress of natural science, it has not yet been able to discover a method of understanding the life of the soul, and this has created a deep gulf between natural science and religious feeling that has never been greater. It is different in ancient cultures and their theologies. In them, this dichotomy does not exist. Theology is nothing other than the expression of their respective scientific thinking. What was presented as a worldview was so noble and great and divine that it was religion translated into sentiment. Today, however, we are faced with the fact that theology and science are two completely separate things, and in this sense, Adolf Harnack says that one feels as if redeemed in the thought that science will never be able to fulfill religious needs.[†] On the other hand, on behalf of natural science, the Englishman Ingersoll says:

> We are so far that for us the expressions of the spirit are only a natural-scientific fact. Our thoughts are nothing else than a transposition of the food we take into our organism. The creation of Hamlet is nothing else than the transformed food substance that Shakespeare took in.[†]

How can we restore the harmony that existed for the ancient religions, even for the early Middle Ages? With St. Augustine,[†] this dichotomy gradually occurred, leading to the two great dualistic currents in the opposition of scholasticism and Galileo[†] and so on. Science is like a son who returns home from a foreign country and can no longer be understood by his father. Protestantism is nothing other than the declaration of the father that he wants to disinherit the son, and Kantianism is the conclusion, the last phase of this process!

The first great attempt to overcome this dichotomy was made by the German idealist philosophers Fichte, Schelling, and Hegel. Three years after Hegel's death, Fichte's son published a book about human self-knowledge.[†] It deals with this as a task that natural science itself has set. I. H. Fichte says something like: If we look at natural beings, we see their eternal laws. But if we regard the human soul itself as a process of nature, we are faced with a change of cognition. The laws of nature lie outside our personality in the basis of nature from which we have emerged. In our soul, we do not see finished laws of nature, but we ourselves are natural law. There, nature becomes our own act. There, we are development. There, we do not merely realize. There, we live. Now we have the task of creating eternal laws of nature, not only of recognizing them. I. H. Fichte then indicates: At this point, man lives not only in his knowledge of nature. At this point, he realizes and lives the divine, the creative. *At this point, philosophy passes over into theosophy.*

Here the concept of theosophy appears in German spiritual life. We see now, perhaps already sooner, that *theosophy is nothing other than the last requirement of a true monism between knowledge of nature and self-knowledge.* This gives us a perspective to balance the opposites between religion and science. We know now: there is no other divine power that transports the worm up to the human being. We know that we ourselves are this divine power.

One will ask: But what is the purpose of such a cognition at all? Well, so I answer, what is the meaning of what one usually calls cognition, the simple registration of the facts? With it, those whom I would like to call cosmic stand-in-the-corner people are content.

Whoever grasps the concept of theosophy in this way will also understand Feuerbach, who says that man created God in his own image. We want to admit that the concept of God is born out of the human heart and that God as a symbol of an inner ideal can develop man beyond man.[†]

We will once more gain a divine wisdom that will pronounce the divinity of nature. Today we live again in a time that can become an important nodal point in the spiritual development of Europe, as was the time in which Copernicus, Giordano Bruno, and Galileo lived and founded modern natural science. But this science did not know how to celebrate its reconciliation with religion. We are faced with this task. We must fulfill it. These attempts may still be insufficient, but we have currents in modern spiritual life that take their start from them. Religions are not founded as such. Religious geniuses in the sense in which there are scientific and artistic geniuses do not exist, but there are personalities who express the cognitive content of their time as religious feeling. I am well aware of the great defects and errors of the theosophical movement. Duboc has called theosophy a feminine philosophy.[†] We can change that by making it a masculine one in the crucial region of Germany.

I know that there can be no salvation outside of natural science, but we must find new methods of soul research on a scientific basis in order to be able to do what all old religious views were able to do: establish a great unity between religious need and science. Theosophy in the sense in which I have characterized it has in itself nothing to do with the reports of hypnotism and somnambulism often thrown together with it. Yes, one could reject these and still be a theosophist, but these phenomena of abnormal soul life are not to be rejected at all. In the scientific interpretation of these facts undertaken especially by French and English scholars, I see the first tentative attempts at real soul research.

Dr. Steiner concluded his programmatic lecture with a reference to a picture by the Belgian painter Wiertz entitled "The Man of the Future."[†] It depicts a giant holding cannons and the other things of today's culture in his hand and smilingly showing them to his wife and children; they have shrunk, pygmy-like, before his large stature. It will be our task not to appear so pygmy-like before future generations.

Summary of the Discussion

Following Rudolf Steiner's Lecture on Monism and Theosophy Along with a Summary of Steiner's Comments

BERLIN, OCTOBER 15, 1902

First, O. Lehmann-Russbüldt† gave a presentation on Dr. R. Steiner's lecture for orientation and added that it would have been his personal wish that not only the two hundred and fifty to three hundred members of the audience had been present but the two to three thousand individuals who make up the spiritual-public life in Germany. Dr. Steiner's call to make theosophy, a feminine philosophy according to Duboc, into a masculine one in the crucial region of Germany should be underlined thickly so as to occupy an entire page by itself, for there is certainly no danger in the theosophical movement. The speaker acknowledged that our spiritual culture, in spite of electricity and precision mechanics, can be called crude compared to the harmony that existed in the great cultures of antiquity between science and the religious world, but, he added emphatically, we do not want to despair of ourselves because of this. The obvious superiority of our intelligence, as it expresses itself in the machine age, could be a guarantee for us that we will deepen and expand what the culture of antiquity possessed only as an intimation, albeit in the most magnificent way. In this connection, the speaker [Lehmann-Rußbüldt] quoted a passage from the racial work of Count Gobineau† about the spiritual disposition of the Aryan, which could certainly be applied to the peoples of the Atlantic world (i.e., to Western Europe and North America):

> The Aryan, then, is superior to the rest of mankind chiefly in the measure of his intelligence and his energy. Thanks to these two endowments, if he succeeds in conquering his passions and his material needs, it is likewise granted to him to attain to an infinitely

> higher morality; although in the ordinary course of things one can reprove as many reprehensible actions in him as in the individuals of inferior races.

The speaker [Lehmann-Rußbüldt] concluded with the remark that, according to his view, the science of an extended and refined psychology would develop out of the despised hypnotism and somnambulism, which would mean as much to us for the knowledge of the soul as astronomy and chemistry mean for the knowledge of nature, although these sciences had developed out of astrology and alchemy.

In the discussion, Nicolai raised the objection that it was not explained what theosophy actually wants and can do.

Dr. Steiner replied that his lecture had only sought to emphasize the connection between monism and the worldview that already in the days of the Vedanta philosophy of India was inclined in a modern direction. The dualism that began in the fourth century in Christianity allowed the eye and the senses to be valid for the knowledge of the world of appearances. This fourth-century Christianity did not admit reason as the means for our knowledge but referred us to faith, to the revelations of old books and prophets. Monism, however, promises a development in knowledge, just as it has been able to establish the development of species among living beings. In the writings of Vedanta philosophy, there is a conversation in which a disciple asks the teacher: What happens when I die? The teacher replies: The solid and liquid of your body becomes again the solid and liquid because the human being is like a stone and an animal. Also, the expressions of your thinking and acting dissolve in your environment, but there remains the "development," the cause of that which has formed your personality. Thus, Vedanta philosophy already thinks monistically in germinal form.[†] What lives in the animal only in the unconscious—namely, the urge to the development of his personality—must, in the human being, enter into full consciousness and arise in consciousness as an ideal.

Fritz Sänger polemicized against Dr. Steiner. The theosophists always pretend to have possessed and still possess the results of modern natural science in advance, but they have never given samples of such superiority. He feared that such a movement would be only too apt to undermine again the results of modern natural science. In spite of the calmest observation, he had been able to find in spiritualism only the expression of nonsense, but the fact of hypnotism he had to acknowledge.

After Köhn had interceded in warm and urgent words for Dr. Steiner, O. Lehmann-Rußbüldt remarked that the statements of Mr. Sänger were typical for the representatives of the so-called natural science of all times. Fifteen years ago, Sänger would have declared as nonsense the fact demonstrated by Krafft-Ebing, among others, that a lime leaf laid on a hypnotized person draws a burn like a red-hot piece of iron if the hypnotized person regards it as such (just as a hundred years ago the French materialists declared it to be humbug that meteor stones can fall to the earth from outer space).

Dr. Steiner then once again vigorously opposed the confusion of theosophy and spiritualism. If Mr. Sänger had encountered such theosophists as give rise to this, let him stick to them, because he, Dr. Steiner, resolutely rejects it. He considers it immoral in the philosophical spirit to want to obtain teachings about fate and human nature through the manifestations of so-called spirits. That would be gross materialism. He also does not attach any special importance to the name theosophy. Above all, the high ethics of theosophy in his sense is important to him, which, for example, leads to the most serious consequences in pedagogy. What a perspective for the mind of the educator if he is aware that he has to develop a seed of divinity in the child! *

* Our reporter, Mr. Otto Lehmann-Rußbüldt, the second chairman of the Bruno Association, feels the need to add to the report that he also considers this lecture, along with so many other significant phenomena in spiritual life, as a nucleus of a new noble culture. "Times of great upheaval do not come upon us like a mystical something. If we create them, they are there. The theosophical movement would be welcome to me with a program such as Dr. Steiner formulates. Let us hope that freshly beginning life forces of rejuvenation can create, above all, livelier, poetically inspiring words; what are all *isms* to us anyway!

In any case, the golden wheat of a genuine theosophy has unfortunately been buried under so much chaff of parroting Indian vocabulary that the philosophical hero should be highly welcome who can gather it into a new barn, that is, under a new name."

EDITORIAL AND REFERENCE NOTES

In 1897, Rudolf Steiner moved from Weimar to Berlin and took over the publication and editing of the *Magazin für Literatur* and the *Dramaturgische Blätter*, the organ of the German Stage Association. (The essays from this period are contained in CW volumes 29, 30, 31, 32.) In addition to this activity, he gave countless lectures in various contexts in the following years, of which, however, almost no transcripts are available. Only a few transcripts of Rudolf Steiner's lectures within the "Worker Education School" and the "Independent College" in Berlin are available, which are contained in this volume 51 of the Collected Works.

On part one

In the years 1899–1904, Rudolf Steiner taught at the Worker Education School in Berlin, established by the Social Democrat Wilhelm Liebknecht. In the chapter 28 of his *Autobiography* (CW 28), Rudolf Steiner reported on this period of his life. See also the booklet *Erinnerungen aus Rudolf Steiner und seine Wirksamkeit an der Arbeiterbildungsschule* [Recollections of Rudolf Steiner and his activity at the Worker Education School] by Johanna Mücke and A. A. Rudolph (new edition, Basel, 1979), which gives a vivid picture of Rudolf Steiner's activity in these contexts.

Textual basis for the lectures at the Worker Education School

Views of the World and of Life from Ancient Times to the Present: The short summary of the contents of ten lectures was written by Rudolf Steiner himself.

William Shakespeare: Notes by Johanna Mücke. Johanna Mücke (1864–1949), belonged to the socialist trade union movement and to the board of the Worker Education School in Berlin. She became a member of the Theosophical Society in 1903 and from 1908 to 1935 was managing director of the Philosophical-Anthroposophical Publishing House founded by Marie Steiner-von Sivers in Berlin, later Dornach. The text by Johanna Mücke was elaborated from her handwritten notes, since she did not know stenography.

On Roman History: This lecture is the only one in the present volume that was stenographically recorded by Franz Seiler (1868–1959), member of the Theosophical Society and the stenographer of Rudolf Steiner's early members-only lectures. In Franz Seiler's shorthand notebook, the lecture date of July 19, 1904, is found. Presumably, this is one of the last lectures of the course *History of Early Peoples and Antiquity up to the Fall of Roman Rule*, which according to Hans Schmidt's *Vortragswerk Rudolf Steiners* [Lecture work of Rudolf Steiner] were held from April 5 to June 14, 1904. A correspondence with one of these dates could not be established. Notes by Marie Steiner-von Sivers indicate that another lecture was given at the Worker Education School on July 26, 1904, on the topic "The Relationship of the Germanic Peoples to Christianity." There is no transcript of the other lectures of this course.

History of the Middle Ages up to the Great Inventions and Discoveries (ten lectures): The first edition published in 1936 contained only eight lectures from October 18 to December 20, 1904. The two lectures missing in this earlier publication are placed by Hans Schmidt in *Vortragswerk Rudolf Steiners* on October 4 and 11, 1904. Deviating from this, these two lectures are printed in the present volume as the ninth and tenth lectures with the dates December 28 and 29, 1904. The correctness of this arrangement is indicated by the thematic context.

On part two

In the fall of 1902, Rudolf Steiner took over the teaching of history at the *Freie Hochschule* (Independent College) in Berlin, founded by Wilhelm Bölsche and Bruno Wille, and held lecture courses there during the winter semester until December 1905. Topics included, among others: *German History from the Migration of the Peoples to the Twelfth Century*, *German History from the Founding of the Free Cities to the Great Inventions and Discoveries at the Beginning of the Modern Era*, *History of Mathematics and Physics*, *From Germanism to Citizenship*, and *German Mysticism and Its Preconditions*. Transcripts of only part of the latter course are available.

Text documents for the lectures at the Freie Hochschule (Independent College)

Platonic Mysticism and Docta ignorantia: Notes by Mathilde Scholl (1868–1941). She was a member of the executive committee of the German Section of the Theosophical Society beginning in 1903 and editor of the Society's newsletter *Notices for the Members of the German Section of the Theosophical Society* from 1905 to 1914. She directed anthroposophical work in Cologne until 1914 and later lived in Dornach.

Schiller and Our Age (nine lectures): notes by Marie Steiner-von Sivers and Johanna Mücke.

On part three

The Giordano Bruno Association for a Unified Worldview was founded in 1900 by Dr. Bruno Wille (1860–1928) and other literati of the *Friedrichshagen* circle. Wille was also the director of the journal *Der Freidenker* in which the papers printed here appeared. For Rudolf Steiner's activities within the Giordano Bruno Association, see the detailed account in the series *Beiträge zur Rudolf Steiner-Gesamtausgabe* [Contributions to Rudolf Steiner's Collected Works], issue 79, Easter 1983.

Notes on the text

Works by Rudolf Steiner within the Collected Works (CW) are indicated in the notes with the bibliographic number. See also the overview at the end of the volume.

I. Lectures at the Worker Education School in Berlin

Views of the World and of Life from Ancient Times to the Present

The Greek Worldviews

1 **the human race lives also by art and reasoning**
Aristotle, *Metaphysics*, I. i.

Thinking makes the soul . . . into a spirit
Georg Wilhelm Friedrich Hegel, "Preface to the Second Edition," in *Encyclopedia of the Philosophical Sciences in Basic Outline, Part I: Science of Logic*, trans. Klaus Brinkmann and Daniel O. Dahlstrom (Cambridge, UK: Cambridge University Press, 2010).

It does not ask why it blossoms
Angelus Silesius, *Cherubinischer Wandersmann*. Literally: "The rose is without a why; it blossoms because it blossoms. It does not notice itself, does not ask if it is seen."

3 **What may I hope?**
See Kant, *Critique of Pure Reason*, trans. and ed. Paul Guyer and Allen W. Wood (Cambridge, UK: Cambridge University Press, 1999).

then I name it truth
Goethe, *Maxims and Reflections*, trans. Bailey Saunders (Dumfries and Galloway, UK: Anodos Books, 2017).

Thales
Thales, Anaximander, and Anaximenes are three generations of philosophers from Miletus. They constitute the Milesian School and are considered the first philosophers of the Western tradition. They were active between about 600 and 520 BC.

4 **Heraclitus**
Heraclitus (*c.* 500 BC), Greek philosopher from Ephesus. For more on Rudolf Steiner's view of Heraclitus, see, for example, *Christianity as Mystical Fact and the Mysteries of Antiquity* (CW 8).

5 **combine to become one object or separate again from it**
Metaphysics, Book I.

8 **numbers to be the primary thing in nature**
Metaphysics, Book I.

9 **that they are not**
DK 80B1.

11 **he brought philosophy down from heaven to earth**
Cicero, *The Tusculanae Disputationes*, Book 1, Chapter 4.

12 **Euclid of Megara**
Euclid of Megara (*c.* 435–*c.* 365 BC), Greek philosopher. Not to be confused with Euclid of Alexandria, the famous geometer.

13 **Plato**
Plato (*c.* 429–*c.* 347 BC), Greek philosopher. A disciple of Socrates and the

teacher of Aristotle, he founded the Academy in Athens and is one of the most influential philosophers in history.

17 **Better a day laborer in the light of the sun, than a king over the shadows**
Homer, *Odyssey*, Book 11, verses 489–91.

18 **But man is a political animal**
Quoted from Vincenz Knauer, *Hauptproblem der Philosopie* [Main problems of philosophy], lecture 32 (1892).

19 **master of those who know**
This appellation comes from Dante, who, in his *Divine Comedy*, refers to Aristotle as "the master of those who know."

The Worldviews of the Middle Ages and of Modern Times

22 **the essence of Christianity**
See, regarding this passage on Christianity, Rudolf Steiner, *Autobiography* (CW 28), trans. Rita Stebbing (SteinerBooks, 2005), p. 187:

> Some of what I said and wrote during that period seems to contradict the way I described Christianity later on. This is because, when I wrote the word *Christianity*, I was referring to the teachings of a "world beyond" that was active in all Christian doctrines at the time. The whole meaning of religious experiences pointed to a world of spirit, one that was supposed to be unattainable by human intellect. Whatever religion might have to say and whatever precepts for moral life it might offer arise from what is revealed to human beings from outside. My own direct, inner perception of spirit objected to this; it wanted to experience the worlds of both spirit and the physical in perceptions of the human being and nature. And my ethical individualism also objected to this. It rejected the external support of commandments for morality; such support came instead as the result of spiritual soul development within the human being, where divinity lives.
>
> That was a trying time for my soul as I looked at Christianity. This period lasted from the time I left the Weimar work until I wrote my book *Christianity as Mystical Fact*. These kinds of tests are obstacles, placed in one's path by destiny (or karma), and they must be overcome through spiritual development.

the authority of the Catholic Church
Aurelius Augustine, *Against the Fundamental Epistle of Manichaeus*, chap. 5, quoted from Willmann's *Geschichte des Idealismus* [History of idealism], volume 2, section IX (1896).

23 **in revelation lies the highest truth**
Augustine, in *De trinitate*, Book X, chapter 14, quoted from Willmann's *Geschichte des Idealismus* [History of idealism].

24 **The physician must go through the exams of nature**
Paracelsus, *Opus Paramirum* (1531). The full quote reads: "Now the physician is beyond medical training, but not out of options; therefore, he must go through nature's examination, where nature is the world and all it encompasses."

24 He must needs give up the ghost
Angelus Silesius, *Cherubinic Wanderer* (1657).

25 an open and acknowledged liar, a lecherous goat
From Luther's letter to Johann Eck in 1519, in Ferdinand Bahlow, *Luthers Stellung zur Philosophie* [Luther's position on philosophy] (Berlin, 1891).

nothing but blaspheme and profane what God speaks and does
Martin Luther, *Luther Weimarer Ausgabe* WA XVIII, 164 (and also in Bahlow).

26 learned the signs in which it is written
Galileo Galilei, *Dialogue Concerning Two New Sciences.* Stillman Drake translates the passage:
. . . if Aristotle were now alive, I have no doubt he would change his opinion. This is easily inferred from his own manner of philosophizing, for when he writes of considering the heavens inalterable, etc., because no new thing is seen to be generated there or any old one dissolved, he seems implicitly to let us understand that if he had seen any such event he would have reversed his opinion, and properly preferred the sensible experience to natural reason. Unless he had taken the senses into account, he would not have argued immutability from sensible mutations not being seen." (University of California Press, 1953)

Giordano Bruno
Giordano Bruno (1548–1600), Italian philosopher and mathematician.

René Descartes (Cartesius)
René Descartes (1596–1650), French philosopher, scientist, and mathematician.

27 in Leibniz and in Wolff
Gottfried Wilhelm Leibniz (1646–1716), German philosopher, scientist, mathematician, and diplomat.

Christian von Wolff (1679–1754), German philosopher.

Locke, David Hume, and . . . Immanuel Kant
John Locke (1632–1704), English philosopher; a founder of empiricism and political liberalism.

David Hume (1711–1776), Scottish philosopher, historian, and economist.

Immanuel Kant (1724–1804), German philosopher.

30 Du Bois-Reymond . . . "On the Limits of the Knowledge of Nature."
Emil du Bois-Reymond (1818–1896), German physician and physiologist. Du Bois-Reymond gave his lecture "On the Limits of the Knowledge of Nature" at the second public session of the forty-fifth Congress of German Scientists and Physicians in Leipzig on August 14, 1872. The lecture became famous primarily for its concluding words:

> With regard to the enigma of the physical world, the investigator of Nature has long been wont to utter his "Ignoramus" with manly resignation.

> As he looks back on the victorious career over which he has passed, he is upheld by the quiet consciousness that wherein he now is ignorant, he may at least under certain conditions be enlightened, and that he yet will know. But as regards the enigma of what matter and force are, and how they are to be conceived, he must resign himself once for all to the far more difficult confession—"Ignorabimus!" (from Latin, "we will never know").

Modern Worldviews

32 **never misses his spirit**

J. W. von Goethe, *Maxims and Reflections* 198.

Johann Gottlieb Fichte

Johann Gottlieb Fichte (1762–1814), German philosopher.

33 **Schelling**

Friedrich Wilhelm Joseph Schelling (1775–1854), German philosopher.

Marx really understood Hegel, in a productive sense

The reader should note that this is a very limited endorsement of Marx—a praise of his method that has embedded in it already a critique, as Marx had rejected this Hegelian approach to history in, among other places, his *Theses on Feuerbach* in 1845, despite continuing to employ Hegel's method in his work. For Steiner's views on social questions, see, inter alia, Rudolf Steiner, *Towards Social Renewal: Rethinking the Basis of Society* (CW 23).

Where the facts are, there are also the laws

Georg Wilhelm Friedrich Hegel (1770–1831) wrote about this topic in *Elements of the Philosophy of Right* (1820).

34 **Charles Darwin's *The Origin of Species* (1859)**

Charles Darwin (1809–1882), English natural historian and geologist; proponent of the theory of evolution by natural selection.

Ernst Haeckel

Ernst Haeckel (1834–1919), German biologist and philosopher. He popularized Darwin's theories in Germany. Rudolf Steiner knew him personally and wrote about him often. See, e.g., Rudolf Steiner, *Autobiography* (CW 28).

Carl Vogt, Jacob Moleschott, and Ludwig Büchner

Carl Vogt (1817–1895), German scientist and philosopher.

Jacob Moleschott (1822–1893), philosopher of scientific materialism.

Ludwig Büchner (1824–1899), German physiologist.

the public confession of his secrets of love

Ludwig Feuerbach (1804–1872), quoted from *The Essence of Christianity* (originally published in Leipzig, 1841). Feuerbach was a neo-Hegelian of the materialistic school, and his writings attacked historical religions and advocated atheism. He is the same Feuerbach that Marx attacked for not being materialistic enough, though in later Marxist circles he is seen as a bridge between Hegel and Marx and an important early figure in the development of historical materialism.

35 **Max Stirner**
Johann Kaspar Schmidt (1806–1856), pen name Max Stirner, German philosopher. His work addresses the topics of social alienation and self-consciousness.

Arthur Schopenhauer and Eduard von Hartmann
Arthur Schopenhauer (1788–1860), German philosopher.

Eduard von Hartmann (1842–1906), German philosopher; author of *The Philosophy of the Unconscious* (1869). Rudolf Steiner knew Hartmann personally and wrote about his ideas often. See, e.g., Rudolf Steiner, *The Philosophy of Freedom* (CW 4).

naturally from the materials of the whole building of nature
From Schiller's letter to Goethe, dated August 23, 1794.

36 ***Philosophy of Freedom* and *Views of the World and Life in the Nineteenth Century***
The Philosophy of Freedom (CW 4), published in 1893/94, is Rudolf Steiner's most important epistemological work. Its subtitle, "Results of observing the soul using the methods of natural science," points to its pivotal role as a bridge between natural science and spiritual science, or anthroposophy.

Originally published in 1900 under the title *Views of the World and Life in the Nineteenth Century*, this book was expanded to include an overview of the development of Western philosophy from Ancient Greece through the twentieth century. It was published in two volumes in 1914 under the title *The Riddles of Philosophy* (CW 18).

Adolf Harnack
Carl Gustav Adolf von Harnack (1851–1930), Lutheran liberal theologian and popular writer.

William Shakespeare
Berlin, May 6, 1902

37 **Georg Brandes**
Georg Brandes (1842–1927), Danish writer and cultural critic. He promoted the trend toward naturalism in theater and literature.

Lessing
Gotthold Ephraim Lessing (1729–1781), German writer, philosopher, and dramatist.

Schlegel and Tieck
August Wilhelm Schlegel (1767–1845), German poet, translator, and critic.

Ludwig Tieck (1773–1853), German poet and translator.

Lord Francis Bacon of Verulam
Francis Bacon, Baron Verulam and Viscount St. Albans (1561–1626), English philosopher, statesman, and scientist. See note to page 227.

38 Eugen Reichel
Eugen Reichel (1853–1916), author of an 1887 book entitled *Shakespeare's Literature*. Reichel published a number of essays in the *Magazin für Literature* while Steiner was the editor.

40 Marlowe
Christopher Marlowe (1564–1593), English playwright.

On Roman History
Berlin, July 19, 1904

42 We have seen
Steiner is referring to earlier lectures held at the same venue, for which no records or notes remain.

Caesar Augustus
Caesar Augustus (63 BC–AD 14), first Roman emperor; his reign lasted from 27 BC until his death in AD 14.

43 the ruler who is most mentioned
The reference here is to Charlemagne, who was crowned Holy Roman Emperor in the year 800 by Pope Leo III.

45 the *consul*, the *quaestor*, the *praetor* as substitutes
In the political system of the Roman Republic, the *consul* (of which there were always two) acted as chief executive for a term of one year. *Praetors* served for the same term and exercised judicial power, though they had some subordinate executive authority. *Quaestors* supervised the treasury and conducted audits. There were at various times as many as twelve *praetors* and twenty *quaestors* serving simultaneously.

Incidents could occur during the short reign of a tribune
There were ten tribunes in the Roman Republic, representing the interests of the plebians.

46 Marius
Gaius Marius (157–86 BC), Roman general and statesman.

Gracchus
Tiberius Sempronius Gracchus (163/162–133 BC) was a populist Roman politician best known for his agrarian reform law. At a time of increasing wealth disparities and a long period of middle-class land dispossession, this involved transferring land from the Roman state and wealthy landowners back to the middle class. This legislation passed during his term as tribune of the plebs in 133 BC, despite strong opposition by the Senate and the patrician class. Tiberius Gracchus was killed, along with many supporters, in a riot instigated by his enemies. A decade later his younger brother Gaius attempted similar legislation and suffered a similar fate.

Octavius
Also known as Caesar Augustus. See note to page 42.

48 Hadrian and Caracalla
Hadrian (AD 76–138), Roman emperor AD 117–138; full name Publius

Aelius Hadrianus. Caracalla (AD 188–217), Roman emperor AD 211–217; born Septimius Bassanius; later called Marcus Aurelius Severus Antoninus Augustus.

49 **Caligula—Mr. "little boots"**
Caligula (AD 12–41), Roman emperor AD 37–41; born Gaius Julius Caesar Germanicus. His nickname was Caligula, meaning "little boots," given to him by adoring soldiers when he was a child travelling with his father Germanicus (24 BC–AD 19) on military campaigns. Caligula's reign was notorious for its tyrannical excesses.

50 **Lucian**
Lucian of Samosata (*c.* 125–*c.* 180), a Syrian of Greek descent and a Roman citizen known for his extensive satirical writings.

Apollonius
Apollonius the Apologist (d. 185 AD), Roman philosopher who converted to Christianity and died as a martyr.

52 **Tertullian**
Tertullian (*c.* 160–*c.* 240), early Christian theologian; principal work *Apologeticus pro Christianis.*

53 **put it at the apostles' feet**
Acts 4:32–37 (NIV translation).

forced to recognize the Christians
Emperor Constantine I issued the Edict of Milan in 313, making Christianity officially tolerated in the Roman empire after two centuries of persecution and restoring previously confiscated property, including many churches. Constantine I was succeeded by his son Constantine II in the Western Roman Empire.

54 **the Nicaean Council turned out the way it did**
The Council of Nicaea in northwestern Anatolia (Turkey), convened by Constantine I in 325, resulted in the Nicene Creed and the adoption of the doctrine of the unity of the Son with the Father.

Arius and Athanasius
Arius (*c.* 250–336), Cyrenaic presbyter. He taught that Christ is not God himself, the Son is not the same as the Father.

Athanasius (*c.* 295–373), bishop of Alexandria. He taught that Christ is the same as God the Father.

in the Roman Empire
Athanasius (295–373) in *Orationes contra Arianos.*

at the beginning of the fourth century
See Jakob Burckhardt's *The Age of Constantine* (1853), in particular the chapter "Constantine and the Church."

56 **And new life blossoms from the ruins**
From Schiller's drama *Wilhelm Tell,* Act 4, Scene 2.

History of the Middle Ages up to the Great Inventions and Discoveries

Lecture One

Berlin, October 18, 1904

59 which stirs one to similar deeds
Goethe, *Maxims and Reflections* 779.

60 King Ashoka
Ashoka the Great (died *c.* 232 BC), an Indian emperor of the Maurya Dynasty, ruling most of the Indian subcontinent from *c.* 268 to 232 BC. Rocks carved with his edicts were rediscovered in the nineteenth century. Rock Edicts 6, 7, and 12 emphasize tolerance of all sects.

Tacitus, has preserved for us in his *Germania*
Publius (or Gaius) Cornelius Tacitus (56–*c.* 120 AD), Roman historian. His *Germania*, or *De origine et situ Germanorum*, is the oldest source on the peoples of Germanic tribes. Considered a minor work and largely forgotten until the Renaissance, it became increasingly popular as Central Europeans sought their origins.

61 The Teutons
One of the principal Germanic tribes.

63 in his work on the Czech people in the fifteenth century
Dějiny národu českého v Čechách a v Moravě [The history of the Czech nation in Bohemia and Moravia], first published in 1836.

the Hussite movement
A religious reform movement led by Jan Hus (1369–1415), who was burned at the stake. His followers were persecuted.

64 Marko
Marko Mrnjavčević, a character in southern Slavic oral tradition.

Wycliffe
John Wycliffe (*c.* 1330–1384), English reformer.

Emperor Henry II
Emperor Henry II (973–1024), Holy Roman Emperor from 1014 to 1024.

Milíč
Jan Milíč (died 1372), canon and archdeacon in Prague. He was a predecessor of John Hus. In 1374, he went to the pope in Avignon to clear himself of suspicion of heresy. He died there the same year and his writings were burned.

Herder
Johann Gottfried Herder (1744–1803), German theologian, poet, and philosopher. See his *Letters for the Advancement of Humanity* (1793).

65 the progress of humanity toward the consciousness of freedom
Hegel, in the introduction to *Lectures on the Philosophy of History*. Literally: "World history is the progress of humanity in the consciousness of freedom."

Lecture Two
Berlin, October 25, 1904

67 **As we learn from the *scholia* to the *Iliad***
Scholia (from Ancient Greek: σχόλιον, "comment, interpretation") are comments inserted in the margin of ancient manuscripts as glosses. The practice dates back to antiquity. When the margins got too crowded, some of these notes got copied into their own volumes. So, the *scholia* to the *Illiad* would be works of ancient commentary on the Illiad, eventually appearing as separate volumes, made either in late antiquity or during the Byzantine period. Likely, Steiner is referring to Ernst Maass, *Scholia Graeca in Homeri Iliadem Townleyana* (1887), a collection of *scholia* to Homer's *Iliad* published in Germany. Steiner was fluent in ancient Greek and Latin, having tutored both for years as a young adult.

Aryan
The concept of Aryans originated with linguistics, where it first entered European consciousness in the eighteenth century as the transliterated self-designated name for the ancient Indo-Iranian peoples. As linguists began to explore the ways in which Indo-European languages were related, racists such as Arthur de Gobineau, whose work later influenced Nazi ideology, co-opted the term to describe a purported "race" that included the Brahmin class of India, the Iranians (and people of the Caucuses, where the race was supposed to have originated), and Europeans. Steiner is referring here to the then common view that the peoples of Europe migrated there from Iran.

70 **Athanasian but Arian Christians**
See note to page 54.

71 ***Hufe***
A *Hufe* is an amount of land measured according to the needs of an average farming family (old field measure of 7 to 15 hectares). The general size was determined by the amount of land a typical man could manage with a single plow.

72 **And new life blossoms from the ruins**
From Schiller's drama *Wilhelm Tell*, Act 4, Scene 2. See note to page 56.

Lecture Three
November 1, 1904

77 **Scotus Eriugena in his work *On the Division of Nature***
John Scotus Eriugena (*c.* 800–*c.* 877), Irish philosopher and theologian. One of the few Northern Europeans of his era to be fluent in ancient Greek, his book *De divisione naturae* (*On the Division of Nature*) synthesized fifteen centuries of philosophy and religious thought in the form of dialogues that reintroduced neo-Platonic ideas.

the Walthari song
Waltharius is a Latin epic poem written in the early to mid tenth century and founded on German popular tradition relating the exploits of the Visigothic hero Walter of Aquitaine.

Lecture Four
Berlin, November 8, 1904

81 Copernicus
Nicolaus Copernicus (1473–1543), Polish astronomer.

83 Columbanus, Gall, and Boniface
Columbanus (*c.* 543–615), one of the greatest Irish missionaries to the Frankish and Lombard kingdoms (not to be confused with Columba, the Irish missionary to Scotland).

Gall (*c.* 550–*c.* 645), Irish missionary. Gall was a disciple of Columbanus and travelled with him to continental Europe. He founded a hermitage on the site of the modern Swiss town named after him, Sankt Gallen.

Boniface (*c.* 675–754), English missionary, often referred to as the apostle of Germany because of his profound influence in the Christianization of that region.

84 *Heliand*
The *Heliand* is an epic poem about the life of Jesus, written in Old Saxon alliterative verse, dating from the early ninth century.

A Frankish law book
The *Lex Salica,* written around 500 AD.

86 Humboldt
Wilhelm von Humboldt (1767–1835), German politician, philosopher, and writer.

87 Walther von der Vogelweide
Walther von der Vogelweide (*c.*1170–1230), German poet. He composed his works in Middle High German.

88 the three will never prosper more!
From "The Election Contest," in *Selected Poems of Walther von der Vogelweide: The Minnesinger*, trans. Walter Alison Philips (London: Smith, Elder, and Co., 1896), pp. 95–96.

Lecture Five
Berlin, November 15, 1904

91 Widukind, whose bravery offered the fiercest resistance
Widukind, defeated by Charlemagne in 785. Died 807.

92 counts palatine
Counts palatine: any of various noblemen originally exercising certain royal powers within their own domains, especially a count of the Holy Roman Empire having sovereign powers in his own territories.

Kaiserpfalzen
Kaiserpfalz: a fortified castle that served as temporary, secondary seat of power for a Holy Roman Emperor, of which Charlamagne was the first. The kings of that era had to move their person and court around their territories regularly to maintain control. This practice was widespread in

medieval Europe and is called "itinerant kingship" by modern scholars.

92 ***Wehrgeld* (blood money)**
Wehregeld: blood money—the monetary value assigned to a person, set according to their rank, used to determine the compensation paid by the perpetrator of a crime to the victim or victim's family. This was common practice throughout all medieval Europe.

93 **Wolfram von Eschenbach**
Wolfram von Eschenbach (*c.* 1160/80–*c.* 1220), German poet. His poem *Parsifal* is widely considered one of the greatest epic poems of the Middle Ages.

Hartmann von Aue
Hartmann von Aue (*c.* 1160–*c.* 1210), German poet.

95 **Copernicus was a canon, and Giordano Bruno was a Dominican monk**
Nicolaus Copernicus (1473–1543), Polish astronomer. A canon is a member of certain groups within the Catholic Church subject to an ecclesiastical rule. While not a priest, a canon conducted his life according to the customary discipline and rules of the Church. Being under ecclesiastical rule in the Middle Ages also meant being exempt from secular law and punishment by any body other than the Church.

Giordano Bruno (1548–1600), Italian philosopher.

Charles the Bald
Charles the Bald, or Charles II (823–877), emperor of the Carolingian Empire (875–877), a grandson of Charlemagne.

On the Division of Nature
See note to page 77.

96 **history is nothing other than the education of humanity to freedom**
See note to page 65.

Lecture Six
Berlin, December 6, 1904

99 **enfeoffed**
To enfeoff: under the feudal system, to give someone freehold property or land in exchange for their pledged service.

Gaugericht
Gaugericht: the independent agricultural villages of pre-Carolingian Saxony. Not to be confused with the political districts of the twentieth-century Third Reich, which re-used the name.

100 **seven sciences—three lower and four higher**
That is, the Seven Liberal Arts: grammar, dialectic, rhetoric, arithmetic, geometry, astronomy, and music.

101 **all the monks, doctors, magisters, clerks, and priests**
Goethe, *Faust I*, "Night Scene," lines 366–67.

102 Charles III

Charles III (839–888), called Charles the Fat, Holy Roman Emperor from 881, deposed 887.

Arnulf of Carinthia

Arnulf of Carinthia (*c.* 850–899).

Lecture Seven
Berlin, Devember 13, 1904

104 tribal dukes

The German word here is *Stammherzog*, from *Stammherzogtum*, historically translated as "stem duchy," though "tribal duchy" is a more accurate translation. It is a term dating to the mid-nineteenth century that refers to the constituent duchies of the German Empire circa 1000 AD.

108 St. Adalbert of Prussia

Steiner is referring here to Adalbert of Prague (c. 956–997), Apostle of Prussia, Bishop of Prague since 982, who died a martyr's death in 997 and was a friend of Emperor Otto III

110 In which the times are reflected

Goethe, *Faust I*, Night Scene, lines 577–79.

Lecture Eight
Berlin, December 20, 1904

113 *Heliand*

See note to page 84.

115 Conrad of Marburg

Conrad of Marburg (1180–1233), confessor of St. Elizabeth of Thuringia, papal inquisitor; he was slain by knights in 1233.

Albertus Magnus

Albertus Magnus (1193–1280), Dominican theologian, philosopher, and scientist, known as Doctor Universalis; he was a teacher of Thomas Aquinas.

Emperor Frederick Barbarossa

Emperor Frederick I (1125–1190), known as Frederick Barbarossa ("Redbeard"), Holy Roman Emperor from 1152 to 1190.

116 the Minne service

Minne service (*Minnedienst*): homage rendered by a knight to his lady within the ideology of courtly love in the context of medieval chivalry.

117 Eckhart, Tauler, Suso

Meister Eckhart (*c.* 1260–*c.* 1328).
Johannes Tauler (*c.* 1300–1361).

Heinrich Suso (1295–1366).

Theologia Deutsch

The *Theologia Deutsch* is an anonymous tract written in colloquial German dating from the fourteenth century. The author is believed to be a priest of the Teutonic Order (*Deutschordenskirche*) who presumably resided in Frankfurt am Main. The name goes back to Martin Luther, who first published the writing in print under the title *Eyn deutsch Theologia*: first in 1516 as excerpts, then in 1518, the complete text.

118 History is the history of humanity's development toward freedom
See note to page 65.

Lecture Nine
Berlin, December 28, 1904

120 Vineta
A mythical city on the southern coast of the Baltic Sea.

121 the Hanseatic League
An organization founded by northern German towns and German merchant communities abroad to protect their mutual trading interests.

Titian
Titian, (*c.* 1476–1576), Italian painter.

Kaspar Zöllner
Kaspar Zöllner, invented rifled barrels for rifles in 1498 (according to Reinhold Günther, *Deutsche Kulturgeschichte* [Leipzig, 1902]).

the Brethren of the Common Life
Late fourteenth-century Roman Catholic religious community founded in the Netherlands by Geert Groote.

124 Walter von Habenichts
Also known as Walter Sans Avoir, Peter of Amiens' lieutenant.

the first real Crusade
First Crusade, 1096–1099 under Gottfried von Bouillon, died 1100.

Duke Rudolf of Swabia
Rudolf of Swabia, counter-king to Henry IV, was crowned in 1077.

Bernard of Clairvaux
Bernard of Clairvaux (1090–1153), abbot, crusading preacher.

the Peace of Constance
In 1183.

125 the Kyffhäuser saga
The Kyffhäuser saga: Frederick Barbarossa drowned in Turkey while on crusade, but a later legend claimed that he hadn't really died but was sleeping under the Kyffhäuser mountain (where his castle was located) and would wake on the Day of Judgement, or, in some versions, the day of need—when the ravens stopped flying around the mountain—and save Germany. The Kyffhäuser legend was elaborated by the brothers Grimm in the early nineteenth century, and was very popular in the late nineteenth century, when an enormous monument was constructed at Kyffhäuser to memorialize it.

Emperor Frederick II of the Hohenstaufen dynasty
Emperor Frederick II (1215–1250). Steiner is referring to the Battle of

Liegnitz in 1241. The Mongols were victorious but retreated for reasons that are difficult to understand.

126 **Albert von Bremen**
Commonly known as Albert of Riga (*c.* 1165–1229), bishop and founder of Riga; missionary of the Baltic countries.

127 **Richard of Cornwall**
Richard of Cornwall (1209–1272).

Alfonso of Castile
Alfonso X (1226–1284), known as the Wise.

Count Rudolf of Habsburg
Rudolf of Habsburg (1218–1291), emperor from 1273.

Duke Heinrich Jasomirgott
Henry II (1107–1177), called Jasomirgott, Margrave and Duke of Austria.

Lecture Ten

Berlin, December 29, 1904

129 **Ottokar of Bohemia**
Ottokar II of Bohemia (c. 1233–1278), king of Bohemia from 1253–1278. Rudolf of Habsburg was elected to the imperial throne over Ottokar II.

the Swiss Confederates
The Federal Charter of 1291 established an important alliance between the cantons of Uri, Schwyz, and Unterwalden that was foundational in the formation of the Swiss Confederacy.

Emperor Albrecht I
Albrecht I of Austria, emperor from 1298 until 1308.

Adolf of Nassau
Adolf of Nassau, emperor from 1292 until 1298.

Henry of Luxembourg
Henry VII of Luxembourg, emperor from 1308 until 1313.

130 ***Pfaffengasse*** **[priest alley]**
Historically, the geographical area along the left bank of the Rhine, with its Catholic bishoprics and high monasteries—i.e., the secular domains of the bishops—was called *Pfaffengasse*. The term is composed of two words: *Pfaffen* and *Gasse*. *Pfaffe* is a derogatory name for priests or clergymen, and *Gasse* refers to a narrow path.

Emperor Charles IV
Charles IV (Charles of Luxembourg), reigned 1346–1378, emperor beginning in 1355.

131 **Emperor Sigismund**
Sigismund of Luxemburg, emperor from 1433 until his death in 1437.

Jan Hus of Husinec
Jan Hus (*c.* 1370–1415), central figure of the Bohemian Reformation, inspirer of the Hussites.

131 Wycliffe
John Wycliffe (*c.* 1328–1384), English philosopher, theologian, and dissident Catholic priest.

the Council of Constance was convened
The Council of Constance was held from 1414 to 1418 in the territory of present Germany. Such Councils were called by the Catholic Church whenever important matters of doctrine needed to be decided. In the case of the Council of Constance, it was initially called by the Pope, but the presence of the Emperor and the combined might of several thousand theologians led the Council to declare itself supreme over the Pope, allowing it to end the era of multiple popes by electing Pope Martin V and deposing his rivals. Among other business, the Council condemned Jan Hus as a heretic, facilitating his execution by secular authorities and ruled on a wide range of other issues.

Savonarola
Girolamo Savonarola (1452–1498), Italian Dominican friar. Active in renaissance Florence, he led a popular uprising, established a republic in the city, preached a drastic puritanism, and was ultimately burned at the stake.

132 Gerson
Jean Charlier de Gerson (1363–1429), French scholar and reformer.

Tauler
Johannes Tauler (*c.* 1300–1361), German mystic, Catholic priest and theologian, disciple of Meister Eckhart.

useless emperor
Emperor Frederick III (1415–1493), emperor from 1452 until his death in 1493.

Medici
Cosimo Medici (1389–1464), banker and patron of the arts. His example led his sons, and all the leading families of the next generation—both in Florence and throughout Europe—to support the artists and scholars who became known as the Renaissance generation.

133 Armer Konrad
Armer Konrad (also Armer Kunz) was the name given to an alliance of common people that rebelled in the Duchy of Württemberg in 1514. These were not primarily peasants bound in the feudal system, but rather citizens of the Württemberg country towns supported by some clergymen. Severe inflation, along with the reigning Duke Ulrich's imposition of Roman law in abrogation of traditional feudal privileges, were the immediate causes.

Bundschuh movement
The Bundschuh movement is the name given to a series of peasant rebellions between the years 1493 to 1517 in southwestern Germany. They are considered one of the roots of the German Peasants' War of 1524 to 1526.

134 Reuchlin
Johann Reuchlin (1455–1522), humanist scholar known for advancing a study of ancient Greek and Hebrew in German-speaking lands.

134 Desiderius Erasmus of Rotterdam

Desiderius Erasmus Roterodamus (1466–1536), Dutch philosopher and scholar, leader of the Northern Renaissance. Writing in Latin, among other things he pioneered textual analysis.

Bartolomeu Dias

Bartolomeu Dias (*c.* 1450–1500), Portuguese mariner and explorer.

Vasco da Gama

Vasco da Gama (*c.* 1460–1524), Portuguese navigator, first European to reach India by sea.

Columbus

Christopher Columbus (1451–1506), Italian explorer.

Copernicus

Nicolaus Copernicus (1473–1543), Polish astronomer; he propounded a heliocentric view of the solar system.

Platonic Mysticism and *Docta Ignorantia*
Lecture One
Berlin, October 29, 1904

139 the Gnostics

The Gnostics represent one of the most important schools of esoteric wisdom in the early Christian centuries. See, e.g., Rudolf Steiner, *Christ and the Spiritual World* (CW 149).

mathesis

From Ancient Greek μάθησις, from the same base as μανθάνω ("I learn").

Scotus Eriugena

See note to page 77.

141 Aristotle

Aristotle (384–322 BC), Greek philosopher and scientist. See *Metaphysics*, chapter 11.

142 Augustine

Augustine of Hippo (354–430), doctor of the Church. See Rudolf Steiner, "Augustine and the Church," chap. 13 in *Christianity as Mystical Fact* (CW 8).

Meister Eckhart

Meister Eckhart (*c.* 1260–*c.* 1328), German mystic. See Rudolf Steiner, *Mystics at the Dawn of the Modern Age* (CW 7).

Tauler

Johannes Tauler (*c.* 1300–1361), German mystic, Catholic priest and theologian, disciple of Meister Eckhart. See Rudolf Steiner, *Mystics at the Dawn of the Modern Age* (CW 7).

143 an eye with which He can look at Himself

For example, Meister Eckhart writes: "The eye with which I see God is the same with which God sees me. My eye and God's eye is one eye, and one sight, and one knowledge, and one love" (*Meister Eckhart's Sermons*, trans. Claud Field [New York: Cosimo Classics, 2007]).

Lecture Two
Berlin, November 5, 1904

144 Plato
Plato (*c.* 429–347 BC), Greek philosopher, disciple of Socrates and teacher of Aristotle. He founded the Academy in Athens. See Rudolf Steiner, "Plato as Mystic," chapter 3 in *Christianity as Mystical Fact* (CW 8).

145 *Henosis*
Henosis (ἕνωσις) is classical Greek for "oneness," "union," or "unity" and is a recurring theme in Neo-Platonism.

146 (Angelus Silesius)
Angelus Silesius (1624–1677), German mystic and poet. Author of *The Cherubinic Wanderer.* See Rudolf Steiner, *Mystics at the Dawn of the Modern Age* (CW 7).

147 *Meisterbuch*
The *Meisterbuch* is a collection of sermons and other material attributed to Johannes Tauler. This attribution has been contested in recent decades since the style of writing does not match Tauler's other sermons, and the text of the book does not show up any earlier than about 150 years after Tauler's death. The *Meisterbuch* was particularly popular in protestant circles after Luther endorsed it. There is an active scholarly debate between protestant theologians, who want to claim Tauler and other mystics of his era as proto-reformers, and Catholic theologians whose efforts are to portray them as loyal members of the Church.

He made the greatest impression
Klemens Löffler summarized this episode as related in the *Meisterbuch* in the Catholic Encyclopedia: "When after this he preached again for the first time, the effect was so great that forty of his hearers went into convulsions and twelve could hardly be revived."

you are only a dull guest on the dark earth
Goethe in his poem "Holy Longing."

148 John of Ruusbroec
John of Ruusbroec (1293–1381), Flemish mystic and prior of the Augustinian monastery in Groenendaal. His main work is *The Spiritual Espousals.*

Lecture Three
Berlin, November 12, 1904

149 Cusanus
Nicholas of Cusa (1401–1464), philosopher and cardinal. See Rudolf Steiner, *Mystics at the Dawn of the Modern Age* (CW 7).

Nicolaus Copernicus
See note to page 134.

scholasticism
The medieval philosophical teachings represented most clearly by Thomas Aquinas (1225–1274).

149 the Council of Basel
1431–1443.

150 the Brethren of the Common Life
See note to page 121.

Eckhart, in Tauler, in Suso, and . . . in Giordano Bruno and Paracelsus
Meister Eckhart (*c.* 1260–*c.* 1328), see previous lecture.

Johannes Tauler (*c.* 1300–1361), see previous lecture.

Heinrich Suso (1295–1366), German Dominican friar.

Giordano Bruno (1548–1600, Italian philosopher.

Paracelsus (*c.* 1493–1541), Swiss physician.

De docta ignorantia
Composed 1440.

Johannes Müller
Johannes Peter Müller (1801–1858), professor of anatomy, physiologist, comparative anatomist, ichthyologist, and herpetologist. Steiner is summarizing his book *Zur vergleichenden Physiologie des Gesichtssinns* [On the comparative physiology of sight] (Leipzig, 1826).

Helmholtz
Ludwig Ferdinand von Helmholtz (1821–1894). A student of Müller, Helmholtz trained as a physician and also studied physics. Steiner is referencing a concept from his book *Handbuch der Physiologischen Optik* [Handbook of physiological optics] in three volumes, completed 1867.

151 *pleroma*
Pleroma (Koinē Greek: πλήρωμα, literally "fullness"). The term occurs seventeen times in the New Testament and is common in Gnostic literature. It is taken to refer to the totality of divine powers.

ānanda
Satchitananda, Sanskrit: Compound of *sat* | *chit* | *ānanda* "existence, consciousness, and bliss." *Sat* in Sanskrit means "being, existence," "real, actual," "true, good, right," *chit* means "consciousness," and *ānanda* means "happiness, joy, bliss," "pure happiness."

153 *Theologia Deutsch*
See second note to page 117.

Schiller and Our Age

Lecture One
Schiller's Life and Character
Berlin, January 21, 1905

155 Schröer
Karl Julius Schröer (1825–1900), Austrian professor of literary history at the Vienna Technical University. He was an important figure in Steiner's biography. See Rudolf Steiner, *Autobiography* (CW 28).

155 Herman Grimm

Herman Grimm (1828–1901), German professor of art history and the son of Wilhelm Grimm (one of the two Brothers Grimm of fairytale fame). Steiner also knew Grimm personally and writes about him, among other places, in his *Autobiography* (CW 28).

156 Ibsen

Henrik Ibsen (1828–1906), Norwegian playwright and theatre director. Considered one of the founders of modernism in theater, he pioneered a style of realism.

Zola

Émile Édouard Charles Antoine Zola (1840–1902), French novelist, journalist, and playwright, known as a pioneer of naturalism, especially in theatre.

Tolstoy

Lev Nikolayevich Tolstoy (1828–1910), famous Russian novelist, known for the use of realism in his characters and settings.

157 English sensualism

In philosophy, sensualism is a doctrine whereby sensations and perception are the basic and most important basis for cognition. Major figures associated with this trend were John Locke and David Hume.

La Mettrie

Julien Offray de La Mettrie (1709–1751), French medical doctor and philosopher, and one of the earliest of the French materialists of the Enlightenment. He is best known for his work *Man a Machine.*

Holbach's *Systeme de la nature* [The system of nature]

Paul-Henri Thiry, Baron d'Holbach (1723–1789). An avowed atheist, he wrote energetically against religion. His best-known work was *Systeme de la nature* [The system of nature] (1770).

a few pat concepts

Goethe, in *Poetry and Truth*, Book 11.

Rousseau

Jean-Jacques Rousseau (1712–1778), French Enlightenment philosopher.

Kant

Immanuel Kant (1724–1804), German Enlightenment philosopher.

158 *Karlsschule*

Schiller attended a military academy run by the Duke of Württemberg, his father's employer, for eight years, from age 13 to 21. Upon graduation he was appointed a medical officer to one of the Duke's regiments.

Klopstock's *Messiah*

Friedrich Gottlieb Klopstock (1724–1803), German poet. His major work was the epic poem *The Messiah.*

160 Marquis Posa

Marquis Posa, one of the main characters in Schiller's drama *Don Carlos.*

160 In his letters *On the Aesthetic Education of Man*
In Letters 12–15.

161 "Theater Considered as a Moral Institution"
An address at a public session of the Elector's German Society in Mannheim in the year 1784.

Lecture Two
Schiller's Work and Its Transformations
Berlin, January 28, 1905

164 Herder's *Ideas for the History of the Philosophy of Mankind*
Johann Gottfried Herder (1744–1803), German theologian, poet, and philosopher. *Ideas for the History of the Philosophy of Mankind* was published in 1784.

Kathederphilosophie
Kathederphilosophie: a term from Schopenhauer, who used it to criticize professional philosophers employed by the Church or by universities (as Kant had been). The literal translation would be "cathedral philosophy." Steiner had edited a complete edition of Schopenhauer's works a few years earlier.

One works and lives in the other . . .
Faust I, Night Scene, line 447.

Hymn to Nature
Nature (1782), a fragmentary poem by Georg Christoph Tobler, often attributed to Goethe. Tobler wrote the work following multiple conversations with Goethe, so the attribution is not entirely incorrect. Steiner was aware of the authorship question and maintained that the *Hymn*, though written down by Tobler, reveals what lived in Goethe's spirit at the time.

165 Never misses His power, never misses His spirit
Goethe, *Proömion* in *Weltanschauliche Gedichte*, 1815.

Wolff's philosophy
Christian von Wolff (1679–1754), philosopher, mathematician, and professor at Halle. Wolff's main achievement was a comprehensive presentation encompassing almost every scholarly subject of his time, written and explicated by means of a demonstrative-deductive, mathematical method. He is considered the peak of Enlightenment rationality in Germany.

English sensualists
In philosophy, sensualism is a doctrine whereby sensations and perception are the basic and most important basis for cognition.

166 the laws of your actions may become general laws of mankind
Kant, *Groundwork of the Metaphysic of Morals*, 4:421.

and thus I am frequently pained by my lack of virtue.
From the poem "The Philosopher, Scruples of Conscience." Schiller is cheekily mocking Kant here.

167 you seek the explanatory ground for the individual phenomenon
In *Correspondence between Schiller and Goethe*.

Lecture Three
Schiller and Goethe
Berlin, February 4, 1905

168 *Egmont*

Egmont: Goethe's 1788 tragic drama, which depicts the downfall of a man who overly trusts the goodness of those around him, written in a very Shakespearean mode.

Iphigenia

Goethe's play *Iphigenia in Tauris* is a reworking of the ancient Greek playwright Euripides' tragedy of the same name. Goethe composed three versions, the first in 1779 and the last in 1786.

169 Schiller's essay *On Grace and Dignity*

First published 1783.

Christian Gottfried Körner

Christian Gottfried Körner (1756–1831), Prussian lawyer and government official. He and his wife hosted regular gatherings of significant literary figures of the day and their admirers, and he corresponded with all the leading representatives of German culture.

170 you seek the explanatory ground for the individual phenomenon

See note to page 167.

On Naïve and Sentimental Poetry

On Naïve and Sentimental Poetry, an essay composed between 1795 and 1796. In it, Schiller divides all poetry into either Naïve or Sentimental forms. Naïve poetry is directly descriptive, whereas Sentimental poetry is self-reflective.

171 the opportunity for external actions

France, at that point, had transformed philosophy into the French Revolution (1789–1795).

Goethe's *Wilhelm Meister*

Wilhelm Meister's Apprenticeship, Goethe's 1795 novel about a young man who seeks to escape the dull confines of bourgeoise existence, falls in love with theatre, and plays Hamlet in a professional production of Shakespeare.

Bildungsroman

Bildungsroman: a genre of German novels that focuses on the development of the lead character from youth to maturity.

press on into the land of knowledge

Schiller, in the poem "The Artists." In the Schiller editions, it reads: "Only through the morning door of beauty...." Regarding this, Rudolf Steiner says in a Stuttgart lecture from December 4, 1922, published in *Spirit as Sculptor of the Human Organism* (CW 218): "Schiller is right in saying: 'Only through the dawn (*Morgenrot*) of beauty do you press on into the land of knowledge,' which you generally find quoted in books as, 'Only through the morning door (*Morgentor*) of beauty do you press on into the land of knowledge.' If an artist makes a slip of the pen, it gets handed down to posterity. The right reading, of course, is: 'Only through the dawn (*Morgenrot*) of beauty do you press on into the land of knowledge.' In other words, all knowledge comes through art. Fundamentally, there is no knowledge that is not intimately related to art."

171 the *causal body*

The Sanskrit term *Karana-Sarira*, which H. P. Blavatsky borrowed for theosophy. There is some ambiguity among theosophical authors about what exactly is supposed to be described by the term. The German word Steiner uses is *Ursachenleib* (*causal body* being the literal translation). Steiner only uses this term in one other place in his Collected Works—namely, in his translation of Blavatsky's *The Key to Theosophy*, in the volume *Übersetzungen und freie Übertragungen verschiedener Werke* [Translations and free renderings of various works] (CW 41b), p. 180. There, we read: "This 'I' is the causal body (*Ursachenleib*) that overshadows every personality into whom the karmic forces penetrate."

Wallenstein

A trilogy of dramas completed in 1799.

172 Manso

Johann Kaspar Friedrich Manso (1760–1826), in his *Gegengeschenk an die Sudelköche von Weimar und Jena. Poetische Epistel* [Counter-gift to the sloppy cooks of Weimar and Jena. Poetic epistle] (Leipzig, 1797).

the *Xenien* in 1796

Die Xenien is a work written in rhyming couplets. It was modeled on the structure of some Latin poems by the Roman poet Martial (first century AD) but written in German. A *xenia* in Latin is a gift. Goethe and Schiller's "gifts" criticized some two hundred other literary figures, works, and periodicals over six hundred and seventy-six rhyming couplets.

Lecture Four
Schiller's Worldview and His *Wallenstein*
Berlin, February 11, 1905

174 for the full truth is there for God alone

Lessing, in his 1777 work *Duplik*, section I, writes: "If God had closed all truth in his right hand and in his left hand only the constantly active urge for truth, although with the addition of being always and eternally wrong, and said to me 'Choose!' I would fall with humility into his left hand and say: 'Father, give! The pure truth is for you alone!'"

the independence of the Netherlands

The Dutch War of Independence lasted from 1568 to 1648.

the Thirty Years' War

The Thirty Years' War lasted from 1618 to 1648 and was one of the longest and most devastating conflicts in European history.

174 Wallenstein

Albrecht Wenzel Eusebius von Wallenstein (1583–1634) of Bohemia fought with great success as a mercenary and then as commander of the forces of the Holy Roman Emperor during the Thirty Years' War. His tactical genius lay in his ability to manage the complex logistics required by cannon-based land warfare. Wallenstein was assassinated by the emperor he served when his many success seemed to make him an independent power and after indications he was starting to act like one.

Julius and Rafael in Schiller's *Philosophical Letters*

Julius and Rafael are fictional characters employed by Schiller in the *Philosophical Letters* published in 1786.

his friend Körner

Apparently, the first "Rafael" letter is based on an actual letter from Körner, while the balance of the "letters" was written by Schiller. The final "Rafael" letter reprints another Körner letter. These details of authorship were established in the twentieth century.

175 "Theosophy of Julius"

A chapter in the *Philosophical Letters*.

the Aesthetic Letters

Schiller, O*n the Aesthetic Education of Man.*

176 "The Walk"

"Der Spaziergang," 1795.

177 "that it had to end this way"

Christian Friedrich Hebbel (1813–1863), German poet and dramatist. He makes this statement in his preface to *Maria Magdelana*: ". . . for the tragic must appear as something conditioned by necessity from the outset, as something, like death, that is set with life itself and cannot be bypassed at all."

178 "The dignity of mankind is given into your hands. Preserve it!"

See fourth note to page 171.

Lecture Five
Schiller, Greek Drama, and Nietzsche
Berlin, February 18, 1905

179 then he could reproach you

Letter from Schiller to Goethe dated March 1, 1793.

180 they discussed architecture

Letter from Schiller to Wilhelm von Humboldt dated November 9, 1795.

Wilhelm von Humboldt

Wilhelm von Humboldt (1767–1835), German philosopher, linguist, and diplomat.

saying that only that which is unchangeable is tragic

See note to page 177.

180 the Erinyes
Also known as the Furies.

181 Carlyle
Thomas Carlyle (1795–1881), Scottish historian, essayist, philosopher, and mathematician. He translated Goethe's *Wilhelm Meister's Apprenticeship* into English in the 1820s. In 1825, he published *The Life of Frederick Schiller* that included an extended appreciation of the structure of *Wallenstein.* Steiner owned several of Carlyle's book, both in German translation and in the original English.

182 That Max can leave me
Schiller, *The Death of Wallenstein*, Act III, Scene 18 (trans. Samuel Taylor Coleridge).

183 *daemon*
From Greek, an attendant spirit or inspiring being presiding over the destiny of each individual.

Édouard Schuré
Édouard Schuré (1841–1929), French writer and playwright. *Sanctuaires d'Orient* was written in 1898. It was translated into German in 1923 by Marie Steiner. Rudolf Steiner staged some of Schuré's plays starting in 1907.

The Birth of Tragedy from the Spirit of Music
Friedrich Nietzsche (1844–1900), German philosopher. *The Birth of Tragedy* was published in 1872. See Rudolf Steiner, *Friedrich Nietzsche, Fighter for Freedom* (CW 5).

Lecture Six
Schiller's Late Dramas
Berlin, February 25, 1905

185 that is in a certain way irrational
See note to page 177.

daemonic
See note to page 183.

187 the *daemon* of Socrates
See note to page 183.

Then call on Tell; you shall not find him fail
William Tell, Act 1, Scene 3 (trans. Theodore Martin).

188 Hebbel's *Judith*
Friedrich Hebbel's play *Judith* was written in 1840. See note to page 177.

Vischer, Hartmann, Fechner
Friedrich Theodor Vischer (1807–1887), Eduard von Hartmann (1842–1906), Gustav Theodor Fechner (1801–1887).

Schiller's Aesthetic Letters
Schiller, *On the Aesthetic Education of Man.*

189 does not want to rule over slaves
Demetrius, Act 1: Demetrius in conversation with the king. Literally: "I do not want to rule over the souls of slaves."

the bliss of poetic creation
In the chapter *Vorerinnerung* in *Briefwechsel zwischen Schiller und Wilhelm von Humboldt* [Letters between Schiller and Wilhelm von Humboldt] (Stuttgart, 1900).

190 "Epilogue to Schiller's Bell"
Schiller wrote a poem called "Song of the Bell," among one of his most famous, wherein he lays out in parallel the construction of a large bell with the unfolding of a human life. Goethe wrote an epilogue that was read aloud at the end of a recitation of the poem after a memorial performance of *Mary Stuart* shortly after Schiller's passing.

Karl Gutzkow
Karl Gutzkow (1811–1878), German writer.

Lecture Seven
Schiller's Effect on the Nineteenth Century
Berlin, March 4, 1905

191 Herder
Johann Gottfried Herder (1744–1803), German theologian, poet, and philosopher.

"Song of the Bell"
See note to page 190.

Caroline von Schlegel, the wife of August Wilhelm von Schlegel
Caroline Schelling (1763–1809), noted German intellectual, central figure of German Romanticism. She was the wife of the poet August Wilhelm von Schlegel (1767–1845) and later married the philosopher Friedrich Schelling (1775–1854).

192 *Xenien*
See note to page 172.

Friedrich von Schlegel
Friedrich Schlegel (1772–1829), poet, critic, and philosopher; brother of August Wilhelm von Schlegel.

August Wilhelm Schlegel
August Wilhelm von Schlegel, *Sämtliche Werke* [Complete works], vol. 1 (Leipzig, 1846), p. 303.

Man is only fully man there where he plays
Schiller, *On the Aesthetic Education of Man*, letter 15.

193 says Schiller
In letter 10 of *On the Aesthetic Education of Man*, Schiller writes: "Consequently the true search of the master consists in destroying matter by the form; and the triumph of art is great in proportion as it overcomes matter and maintains its sway over those who enjoy its work."

193 Ludwig Tieck

Johann Ludwig Tieck (1773–1853), German Romantic poet, translator, writer, and critic.

Theodor Körner

Theodor Körner (1791–1813), son of Christian Gottfried Körner, who had encouraged Schiller in his early days. Theodor died a hero's death in the Napoleonic wars. His 1814 posthumous collection of poems, *Sword and Lyre*, were overtly patriotic and enormously popular.

194 Jakob Grimm . . . Ernst Curtius, Moriz Carriere, and many others

Jakob Grimm (1785–1863), of the Brothers Grimm; linguist, historian, and philologist.

Ernst Curtius (1814–1896), archeologist and historian.

Moriz Philipp Carrière (1817–1895), philosopher and writer.

Charles Darwin's *On the Origin of Species* and Fechner's *Vorschule der Ästhetik* [Elements of aesthetics]

Charles Darwin (1809–1882), English natural historian and geologist; a proponent of the theory of evolution by natural selection as expressed in his *On the Origin of Species.*

Gustav Theodor Fechner (180–1887), one of the founders of modern experimental psychology. Steiner, or the note-taker, appears to have mixed up Fechner's 1860 book *Elemente der Psychophysik* [Elements of psycho-physics] with his 1878 book *Vorschule der Ästhetik* [Elements of aesthetics]. Neither book has ever been translated to English, though both are monumental in the history of science.

But, friends, the sublime does not dwell in space

Schiller, *Sämtliche Werke* [Complete works], vol. 1 (Munich, 1962), pp. 253, 257.

Kirchhoff and Bunsen

Gustav Robert Kirchhoff (1824–1887) and Robert Wilhelm Eberhard Bunsen (1811–1899), both enormously accomplished practical experimental scientists; their collaborative development of spectroscopy is but one of each of their several significant contributions to the advancement of the fields of physics and chemistry.

Karl Marx's *Critique of Political Economy*

Karl Marx (1818–1883), German revolutionary socialist thinker. Together with Friedrich Engels, he wrote *The Communist Manifesto* (1848), which he then expanded into the highly influential three-volume work *Das Kapital.*

Winckelmann

Johann Joachim Winckelmann (1717–1768), German art historian and archaeologist. He was the first modern art historian to draw attention to the differences between Greek, Greco-Roman, and Roman art.

Lecture Eight
What Can the Present Time Learn from Schiller?
Berlin, March 5, 1905

196 **press on into the land of knowledge**

See note to page 171.

Ludwig Büchner

Friedrich Karl Christian Ludwig Büchner (1824–1899), physician and philosopher; one of the best-known proponents of scientific materialism in the nineteenth century.

197 **Otto Brahm**

Otto Brahm (1856–1912), drama and literary critic, theater manager and director; known for pioneering the style of naturalism in German theater.

the Scherer school

Scherer school, named after Wilhelm Scherer (1841–1886), a German philologist and historian of literature. In his pioneering study of the development of the German language, he labeled the phases (such as Middle High German) that are still accepted as definitive today. He also labeled waxing and waning phases in German literary history.

Peter Cornelius

Peter von Cornelius (1784–1867), German painter who attempted to revive the Renaissance style; known for grand and elegant designs and a somewhat inept technical execution.

Jakob Minor

Jakob Minor (1855–1912), German literary historian.

Vischer

Friedrich Theodor Vischer (1807–1887), German novelist, poet, and writer on aesthetics. Steiner is referring to his *Ästhetik oder Wissenschaft des Schönen* [Aesthetics, or the science of the beautiful] (Reutlingen and Leipzig, 1846). See also, Rudolf Steiner, *Art and Theory of Art* (CW 271).

198 **Emil Du Bois-Reymond**

Emil Du Bois-Reymond (1818–1896), physician and physiologist. He dabbled in philosophy and literary criticism.

199 **Eduard von Hartmann's *Philosophy of the Unconscious***

Eduard von Hartmann (1842–1906), German philosopher. His *Philosophy of the Unconscious*, published in 1869, was widely read. Rudolf Steiner spoke about von Hartmann in many places in his work (see, e.g., *The Philosophy of Freedom*) and also knew him personally. Their correspondence is collected in *Briefe* [Letters] (GA 38 and 39).

Out of religion

Schiller, *Votivetafeln*, number 30, "My Belief."

200 **Max Stirner**

Johann Kaspar Schmidt (1806–1856), pen name Max Stirner, German philosopher whose work addressed social alienation and self-consciousness.

Stirner's *The Ego and Its Own*
German title: *Der Einzige und sein Eigentum*; also translated as *The Only One and His Property*. Stirner's 1845 book was radical in its time and has remained a bit of a cult classic among philosophers ever since. Stirner critiqued just about every aspect of modern Western society and argued that every ideology and religion is based on empty concepts.

Schiller's Aesthetic Letters
Full title: *On the Aesthetic Education of Man.*

His work formed the basis of what is floating around as individualism
About ten years earlier, Steiner had published his *Philosophy of Freedom* (1894), which argues for a morality based on ethical individualism. The cultural currents of individualism among philosophers of the 1890s was something he was intimately familiar with. Steiner had discussed Stirner in multiple essays and letters over the previous decade.

Lecture Nine
Schiller and Idealism (Aesthetics and Morals)
Berlin, March 25, 1905

202 Wolffian philosophy
Christian von Wolff (1679–1754); he summarized all the sciences of his age.

Baumgarten
Alexander Gottlieb Baumgarten (1714–1762), German philosopher known for advances in the field of aesthetics.

Critique of Judgment
Published in 1790.

Aesthetic Letters
Schiller, *On the Aesthetic Education of Man.*

203 "The Gods of Greece"
Composed in 1788.

fear and pity
In chapter 6 of his Poetics, Aristotle writes: "Tragedy is an imitation of an action that is serious, complete, and of a certain magnitude . . . through pity and fear effecting the proper purgation [*catharsis*] of these emotions."

the drama of Aeschylus
Aeschylus (*c.* 525–*c.* 456 BC), Greek playwright. He is best known for his trilogy the *Oresteia* (458 BC), consisting of the tragedies *Agamemnon*, *Choephoroe*, and *Eumenides*.

Édouard Schuré
See note to page 183.

Preaching morality is easy; establishing morality is difficult
Arthur Schopenhauer (1788–1860). The quoted sentence is the motto of his "Prize Paper on the Basis of Morality," January 30, 1840, and is treated in "On the Will in Nature" in *Schopenhauer's Complete Works in Twelve Volumes*, ed. Rudolf Steiner, vol. 6, p. 361, and vol. 7, p. 133.

204 "Theater Considered as a Moral Institution"
See note to page 161.

the overcoming of matter by form
See first note to page 193.

"Consider *what*, but more, consider *how*!"
Goethe, *Faust II*, Laboratory Scene, line 6992. The character Homunculus is speaking.

205 *Der Groß-Cophta* [The Grand Kofta]
Der Groß-Cophta [The Grand Kofta], a 1792 play.

The Ghost-Seer
The Ghost-Seer (*Der Geistseher*), a fragment of a novel that Schiller worked on between 1787 and 1789. He published the initial section in 1787, and it proved popular, spawning an entire genre of "manifestation literature."

207 as Goethe recollected of him
See note to page 190.

Who must conquer it daily
Goethe, *Faust II*, Palace Scene, line 11575.

Appendix: Discussions and Lectures by Rudolf Steiner in the "Giordano Bruno Association for a unified worldview" in 1902

The Unity of the World
Berlin, March 1902

211 Wolfgang Kirchbach
Wolfgang Kirchbach (1857–1906), writer, one of the leading personalities of the Giordano Bruno Association.

212 Robert Mayer's discovery
Robert Mayer (1814–1878), German scientist, one of the founders of thermodynamics.

216 Professor Ostwald
Wilhelm Ostwald, (1853–1932), German physicist, chemist, and philosopher. At the Natural Scientists' Congress in Lübeck in 1895, he delivered a speech on "Overcoming Materialism."

a journal
This was *Annalen der Naturphilosophie*, edited by professor Wilhelm Ostwald, 14 volumes (1901–1921).

through the forms of the species from which it descends
This is Ernst Haeckel's (1834–1919) Biogenetic Law, which states that ontogeny recapitulates phylogeny. He proposed it in his 1866 book *Generelle morphologie der organismen* [General morphology of organisms].

we have been offered a clear path to unity
For a long time, scientists doubted that it would be possible to synthesize organic molecules (that is, complex substances that are produced by living

organisms) in the laboratory. Matter was initially seen as of two entirely separate types, that produced by organic beings, which was endowed with a vital force, and that which was by nature inorganic. Synthesizing organic compounds was eventually accomplished by the 1860s. Steiner is not claiming that life itself can be synthesized in a laboratory.

217 Dr. Bruno Wille

Bruno Wille (1860–1928) founded the Giordano Bruno Association in 1900. He was a liberal writer on religion and editor of *Der Freidenker* (Berlin, 1892) after creating The Free People's Theater in Berlin. With Wilhelm Bölsche, he established the Independent College in Berlin, 1901. Bölsche was a romantic lyricist, philosopher, critic, socialist, and novelist. He wrote a Faustian, monistic novel, *Revelations of the Juniper Tree.*

Truth and Science

Berlin, May 7, 1902

221 Haeckel's *The Riddle of the Universe*

Ernst Haeckel (1834–1919) had published his book *Die Welträthsel* three years earlier in 1899. It was translated into English as *The Riddle of the Universe* in 1901. After he establishing his reputation in the realm of science as a major supporter of Darwinism, in his later years he turned to larger questions of philosophy.

a "falsification" of the available facts

Copernicus is famous for championing the heliocentric solar system, yet his presentation had the planets in circular orbits, in contradiction to their observed paths. Kepler, relying on observations by Tycho Brahe, finally resolved observation with theory in describing the elliptical orbits of the planets in a heliocentric system.

Tycho Brahe

Tycho Brahe (1546–1601), Danish astronomer.

224 Maeterlinck

Maurice Maeterlinck (1862–1949), Belgian writer who wrote in French. Most famous for his symbolist plays, he won the Nobel Prize for Literature in 1911. His book *The Life of the Bee* was published in German in 1901 and in English in 1914.

225 if I became nothing, it, too, would have to crumble into nothingness.

Angelus Silesius (pen name of Johannes Scheffler, 1624–1677) in *Der Cherubinische Wandersmann.*

226 philosophy has happily arrived again where it started out, in hylozoism

Hylozoism, in philosophy, is the doctrine that all matter has life.

227 his conception of the *perceptiones*

Francis Bacon (1561–1626), famous English philosopher of science. An early champion of empiricism, his most famous work is the *Novum Organum* (*The New Method*, 1620) in which he argued for empiricism, the primacy of perceptions of the senses—*perceptionibus sensum.* Like most scientific tracts of the day, it was written in Latin. In another work published that same year, *Instauratio Magna* (*The Great Instauration*), Bacon criticized Copernicus and his followers and tried to advance a geocentric universe with a chemical mechanism behind planetary motion. This was fifty years before Newton developed a theory of gravity.

228 Büchner
Friedrich Karl Christian Ludwig Büchner (1824–1899) was a major proponent of philosophical materialism. His best-known work is his 1855 book *Force and Matter.*

Monism and Theosophy
Berlin, October 8, 1902

231 *Rudolf Steiner's lecture at the Giordano Bruno Association*
Concerning this lecture, Rudolf Steiner wrote to the German theosophist Wilhelm Hübbe-Schleiden on October 13, 1902, (contained in *Letters Volume II* [CW 39]):

> It was surprising to me how much interest I found with my lecture "Monism and Theosophy" (in the Giordano Bruno Association). Wolfgang Kirchbach chaired the evening of the lecture, and he too was interested to the highest degree. This was an audience accustomed to hearing about monism on the basis of Haeckel's views. The day after tomorrow, there will be a public discussion about my lecture. In the course of the lecture, I also characterized Mrs. Besant and her whole way of thinking. Everything will now depend on whether we are able to work in such a way that we will not be found compromised by joining the theosophical movement. I knew what I was risking that evening. But we need a strong either-or. Count Hoensbroech left the hall after my first sentences. In front of the remaining more than three hundred people, I spoke for 1¾ hours under—I may well say—the most rapt attention.
>
> I am certainly under no illusions, but I think that most of those who were present were aware that they were standing in front of something they could not ignore. And this audience of the Giordano Bruno Association knows me as a person who is well informed in the natural sciences. Also on this day, by the way, as I am told, [Franz] Hartmann had a meeting with his Berlin followers at Raatz on the Plan-Ufer, so there was nothing of what in Berlin could be called the majority of theosophists.
>
> And I came to the people with genuine German theosophy. The middle part of my lecture was an interpretation of the sentence, which I. H. Fichte wrote in 1833 in his book about self-knowledge:
>
> "When the eternal has shown itself as the infinitely revealing spirit, then at the same time the highest mediation of all levels of cognition and opposite points of view of consciousness is won. Philosophy has become theosophy. . . . Now let us see what will become. . . ."

in the 22nd part of his *Organic Ancestry*, it stopped
See Haeckel, *The History of Creation*, vol. 2, part 2, "General tribal history, animal ancestral series or ancestral chain of man" (Berlin, 1898) and "Über

den Stammbaum des Menschengeschlechts" [On the family tree of the human race], lecture in Jena, 1865.

231 David Friedrich Strauss

David Friedrich Strauss (1808–1874), liberal protestant theologian. In his writings he denied the divinity of Jesus, emphasizing instead the "historical Jesus." In his later works, he fully embraced scientific materialism and evolutionary theory, including *The Old Faith and the New)* in 1881.

232 "so many miracles are there"

Carl von Linné (1707–1778), a scientist who, like most others of his age wrote in Latin and is thus known by his Latin name Carolus Linnæus, invented the classification still used by scientists today to label every species. The sentence on miracles is from his book *Genera planetarium*, volume I, page iv.

his basic biogenetic law

Ernst Haeckel's Biogenetic Law states that ontogeny recapitulates phylogeny. He proposed it in his 1866 book *Generelle morphologie der organismen* [General morphology of organisms].

science will never be able to fulfill religious needs

Adolf von Harnack (1851–1930), German theologian. He makes this statement in his 1901 book *Das Wesen Des Christentums* [The essence of Christianity], page 111.

the transformed food substance that Shakespeare took in

Robert G. Ingersoll (1833–1899), American lawyer, writer, and staunch defender of agnosticism, nicknamed "The Great Agnostic." Steiner would likely have read the German edition, published in German as *Moderne Götterdämmerung* with no date (likely in the early 1890s). In the *Preface to Dr. Edgar C. Beall's "The Brain and The Bible"* (as printed in Volume 12 of his 1901 Collected Works), Ingersoll writes:

> Nothing seems more certain than that the capacity of a human being depends, other things being equal, upon the amount, form, and quality of his brain. We also know that health, disposition, temperament, occupation, food, surroundings, ancestors, quality, form, and texture of the brain, determine what we call character. Man is, collectively and individually, what his surroundings have made him. Nations differ from each other as greatly as individuals in the same nation. Nations depend upon soil, climate, geographical position, and countless other facts. Shakespeare would have been impossible without the climate of England. There is a direct relation between Hamlet and the Gulf Stream. Dr. Draper has shown that the great desert of Sahara made negroes possible in Africa. If the Caribbean Sea had been a desert, negroes might have been produced in America. Are the effects of climate upon man necessary effects? Is it possible for man to escape them? Is he responsible for what he does as a consequence of his surroundings? Is the mind dependent upon causes?

Does it act without cause? Is every thought a necessity? Can man choose without reference to any quality in the thing chosen?

233 St. Augustine

Augustine of Hippo (354–430), doctor of the Church. See Rudolf Steiner, "Augustine and the Church," chap. 13 in *Christianity as Mystical Fact* (CW 8).

Galileo

Galileo Galilei (1564–1642), Italian astronomer and physicist.

Fichte's son published a book about human self-knowledge

Immanuel Hermann Fichte (1797–1879), philosopher and psychologist, published *Grundzüge zum Systeme der Philosophie* [Basic features of the systems of philosophy] in three volumes between 1833 and 1846. Steiner is summarizing volume one, *Das Erkennen als Selbsterkennen* [Knowledge as self-knowledge].

234 an inner ideal can develop man beyond man

Ludwig Feuerbach (1804–1872) in *Das Wesen der Religion* [The essence of religion] (1851), p. 224: "For it was not God who created man in His image, as the Bible says, but man who created . . . God in his image."

Duboc has called theosophy a feminine philosophy

Charles Edouard Duboc (1822–1910), German painter and author, in the periodical *Zukunft*, volume 1 (March 1901).

"The Man of the Future"

Antoine Wiertz (1806–1865), Belgian painter who lived in Brussels. The painting is in the Wiertz Museum in Brussels.

Summary of the Discussion
Berlin, October 15, 1902

235 O. Lehmann-Rußbüldt

Otto Lehmann-Rußbüldt, writer, executive director and temporarily Second Chairman of the Giordano Bruno Association.

Count Gobineau

Joseph Arthur de Gobineau (1816–1882), founder and publicist of materialistic scientific racism and the theory of the Aryan master race, in his 1855 book *An Essay on the Inequality of the Human Races*. Gobineau was extremely popular in the United States and in Europe in the late nineteenth and early twentieth centuries.

236 Thus, Vedanta philosophy already thinks monistically in germinal form

This conversation appears in the Brihadaranyaka Upanishad (trans. Max Müller, 1879), chapter 3, section 2, verse 13:

> "Yagnavalkya," he said, "when the speech of this dead person enters into the fire, breath into the air, the eye into the sun, the mind into the moon, the hearing into space, into the earth the body, into the ether the self, into the shrubs the hairs of the body, into the trees the hairs of the head,

when the blood and the seed are deposited in the water, where is then that person?"

Yagnavalkya said: "Take my hand, my friend. We two alone shall know of this; let this question of ours not be (discussed) in public." Then these two went out and argued, and what they said was *karman* (work), what they praised was *karman*, viz. that a man becomes good by good work, and bad by bad work. After that Garatkarava Artabhaga held his peace.

RUDOLF STEINER'S COLLECTED WORKS

The German Edition of Rudolf Steiner's Collected Works (the *Gesamtausgabe* [GA] published by Rudolf Steiner Verlag, Dornach, Switzerland) presently runs to 354 titles, organized either by type of work (written or spoken), chronology, audience (public or other), or subject (education, art, etc.). For ease of comparison, the Collected Works in English [CW] follows the German organization. A complete listing of the CWs follows with *literal translations* of the German titles. Other than in the case of the books published in his lifetime, titles were rarely given by Rudolf Steiner himself, and were often provided by the editors of the German editions. The titles in English are not necessarily the same as the German; and, indeed, over the past seventy-five years have frequently been different, with the same book sometimes appearing under different titles.

For ease of identification and to avoid confusion, we suggest that readers looking for a title should do so by CW number. Because the work of creating the Collected Works of Rudolf Steiner is an ongoing process, with new titles being published every year, we have not indicated in this listing which books are presently available. To find out what titles in the Collected Works are currently in print, please check our website at www.steinerbooks.org.

A. Written Works

I. Writings 1884–1925

CW 1	Goethe: Natural-Scientific Writings, Introduction, with Footnotes and Explanations in the text by Rudolf Steiner
CW 2	Outlines of an Epistemology of the Goethean World View, with Special Consideration of Schiller
CW 3	Truth and Science
CW 4	The Philosophy of Freedom
CW 4a	Documents to "The Philosophy of Freedom"
CW 5	Friedrich Nietzsche, A Fighter against His Own Time
CW 6	Goethe's Worldview
CW 6a	*[Now in CW 30]*
CW 7	Mysticism at the Dawn of Modern Spiritual Life and Its Relationship with Modern Worldviews
CW 8	Christianity as Mystical Fact and the Mysteries of Antiquity
CW 9	Theosophy: An Introduction into Supersensible World Knowledge and Human Purpose
CW 10	How Does One Attain Knowledge of Higher Worlds?
CW 11	From the Akasha-Chronicle
CW 12	Levels of Higher Knowledge
CW 13	Occult Science in Outline
CW 14	Four Mystery Dramas
CW 15	The Spiritual Guidance of the Individual and Humanity

CW 16	A Way to Human Self-Knowledge: Eight Meditations
CW 17	The Threshold of the Spiritual World. Aphoristic Comments
CW 18	The Riddles of Philosophy in Their History, Presented as an Outline
CW 19	*[Contained in CW 24]*
CW 20	The Riddles of the Human Being: Articulated and Unarticulated in the Thinking, Views and Opinions of a Series of German and Austrian Personalities
CW 21	The Riddles of the Soul
CW 22	Goethe's Spiritual Nature and Its Revelation in "Faust" and through the "Fairy Tale of the Snake and the Lily"
CW 23	The Central Points of the Social Question in the Necessities of Life in the Present and the Future
CW 24	Essays Concerning the Threefold Division of the Social Organism and the Period 1915-1921
CW 25	Cosmology, Religion and Philosophy
CW 26	Anthroposophical Leading Thoughts
CW 27	Fundamentals for Expansion of the Art of Healing according to Spiritual-Scientific Insights
CW 28	The Course of My Life

II. Collected Essays

CW 29	Collected Essays on Dramaturgy, 1889-1900
CW 30	Methodical Foundations of Anthroposophy: Collected Essays on Philosophy, Natural Science, Aesthetics and Psychology, 1884-1901
CW 31	Collected Essays on Culture and Current Events, 1887-1901
CW 32	Collected Essays on Literature, 1884-1902
CW 33	Biographies and Biographical Sketches, 1894-1905
CW 34	Lucifer-Gnosis: Foundational Essays on Anthroposophy and Reports from the Periodicals "Lucifer" and "Lucifer-Gnosis," 1903-1908
CW 35	Philosophy and Anthroposophy: Collected Essays, 1904-1923
CW 36	The Goetheanum-Idea in the Middle of the Cultural Crisis of the Present: Collected Essays from the Periodical "Das Goetheanum," 1921-1925
CW 37	*[Now in CWs 251 and 260a]*

III. Publications from the Literary Estate

CW 38	Letters, Vol. 1: 1881-1890
CW 39	Letters, Vol. 2: 1890-1925
CW 40	Truth-Wrought Words
CW 40a	Sayings, Poems and Mantras; Supplementary Volume

CW 42 *[Now in CWs 264-266]*
CW 43 Stage Adaptations
CW 44 On the Four Mystery Dramas. Sketches, Fragments and Paralipomena on the Four Mystery Dramas
CW 45 Anthroposophy: A Fragment from the Year 1910

B. Lectures

I. Public Lectures

CW 51 On Philosophy, History and Literature
CW 52 Spiritual Teachings Concerning the Soul and Observation of the World
CW 53 The Origin and Goal of the Human Being
CW 54 The Riddles of the World and Anthroposophy
CW 55 Knowledge of the Supersensible in Our Times and Its Meaning for Life Today
CW 56 Knowledge of the Soul and of the Spirit
CW 57 Where and How Does One Find the Spirit?
CW 58 The Metamorphoses of the Soul Life. Paths of Soul Experiences: Part One
CW 59 The Metamorphoses of the Soul Life. Paths of Soul Experiences: Part Two
CW 60 The Answers of Spiritual Science to the Biggest Questions of Existence
CW 61 Human History in the Light of Spiritual Research
CW 62 Results of Spiritual Research
CW 63 Spiritual Science as a Treasure for Life
CW 64 Out of Destiny-Burdened Times
CW 65 Out of Central European Spiritual Life
CW 66 Spirit and Matter, Life and Death
CW 67 The Eternal in the Human Soul. Immortality and Freedom
CW 68 Public lectures in various cities, 1906-1918
CW 69 Public lectures in various cities, 1906-1918
CW 70 Public lectures in various cities, 1906-1918
CW 71 Public lectures in various cities, 1906-1918
CW 72 Freedom – Immortality – Social Life
CW 73 The Supplementing of the Modern Sciences through Anthroposophy
CW 73a Specialized Fields of Knowledge and Anthroposophy
CW 74 The Philosophy of Thomas Aquinas
CW 75 Anthroposophy and the Natural Sciences. Foundations and Methods
CW 76 The Fructifying Effect of Anthroposophy on Specialized Fields

CW 77a The Task of Anthroposophy in Relation to Science and Life: The Darmstadt College Course
CW 77b Art and Anthroposophy. The Goetheanum-Impulse
CW 78 Anthroposophy, Its Roots of Knowledge and Fruits for Life
CW 79 The Reality of the Higher Worlds
CW 80 Public lectures in various cities, 1922
CW 81 Renewal-Impulses for Culture and Science–Berlin College Course
CW 82 So That the Human Being Can Become a Complete Human Being
CW 83 Western and Eastern World-Contrast. Paths to Understanding It through Anthroposophy
CW 84 What Did the Goetheanum Intend and What Should Anthroposophy Do?

II. Lectures to the Members of the Anthroposophical Society

CW 88 Concerning the Astral World and Devachan
CW 89 Consciousness – Life – Form. Fundamental Principles of a Spiritual-Scientific Cosmology
CW 90 Participant Notes from the Lectures during the Years 1903-1905
CW 91 Participant Notes from the Lectures during the Years 1903-1905
CW 92 The Occult Truths of Ancient Myths and Sagas
CW 93 The Temple Legend and the Golden Legend
CW 93a Fundamentals of Esotericism
CW 94 Cosmogony. Popular Occultism. The Gospel of John. The Theosophy in the Gospel of John
CW 95 At the Gates of Theosophy
CW 96 Origin-Impulses of Spiritual Science. Christian Esotericism in the Light of New Spirit-Knowledge
CW 97 The Christian Mystery
CW 98 Nature Beings and Spirit Beings – Their Effects in Our Visible World
CW 99 The Theosophy of the Rosicrucians
CW 100 Human Development and Christ-Knowledge
CW 101 Myths and Legends. Occult Signs and Symbols
CW 102 The Working into Human Beings by Spiritual Beings
CW 103 The Gospel of John
CW 104 The Apocalypse of John
CW 104a From the Picture-Script of the Apocalypse of John
CW 105 Universe, Earth, the Human Being: Their Being and Development, as well as Their Reflection in the Connection between Egyptian Mythology and Modern Culture
CW 106 Egyptian Myths and Mysteries in Relation to the Active Spiritual

	Forces of the Present
CW 107	Spiritual-Scientific Knowledge of the Human Being
CW 108	Answering the Questions of Life and the World through Anthroposophy
CW 109	The Principle of Spiritual Economy in Connection with the Question of Reincarnation. An Aspect of the Spiritual Guidance of Humanity
CW 110	The Spiritual Hierarchies and Their Reflection in the Physical World. Zodiac, Planets and Cosmos
CW 111	*[Contained in CW 109]*
CW 112	The Gospel of John in Relation to the Three Other Gospels, Especially the Gospel of Luke
CW 113	The Orient in the Light of the Occident. The Children of Lucifer and the Brothers of Christ
CW 114	The Gospel of Luke
CW 115	Anthroposophy – Psychosophy – Pneumatosophy
CW 116	The Christ-Impulse and the Development of "I"- Consciousness
CW 117	The Deeper Secrets of the Development of Humanity in Light of the Gospels
CW 118	The Event of the Christ-Appearance in the Etheric World
CW 119	Macrocosm and Microcosm. The Large World and the Small World. Soul-Questions, Life-Questions, Spirit-Questions
CW 120	The Revelation of Karma
CW 121	The Mission of Individual Folk-Souls in Connection with Germanic-Nordic Mythology
CW 122	The Secrets of the Biblical Creation-Story. The Six-Day Work in the First Book of Moses
CW 123	The Gospel of Matthew
CW 124	Excursus in the Area of the Gospel of Mark
CW 125	Paths and Goals of the Spiritual Human Being. Life Questions in the Light of Spiritual Science
CW 126	Occult History. Esoteric Observations of the Karmic Relationships of Personalities and Events of World History
CW 127	The Mission of the New Spiritual Revelation. The Christ-Event as the Middle-Point of Earth Evolution
CW 128	An Occult Physiology
CW 129	Wonders of the World, Trials of the Soul, and Revelations of the Spirit
CW 130	Esoteric Christianity and the Spiritual Guidance of Humanity
CW 131	From Jesus to Christ
CW 132	Evolution from the View Point of the Truth
CW 133	The Earthly and the Cosmic Human Being
CW 134	The World of the Senses and the World of the Spirit

CW 135	Reincarnation and Karma and their Meaning for the Culture of the Present
CW 136	The Spiritual Beings in Celestial Bodies and the Realms of Nature
CW 137	The Human Being in the Light of Occultism, Theosophy and Philosophy
CW 138	On Initiation. On Eternity and the Passing Moment. On the Light of the Spirit and the Darkness of Life
CW 139	The Gospel of Mark
CW 140	Occult Investigation into the Life between Death and New Birth. The Living Interaction between Life and Death
CW 141	Life between Death and New Birth in Relationship to Cosmic Facts
CW 142	The Bhagavad Gita and the Letters of Paul
CW 143	Experiences of the Supersensible. Three Paths of the Soul to Christ
CW 144	The Mysteries of the East and of Christianity
CW 145	What Significance Does Occult Development of the Human Being Have for the Sheaths – Physical Body, Etheric Body, Astral Body, and Self?
CW 146	The Occult Foundations of the Bhagavad Gita
CW 147	The Secrets of the Threshold
CW 148	The Fifth Gospel
CW 149	Christ and the Spiritual World. Concerning the Search for the Holy Grail
CW 150	The World of the Spirit and Its Extension into Physical Existence; The Influence of the Dead in the World of the Living
CW 151	Human Thought and Cosmic Thought
CW 152	Preliminary Stages to the Mystery of Golgotha
CW 153	The Inner Being of the Human Being and Life Between Death and New Birth
CW 154	How does One Gain an Understanding of the Spiritual World? The Flowing in of Spiritual Impulses from out of the World of the Deceased
CW 155	Christ and the Human Soul. Concerning the Meaning of Life. Theosophical Morality. Anthroposophy and Christianity
CW 156	Occult Reading and Occult Hearing
CW 157	Human Destinies and the Destiny of Peoples
CW 157a	The Formation of Destiny and the Life after Death
CW 158	The Connection Between the Human Being and the Elemental World. Kalevala – Olaf Asteson – The Russian People – The World as the Result of the Influences of Equilibrium
CW 159	The Mystery of Death. The Nature and Significance of Middle Europe and the European Folk Spirits
CW 160	*[In CW 159]*

CW 161 Paths of Spiritual Knowledge and the Renewal of the Artistic Worldview
CW 162 Questions of Art and Life in Light of Spiritual Science
CW 163 Coincidence, Necessity and Providence. Imaginative Knowledge and the Processes after Death
CW 164 The Value of Thinking for a Knowledge That Satisfies the Human Being. The Relationship of Spiritual Science to Natural Science
CW 165 The Spiritual Unification of Humanity through the Christ-Impulse
CW 166 Necessity and Freedom in World Events and in Human Action
CW 167 The Present and the Past in the Human Spirit
CW 168 The Connection between the Living and the Dead
CW 169 World-being and Selfhood
CW 170 The Riddle of the Human Being. The Spiritual Background of Human History. Cosmic and Human History, Vol. 1
CW 171 Inner Development-Impulses of Humanity. Goethe and the Crisis of the 19th Century. Cosmic and Human History, Vol. 2
CW 172 The Karma of the Vocation of the Human Being in Connection with Goethe's Life. Cosmic and Human History, Vol. 3
CW 173 Contemporary-Historical Considerations: The Karma of Untruthfulness, Part One. Cosmic and Human History, Vol. 4
CW 174 Contemporary-Historical Considerations: The Karma of Untruthfulness, Part Two. Cosmic and Human History, Vol. 5
CW 174a Middle Europe between East and West. Cosmic and Human History, Vol. 6
CW 174b The Spiritual Background of the First World War. Cosmic and Human History, Vol. 7
CW 175 Building Stones for an Understanding of the Mystery of Golgotha. Cosmic and Human Metamorphoses
CW 176 Truths of Evolution of the Individual and Humanity. The Karma of Materialism
CW 177 The Spiritual Background of the Outer World. The Fall of the Spirits of Darkness. Spiritual Beings and Their Effects, Vol. 1
CW 178 Individual Spiritual Beings and their Influence in the Soul of the Human Being. Spiritual Beings and their Effects, Vol. 2
CW 179 Spiritual Beings and Their Effects. Historical Necessity and Freedom. The Influences on Destiny from out of the World of the Dead. Spiritual Beings and Their Effects, Vol. 3
CW 180 Mystery Truths and Christmas Impulses. Ancient Myths and their Meaning. Spiritual Beings and Their Effects, Vol. 4
CW 181 Earthly Death and Cosmic Life. Anthroposophical Gifts for Life. Necessities of Consciousness for the Present and the Future.
CW 182 Death as Transformation of Life
CW 183 The Science of the Development of the Human Being

CW 184	The Polarity of Duration and Development in Human Life. The Cosmic Pre-History of Humanity
CW 185	Historical Symptomology
CW 185a	Historical-Developmental Foundations for Forming a Social Judgment
CW 186	The Fundamental Social Demands of Our Time–In Changed Situations
CW 187	How Can Humanity Find the Christ Again? The Threefold Shadow-Existence of our Time and the New Christ-Light
CW 188	Goetheanism, a Transformation-Impulse and Resurrection-Thought. Science of the Human Being and Science of Sociology
CW 189	The Social Question as a Question of Consciousness. The Spiritual Background of the Social Question, Vol. 1
CW 190	Impulses of the Past and the Future in Social Occurrences. The Spiritual Background of the Social Question, Vol. 2
CW 191	Social Understanding from Spiritual-Scientific Cognition. The Spiritual Background of the Social Question, Vol. 3
CW 192	Spiritual-Scientific Treatment of Social and Pedagogical Questions
CW 193	The Inner Aspect of the Social Riddle. Luciferic Past and Ahrimanic Future
CW 194	The Mission of Michael. The Revelation of the Actual Mysteries of the Human Being
CW 195	Cosmic New Year and the New Year Idea
CW 196	Spiritual and Social Transformations in the Development of Humanity
CW 197	Polarities in the Development of Humanity: West and East, Materialism and Mysticism, Knowledge and Belief
CW 198	Healing Factors for the Social Organism
CW 199	Spiritual Science as Knowledge of the Foundational Impulses of Social Formation
CW 200	The New Spirituality and the Christ-Experience of the 20th Century
CW 201	The Correspondences Between Microcosm and Macrocosm. The Human Being – A Hieroglyph of the Universe. The Human Being in Relationship with the Cosmos: 1
CW 202	The Bridge between the World-Spirituality and the Physical Aspect of the Human Being. The Search for the New Isis, the Divine Sophia. The Human Being in Relationship with the Cosmos: 2
CW 203	The Responsibility of Human Beings for the Development of the World through their Spiritual Connection with the Planet Earth and the World of the Stars. The Human Being in Relationship with the Cosmos: 3
CW 204	Perspectives of the Development of Humanity. The Materialistic

Knowledge-Impulse and the Task of Anthroposophy. The Human Being in Relationship with the Cosmos: 4

CW 205 Human Development, World-Soul, and World-Spirit. Part One: The Human Being as a Being of Body and Soul in Relationship to the World. The Human Being in Relationship with the Cosmos: 5

CW 206 Human Development, World-Soul, and World-Spirit. Part Two: The Human Being as a Spiritual Being in the Process of Historical Development. The Human Being in Relationship with the Cosmos: 6

CW 207 Anthroposophy as Cosmosophy. Part One: Characteristic Features of the Human Being in the Earthly and the Cosmic Realms. The Human Being in Relationship with the Cosmos: 7

CW 208 Anthroposophy as Cosmosophy. Part Two: The Forming of the Human Being as the Result of Cosmic Influence. The Human Being in Relationship with the Cosmos: 8

CW 209 Nordic and Central European Spiritual Impulses. The Festival of the Appearance of Christ. The Human Being in Relationship with the Cosmos: 9

CW 210 Old and New Methods of Initiation. Drama and Poetry in the Change of Consciousness in the Modern Age

CW 211 The Sun Mystery and the Mystery of Death and Resurrection. Exoteric and Esoteric Christianity

CW 212 Human Soul Life and Spiritual Striving in Connection with World and Earth Development

CW 213 Human Questions and World Answers

CW 214 The Mystery of the Trinity: The Human Being in Relationship with the Spiritual World in the Course of Time

CW 215 Philosophy, Cosmology, and Religion in Anthroposophy

CW 216 The Fundamental Impulses of the World-Historical Development of Humanity

CW 217 Spiritually Active Forces in the Coexistence of the Older and Younger Generations. Pedagogical Course for Youth

CW 217a Youth's Cognitive Task

CW 218 Spiritual Connections in the Forming of the Human Organism

CW 219 The Relationship of the World of the Stars to the Human Being, and of the Human Being to the World of the Stars. The Spiritual Communion of Humanity

CW 220 Living Knowledge of Nature. Intellectual Fall and Spiritual Redemption

CW 221 Earth-Knowing and Heaven-Insight

CW 222 The Imparting of Impulses to World-Historical Events through Spiritual Powers

CW 223 The Cycle of the Year as Breathing Process of the Earth and the

	Four Great Festival-Seasons. Anthroposophy and the Human Heart (*Gemüt*)
CW 224	The Human Soul and its Connection with Divine-Spiritual Individualities. The Internalization of the Festivals of the Year
CW 225	Three Perspectives of Anthroposophy. Cultural Phenomena Observed from a Spiritual-Scientific Perspective
CW 226	Human Being, Human Destiny, and World Development
CW 227	Initiation-Knowledge
CW 228	Science of Initiation and Knowledge of the Stars. The Human Being in the Past, the Present, and the Future from the Viewpoint of the Development of Consciousness
CW 229	The Experiencing of the Course of the Year in Four Cosmic Imaginations
CW 230	The Human Being as Harmony of the Creative, Building, and Formative World-Word
CW 231	The Supersensible Human Being, Understood Anthroposophically
CW 232	The Forming of the Mysteries
CW 233	World History Illuminated by Anthroposophy and as the Foundation for Knowledge of the Human Spirit
CW 233a	Mystery Sites of the Middle Ages: Rosicrucianism and the Modern Initiation-Principle. The Festival of Easter as Part of the History of the Mysteries of Humanity
CW 234	Anthroposophy. A Summary after 21 Years
CW 235	Esoteric Observations of Karmic Relationships in 6 Volumes, Vol. 1
CW 236	Esoteric Observations of Karmic Relationships in 6 Volumes, Vol. 2
CW 237	Esoteric Observations of Karmic Relationships in 6 Volumes, Vol. 3: The Karmic Relationships of the Anthroposophical Movement
CW 238	Esoteric Observations of Karmic Relationships in 6 Volumes, Vol. 4: The Spiritual Life of the Present in Relationship to the Anthroposophical Movement
CW 239	Esoteric Observations of Karmic Relationships in 6 Volumes, Vol. 5
CW 240	Esoteric Observations of Karmic Relationships in 6 Volumes, Vol. 6
CW 243	The Consciousness of the Initiate
CW 245	Instructions for an Esoteric Schooling
CW 250	The Building-Up of the Anthroposophical Society. From the Beginning to the Outbreak of the First World War
CW 251	The History of the Goetheanum Building-Association
CW 252	Life in the Anthroposophical Society from the First World War to the Burning of the First Goetheanum
CW 253	The Problems of Living Together in the Anthroposophical Society. On the Dornach Crisis of 1915. With Highlights on Swedenborg's Clairvoyance, the Views of Freudian Psychoanalysts, and the Concept of Love in Relation to Mysticism
CW 254	The Occult Movement in the 19th Century and Its Relationship

to World Culture. Significant Points from the Exoteric Cultural Life around the Middle of the 19th Century

CW 255 Rudolf Steiner during the First World War

CW 255a Anthroposophy and the Reformation of Society. On the History of the Threefold Movement

CW 255b Anthroposophy and Its Opponents, 1919-1921

CW 256 How Can the Anthroposophical Movement Be Financed?

CW 256a Futurum, Inc. / International Laboratories, Inc.

CW 256b The Coming Day, Inc.

CW 257 Anthroposophical Community-Building

CW 258 The History of and Conditions for the Anthroposophical Movement in Relationship to the Anthroposophical Society. A Stimulus to Self-Contemplation

CW 259 The Year of Destiny 1923 in the History of the Anthroposophical Society. From the Burning of the Goetheanum to the Christmas Conference

CW 260 The Christmas Conference for the Founding of the General Anthroposophical Society

CW 260a The Constitution of the General Anthroposophical Society and the School for Spiritual Science. The Rebuilding of the Goetheanum

CW 261 Our Dead. Addresses, Words of Remembrance, and Meditative Verses, 1906-1924

CW 262 Rudolf Steiner and Marie Steiner-von Sivers: Correspondence and Documents, 1901-1925

CW 263/1 Rudolf Steiner and Edith Maryon: Correspondence: Letters, Verses, Sketches, 1912-1924

CW 264 On the History and the Contents of the First Section of the Esoteric School from 1904 to 1914. Letters, Newsletters, Documents, Lectures

CW 265 On the History and from the Contents of the Ritual-Knowledge Section of the Esoteric School from 1904 to 1914. Documents, and Lectures from the Years 1906 to 1914, as Well as on New Approaches to Ritual-Knowledge Work in the Years 1921-1924

CW 266/1 From the Contents of the Esoteric Lessons. Volume 1: 1904-1909. Notes from Memory of Participants. Meditation texts from the notes of Rudolf Steiner

CW 266/2 From the Contents of the Esoteric Lessons. Volume 2: 1910-1912. Notes from Memory of Participants

CW 266/3 From the Contents of the Esoteric Lessons. Volume 3: 1913, 1914 and 1920-1923. Notes from Memory of Participants. Meditation texts from the notes of Rudolf Steiner

CW 267 Soul-Exercises: Vol. 1: Exercises with Word and Image Meditations for the Methodological Development of Higher Powers of

Knowledge, 1904-1924

CW 268 Soul-Exercises: Vol. 2: Mantric Verses, 1903-1925

CW 269 Ritual Texts for the Celebration of the Free Christian Religious Instruction. The Collected Verses for Teachers and Students of the Waldorf School

CW 270 Esoteric Instructions for the First Class of the School for Spiritual Science at the Goetheanum 1924, 4 Volumes

III. Lectures and Courses on Specific Realms of Life

Lectures on Art

CW 271 Art and Theory of Art. Foundations of a New Aesthetics

CW 272 Spiritual-Scientific Commentary on Goethe's "Faust" in Two Volumes. Vol. 1: Faust, the Striving Human Being

CW 273 Spiritual-Scientific Commentary on Goethe's "Faust" in Two Volumes. Vol. 2: The Faust-Problem

CW 274 Addresses for the Christmas Plays from the Old Folk Traditions

CW 275 Art in the Light of Mystery Wisdom

CW 276 The Artistic in Its Mission in the World. The Genius of Language. The World of Self-Revealing Radiant Appearances – Anthroposophy and Art. Anthroposophy and Poetry

CW 277 Eurythmy. The Revelation of the Speaking Soul

CW 277a The Origin and Development of Eurythmy

CW 278 Eurythmy as Visible Song

CW 279 Eurythmy as Visible Speech

CW 280 The Method and Nature of Speech Formation

CW 281 The Art of Recitation and Declamation

CW 282 Speech Formation and Dramatic Art

CW 283 The Nature of Things Musical and the Experience of Tone in the Human Being

CW 284/285 Images of Occult Seals and Pillars. The Munich Congress of Whitsun 1907 and Its Consequences

CW 286 Paths to a New Style of Architecture. "And the Building Becomes Human"

CW 287 The Building at Dornach as a Symbol of Historical Becoming and an Artistic Transformation Impulse

CW 288 Style-Forms in the Living Organic

CW 289 The Building-Idea of the Goetheanum: Lectures with Slides from the Years 1920-1921

CW 290 Toward a New Theory of Architecture: The Goetheanum in Pictures [no longer in the German GA]

CW 291 The Nature of Colors

CW 291a Knowledge of Colors. Supplementary Volume to "The Nature of Colors"

CW 292 Art History as Image of Inner Spiritual Impulses

Lectures on Education

CW 293 General Knowledge of the Human Being as the Foundation of Pedagogy
CW 294 The Art of Education: Methodology and Didactics
CW 295 The Art of Education: Seminar Discussions and Lectures on Lesson Planning
CW 296 The Question of Education as a Social Question
CW 297 The Idea and Practice of the Waldorf School
CW 297a Education for Life: Self-Education and the Practice of Pedagogy
CW 298 Rudolf Steiner in the Waldorf School
CW 299 Spiritual-Scientific Observations on Speech
CW 300a Conferences with the Teachers of the Free Waldorf School in Stuttgart, 1919 to 1924, in 3 Volumes, Vol. 1
CW 300b Conferences with the Teachers of the Free Waldorf School in Stuttgart, 1919 to 1924, in 3 Volumes, Vol. 2
CW 300c Conferences with the Teachers of the Free Waldorf School in Stuttgart, 1919 to 1924, in 3 Volumes, Vol. 3
CW 301 The Renewal of Pedagogical-Didactical Art through Spiritual Science
CW 302 Knowledge of the Human Being and the Forming of Class Lessons
CW 302a Education and Teaching from a Knowledge of the Human Being
CW 303 The Healthy Development of the Human Being
CW 304 Methods of Education and Teaching Based on Anthroposophy
CW 304a Anthroposophical Knowledge of the Human Being and Pedagogy
CW 305 The Soul-Spiritual Foundational Forces of the Art of Education. Spiritual Values in Education and Social Life
CW 306 Pedagogical Praxis from the Viewpoint of a Spiritual-Scientific Knowledge of the Human Being. The Education of the Child and Young Human Beings
CW 307 The Spiritual Life of the Present and Education
CW 308 The Method of Teaching and the Life-Requirements for Teaching
CW 309 Anthroposophical Pedagogy and Its Prerequisites
CW 310 The Pedagogical Value of a Knowledge of the Human Being and the Cultural Value of Pedagogy
CW 311 The Art of Education from an Understanding of the Being of Humanity

Lectures on Medicine

CW 312 Spiritual Science and Medicine
CW 313 Spiritual-Scientific Viewpoints on Therapy
CW 314 Physiology and Therapy Based on Spiritual Science

CW 315 Curative Eurythmy
CW 316 Meditative Observations and Instructions for a Deepening of the Art of Healing
CW 317 The Curative Education Course
CW 318 The Working Together of Doctors and Pastors
CW 319 Anthroposophical Knowledge of the Human Being and Medicine

Lectures on Natural Science

CW 320 Spiritual-Scientific Impulses for the Development of Physics 1: The First Natural-Scientific Course: Light, Color, Tone, Mass, Electricity, Magnetism
CW 321 Spiritual-Scientific Impulses for the Development of Physics 2: The Second Natural-Scientific Course: Warmth at the Border of Positive and Negative Materiality
CW 322 The Borders of the Knowledge of Nature
CW 323 The Relationship of the Various Natural-Scientific Fields to Astronomy
CW 324 Nature Observation, Mathematics, and Scientific Experimentation and Results from the Viewpoint of Anthroposophy
CW 324a The Fourth Dimension in Mathematics and Reality
CW 325 Natural Science and the World-Historical Development of Humanity since Ancient Times
CW 326 The Moment of the Coming Into Being of Natural Science in World History and Its Development Since Then
CW 327 Spiritual-Scientific Foundations for Success in Farming. The Agricultural Course

Lectures on Social Life and the Threefold Arrangement of the Social Organism

CW 328 The Social Question
CW 329 The Liberation of the Human Being as the Foundation for a New Social Form
CW 330 The Renewal of the Social Organism
CW 331 Work-Council and Socialization
CW 332 The Alliance for Threefolding and the Total Reform of Society. The Council on Culture and the Liberation of the Spiritual Life
CW 332a The Social Future
CW 333 Freedom of Thought and Social Forces
CW 334 From the Unified State to the Threefold Social Organism
CW 335 The Crisis of the Present and the Path to Healthy Thinking
CW 336 The Great Questions of the Times and Anthroposophical Spiritual Knowledge
CW 337a Social Ideas, Social Realities, Social Practice, Vol. 1: Question-and-Answer Evenings and Study Evenings of the Alliance for the

	Threefold Social Organism in Stuttgart, 1919-1920
CW 337b	Social Ideas, Social Realities, Social Practice, Vol. 2: Discussion Evenings of the Swiss Alliance for the Threefold Social Organism
CW 338	How Does One Work on Behalf of the Impulse for the Threefold Social Organism?
CW 339	Anthroposophy, Threefold Social Organism, and the Art of Public Speaking
CW 340	The National-Economics Course. The Tasks of a New Science of Economics, Volume 1
CW 341	The National-Economics Seminar. The Tasks of a New Science of Economics, Volume 2

Lectures and Courses on Christian Religious Work

CW 342	Lectures and Courses on Christian Religious Work, Vol. 1: Anthroposophical Foundations for a Renewed Christian Religious Working
CW 343	Lectures and Courses on Christian Religious Work, Vol. 2: Spiritual Knowledge – Religious Feeling – Cultic Doing
CW 344	Lectures and Courses on Christian Religious Work, Vol. 3: Lectures at the Founding of the Christian Community
CW 345	Lectures and Courses on Christian Religious Work, Vol. 4: Concerning the Nature of the Working Word
CW 346	Lectures and Courses on Christian Religious Work, Vol. 5: The Apocalypse and the Work of the Priest

Lectures for Workers at the Goetheanum

CW 347	The Knowledge of the Nature of the Human Being According to Body, Soul and Spirit. On Earlier Conditions of the Earth
CW 348	On Health and Illness. Foundations of a Spiritual-Scientific Doctrine of the Senses
CW 349	On the Life of the Human Being and of the Earth. On the Nature of Christianity
CW 350	Rhythms in the Cosmos and in the Human Being. How Does One Come To See the Spiritual World?
CW 351	The Human Being and the World. The Influence of the Spirit in Nature. On the Nature of Bees
CW 352	Nature and the Human Being Observed Spiritual-Scientifically
CW 353	The History of Humanity and the World-Views of the Folk Cultures
CW 354	The Creation of the World and the Human Being. Life on Earth and the Influence of the Stars

SIGNIFICANT EVENTS IN THE LIFE OF RUDOLF STEINER

1829: June 23: birth of Johann Steiner (1829–1910)—Rudolf Steiner's father—in Geras, Lower Austria.

1834: May 8: birth of Franciska Blie (1834–1918)—Rudolf Steiner's mother—in Horn, Lower Austria. "My father and mother were both children of the glorious Lower Austrian forest district north of the Danube."

1860: May 16: marriage of Johann Steiner and Franciska Blie.

1861: February 25: birth of *Rudolf Joseph Lorenz Steiner* in Kraljevec, Croatia, near the border with Hungary, where Johann Steiner works as a telegrapher for the South Austria Railroad. Rudolf Steiner is baptized two days later, February 27, the date usually given as his birthday.

1862: Summer: the family moves to Mödling, Lower Austria.

1863: The family moves to Pottschach, Lower Austria, near the Styrian border, where Johann Steiner becomes stationmaster. "The view stretched to the mountains...majestic peaks in the distance and the sweet charm of nature in the immediate surroundings."

1864: November 15: birth of Rudolf Steiner's sister, Leopoldine (d. November 1, 1927). She will become a seamstress and live with her parents for the rest of her life.

1866: July 28: birth of Rudolf Steiner's deaf-mute brother, Gustav (d. May 1, 1941).

1867: Rudolf Steiner enters the village school. Following a disagreement between his father and the schoolmaster, whose wife falsely accused the boy of causing a commotion, Rudolf Steiner is taken out of school and taught at home.

1868: A critical experience. Unknown to the family, an aunt dies in a distant town. Sitting in the station waiting room, Rudolf Steiner sees her "form," which speaks to him, asking for help. "Beginning with this experience, a new soul life began in the boy, one in which not only the outer trees and mountains spoke to him, but also the worlds that lay behind them. From this moment on, the boy began to live with the spirits of nature...."

1869: The family moves to the peaceful, rural village of Neudorfl, near Wiener-Neustadt in present-day Austria. Rudolf Steiner attends the village school. Because of the "unorthodoxy" of his writing and spelling, he has to do "extra lessons."

1870: Through a book lent to him by his tutor, he discovers geometry: "To grasp something purely in the spirit brought me inner happiness. I know that I first learned happiness through geometry." The same tutor allows him to draw, while other students still struggle with their reading and writing. "An artistic element" thus enters his education.

1871: Though his parents are not religious, Rudolf Steiner becomes a "church child," a favorite of the priest, who was "an exceptional character." "Up to the age of ten or eleven, among those I came to know, he was far and away the most significant." Among other things, he introduces Steiner to Copernican, heliocentric cosmology. As an altar boy, Rudolf Steiner serves at Masses, funerals, and Corpus Christi processions. At year's end, after an incident in which he escapes a thrashing, his father forbids him to go to church.

1872: Rudolf Steiner transfers to grammar school in Wiener-Neustadt, a five-mile walk from home, which must be done in all weathers.

1873–75: Through his teachers and on his own, Rudolf Steiner has many wonderful experiences with science and mathematics. Outside school, he teaches himself analytic geometry, trigonometry, differential equations, and calculus.

1876: Rudolf Steiner begins tutoring other students. He learns bookbinding from his father. He also teaches himself stenography.

1877: Rudolf Steiner discovers Kant's *Critique of Pure Reason*, which he reads and rereads. He also discovers and reads von Rotteck's *World History*.

1878: He studies extensively in contemporary psychology and philosophy.

1879: Rudolf Steiner graduates from high school with honors. His father is transferred to Inzersdorf, near Vienna. He uses his first visit to Vienna "to purchase a great number of philosophy books"—Kant, Fichte, Schelling, and Hegel, as well as numerous histories of philosophy. His aim: to find a path from the "I" to nature.

October 1879–1883: Rudolf Steiner attends the Technical College in Vienna—to study mathematics, chemistry, physics, mineralogy, botany, zoology, biology, geology, and mechanics—with a scholarship. He also attends lectures in history and literature, while avidly reading philosophy on his own. His two favorite professors are Karl Julius Schröer (German language and literature) and Edmund Reitlinger (physics). He also audits lectures by Robert Zimmerman on aesthetics and Franz Brentano on philosophy. During this year he begins his friendship with Moritz Zitter (1861–1921), who will help support him financially when he is in Berlin.

1880: Rudolf Steiner attends lectures on Schiller and Goethe by Karl Julius Schröer, who becomes his mentor. Also "through a remarkable combination of circumstances," he meets Felix Koguzki, an "herb gatherer" and healer, who could "see deeply into the secrets of nature." Rudolf Steiner will meet and study with this "emissary of the Master" throughout his time in Vienna.

1881: January: "… I didn't sleep a wink. I was busy with philosophical problems until about 12:30 a.m. Then, finally, I threw myself down on my couch. All my striving during the previous year had been to research whether the following statement by Schelling was true or not: *Within everyone dwells a secret, marvelous capacity to draw back from the stream of time—out of the self clothed in all that comes to us from outside—into our innermost being and there, in the immutable form of the Eternal, to look into ourselves.* I believe, and I am still quite certain of it, that I discovered this capacity in myself; I had long had an inkling of it. Now the whole of idealist philosophy stood before me in modified form. What's a sleepless night compared to that!"

Rudolf Steiner begins communicating with leading thinkers of the day, who send him books in return, which he reads eagerly.

July: "I am not one of those who dives into the day like an animal in human form. I pursue a quite specific goal, an idealistic aim—knowledge of the truth! This cannot be done offhandedly. It requires the greatest striving in the world, free of all egotism, and equally of all resignation."

August: Steiner puts down on paper for the first time thoughts for a "Philosophy of Freedom." "The striving for the absolute: this human yearning is freedom." He also seeks to outline a "peasant philosophy," describing what the worldview of a "peasant"—one who lives close to the earth and the old ways—really is.

1881–1882: Felix Koguzki, the herb gatherer, reveals himself to be the envoy of another, higher initiatory personality, who instructs Rudolf Steiner to penetrate Fichte's philosophy and to master modern scientific thinking as a preparation for right entry into the spirit. This "Master" also teaches him the double (evolutionary and involutionary) nature of time.

1882: Through the offices of Karl Julius Schröer, Rudolf Steiner is asked by Joseph Kurschner to edit Goethe's scientific writings for the *Deutschen National-Literatur* edition. He writes "A Possible Critique of Atomistic Concepts" and sends it to Friedrich Theodor Vischer.

1883: Rudolf Steiner completes his college studies and begins work on the Goethe project.

1884: First volume of Goethe's *Scientific Writings* (CW 1) appears (March). He lectures on Goethe and Lessing, and Goethe's approach to science. In July, he enters the household of Ladislaus and Pauline Specht as tutor to the four Specht boys. He will live there until 1890. At this time, he meets Josef Breuer (1842–1925), the coauthor with Sigmund Freud of *Studies in Hysteria*, who is the Specht family doctor.

1885: While continuing to edit Goethe's writings, Rudolf Steiner reads deeply in contemporary philosophy (Edouard von Hartmann, Johannes Volkelt, and Richard Wahle, among others).

1886: May: Rudolf Steiner sends Kurschner the manuscript of *Outlines of Goethe's Theory of Knowledge* (CW 2), which appears in October, and which he sends out widely. He also meets the poet Marie Eugenie Delle Grazie and writes "Nature and Our Ideals" for her. He attends her salon, where he meets many priests, theologians, and philosophers, who will become his friends. Meanwhile, the director of the Goethe Archive in Weimar requests his collaboration with the *Sophien* edition of Goethe's works, particularly the writings on color.

1887: At the beginning of the year, Rudolf Steiner is very sick. As the year progresses and his health improves, he becomes increasingly "a man of letters," lecturing, writing essays, and taking part in Austrian cultural life. In August–September, the second volume of Goethe's *Scientific Writings* appears.

1888: January–July: Rudolf Steiner assumes editorship of the "German

Weekly" (*Deutsche Wochenschrift*). He begins lecturing more intensively, giving, for example, a lecture titled "Goethe as Father of a New Aesthetics." He meets and becomes soul friends with Friedrich Eckstein (1861–1939), a vegetarian, philosopher of symbolism, alchemist, and musician, who will introduce him to various spiritual currents (including Theosophy) and with whom he will meditate and interpret esoteric and alchemical texts.

1889: Rudolf Steiner first reads Nietzsche (*Beyond Good and Evil*). He encounters Theosophy again and learns of Madame Blavatsky in the Theosophical circle around Marie Lang (1858–1934). Here he also meets well-known figures of Austrian life, as well as esoteric figures like the occultist Franz Hartman and Karl Leinigen-Billigen (translator of C.G. Harrison's *The Transcendental Universe*). During this period, Steiner first reads A.P. Sinnett's *Esoteric Buddhism* and Mabel Collins's *Light on the Path*. He also begins traveling, visiting Budapest, Weimar, and Berlin (where he meets philosopher Edouard von Hartman).

1890: Rudolf Steiner finishes volume 3 of Goethe's scientific writings. He begins his doctoral dissertation, which will become *Truth and Science* (CW 3). He also meets the poet and feminist Rosa Mayreder (1858–1938), with whom he can exchange his most intimate thoughts. In September, Rudolf Steiner moves to Weimar to work in the Goethe-Schiller Archive.

1891: Volume 3 of the Kurschner edition of Goethe appears. Meanwhile, Rudolf Steiner edits Goethe's studies in mineralogy and scientific writings for the *Sophien* edition. He meets Ludwig Laistner of the Cotta Publishing Company, who asks for a book on the basic question of metaphysics. From this will result, ultimately, *The Philosophy of Freedom* (CW 4), which will be published not by Cotta but by Emil Felber. In October, Rudolf Steiner takes the oral exam for a doctorate in philosophy, mathematics, and mechanics at Rostock University, receiving his doctorate on the twenty-sixth. In November, he gives his first lecture on Goethe's "Fairy Tale" in Vienna.

1892: Rudolf Steiner continues work at the Goethe-Schiller Archive and on his *Philosophy of Freedom*. *Truth and Science*, his doctoral dissertation, is published. Steiner undertakes to write introductions to books on Schopenhauer and Jean Paul for Cotta. At year's end, he finds lodging with Anna Eunike, née Schulz (1853–1911), a widow with four daughters and a son. He also develops a friendship with Otto Erich Hartleben (1864–1905) with whom he shares literary interests.

1893: Rudolf Steiner begins his habit of producing many reviews and articles. In March, he gives a lecture titled "Hypnotism, with Reference to Spiritism." In September, volume 4 of the Kurschner edition is completed. In November, *The Philosophy of Freedom* appears. This year, too, he meets John Henry Mackay (1864–1933), the anarchist, and Max Stirner, a scholar and biographer.

1894: Rudolf Steiner meets Elisabeth Förster Nietzsche, the philosopher's sister, and begins to read Nietzsche in earnest, beginning with the as yet unpublished *Antichrist*. He also meets Ernst Haeckel (1834–1919). In the fall, he begins to write *Nietzsche, A Fighter against His Time* (CW 5).

1895: May: *Nietzsche, A Fighter against His Time* appears.

1896: January 22: Rudolf Steiner sees Friedrich Nietzsche for the first and only time. Moves between the Nietzsche and the Goethe-Schiller Archives, where he completes his work before year's end. He falls out with Elisabeth Förster Nietzsche, thus ending his association with the Nietzsche Archive.

1897: Rudolf Steiner finishes the manuscript of *Goethe's Worldview* (CW 6). He moves to Berlin with Anna Eunike and begins editorship of the *Magazin fur Literatur*. From now on, Steiner will write countless reviews, literary and philosophical articles, and so on. He begins lecturing at the "Free Literary Society." In September, he attends the Zionist Congress in Basel. He sides with Dreyfus in the Dreyfus affair.

1898: Rudolf Steiner is very active as an editor in the political, artistic, and theatrical life of Berlin. He becomes friendly with John Henry Mackay and poet Ludwig Jacobowski (1868–1900). He joins Jacobowski's circle of writers, artists, and scientists—"The Coming Ones" (*Die Kommenden*)—and contributes lectures to the group until 1903. He also lectures at the "League for College Pedagogy." He writes an article for Goethe's sesquicentennial, "Goethe's Secret Revelation," on the "Fairy Tale of the Green Snake and the Beautiful Lily."

1898–99: "This was a trying time for my soul as I looked at Christianity. . . . I was able to progress only by contemplating, by means of spiritual perception, the evolution of Christianity. . . . Conscious knowledge of real Christianity began to dawn in me around the turn of the century. This seed continued to develop. My soul trial occurred shortly before the beginning of the twentieth century. It was decisive for my soul's development that I stood spiritually before the Mystery of Golgotha in a deep and solemn celebration of knowledge."

1899: Rudolf Steiner begins teaching and giving lectures and lecture cycles at the Workers' College, founded by Wilhelm Liebknecht (1826–1900). He will continue to do so until 1904. Writes: *Literature and Spiritual Life in the Nineteenth Century; Individualism in Philosophy; Haeckel and His Opponents; Poetry in the Present;* and begins what will become (fifteen years later) *The Riddles of Philosophy* (CW 18). He also meets many artists and writers, including Käthe Kollwitz, Stefan Zweig, and Rainer Maria Rilke. On October 31, he marries Anna Eunike.

1900: "I thought that the turn of the century must bring humanity a new light. It seemed to me that the separation of human thinking and willing from the spirit had peaked. A turn or reversal of direction in human evolution seemed to me a necessity." Rudolf Steiner finishes *World and Life Views in the Nineteenth Century* (the second part of what will become *The Riddles of Philosophy*) and dedicates it to Ernst Haeckel.

It is published in March. He continues lecturing at *Die Kommenden*, whose leadership he assumes after the death of Jacobowski. Also, he gives the Gutenberg Jubilee lecture before 7,000 typesetters and printers. In September, Rudolf Steiner is invited by Count and Countess Brockdorff to lecture in the Theosophical Library. His first lecture is on Nietzsche. His second lecture is titled "Goethe's Secret Revelation." October 6, he begins a lecture cycle on the mystics that will become *Mystics after Modernism* (CW 7). November–December: "Marie von Sivers appears in the audience...." Also in November, Steiner gives his first lecture at the Giordano Bruno Bund (where he will continue to lecture until May, 1905). He speaks on Bruno and modern Rome, focusing on the importance of the philosophy of Thomas Aquinas as monism.

1901: In continual financial straits, Rudolf Steiner's early friends Moritz Zitter and Rosa Mayreder help support him. In October, he begins the lecture cycle *Christianity as Mystical Fact* (CW 8) at the Theosophical Library. In November, he gives his first "Theosophical lecture" on Goethe's "Fairy Tale" in Hamburg at the invitation of Wilhelm Hubbe-Schleiden. He also attends a tea to celebrate the founding of the Theosophical Society at Count and Countess Brockdorff's. He gives a lecture cycle, "From Buddha to Christ," for the circle of the *Kommenden*. November 17, Marie von Sivers asks Rudolf Steiner if Theosophy does not need a Western-Christian spiritual movement (to complement Theosophy's Eastern emphasis). "The question was posed. Now, following spiritual laws, I could begin to give an answer...." In December, Rudolf Steiner writes his first article for a Theosophical publication. At year's end, the Brockdorffs and possibly Wilhelm Hubbe-Schleiden ask Rudolf Steiner to join the Theosophical Society and undertake the leadership of the German section. Rudolf Steiner agrees, on the condition that Marie von Sivers (then in Italy) work with him.

1902: Beginning in January, Rudolf Steiner attends the opening of the Workers' School in Spandau with Rosa Luxemberg (1870–1919). January 17, Rudolf Steiner joins the Theosophical Society. In April, he is asked to become general secretary of the German Section of the Theosophical Society, and works on preparations for its founding. In July, he visits London for a Theosophical congress. He meets Bertram Keightly, G.R.S. Mead, A.P. Sinnett, and Annie Besant, among others. In September, *Christianity as Mystical Fact* appears. In October, Rudolf Steiner gives his first public lecture on Theosophy ("Monism and Theosophy") to about three hundred people at the Giordano Bruno Bund. From October 19–21, the German Section of the Theosophical Society has its first meeting; Rudolf Steiner is the general secretary, and Annie Besant attends. Steiner lectures on practical karma studies. On October 23, Annie Besant inducts Rudolf Steiner into the Esoteric School of the Theosophical Society. On October 25, Steiner begins a weekly series of lectures: "The Field of Theosophy." During this year, Rudolf Steiner also first meets Ita Wegman (1876–1943), who will become his close collaborator in his final years.

1903: Rudolf Steiner holds about 300 lectures and seminars. In May, the first issue of the periodical *Luzifer* appears. In June, Rudolf Steiner visits London for the first meeting of the Federation of the European Sections of the Theosophical Society, where he meets Colonel Olcott. He begins to write *Theosophy* (CW 9).

1904: Rudolf Steiner continues lecturing at the Workers' College and elsewhere (about 90 lectures), while lecturing intensively all over Germany among Theosophists (about 140 lectures). In February, he meets Carl Unger (1878–1929), who will become a member of the board of the Anthroposophical Society (1913). In March, he meets Michael Bauer (1871–1929), a Christian mystic, who will also be on the board. In May, *Theosophy* appears, with the dedication: "To the spirit of Giordano Bruno." Rudolf Steiner and Marie von Sivers visit London for meetings with Annie Besant. In June, Rudolf Steiner and Marie von Sivers attend the meeting of the Federation of European Sections of the Theosophical Society in Amsterdam. In July, Steiner begins the articles in *Luzifer-Gnosis* that will become *How to Know Higher Worlds* (CW 10) and *Cosmic Memory* (CW 11). In September, Annie Besant visits Germany. In December, Steiner lectures on Freemasonry. He mentions the High Grade Masonry derived from John Yarker and represented by Theodore Reuss and Karl Kellner as a blank slate "into which a good image could be placed."

1905: This year, Steiner ends his non-Theosophical lecturing activity. Supported by Marie von Sivers, his Theosophical lecturing—both in public and in the Theosophical Society—increases significantly: "The German Theosophical Movement is of exceptional importance." Steiner recommends reading, among others, Fichte, Jacob Boehme, and Angelus Silesius. He begins to introduce Christian themes into Theosophy. He also begins to work with doctors (Felix Peipers and Ludwig Noll). In July, he is in London for the Federation of European Sections, where he attends a lecture by Annie Besant: "I have seldom seen Mrs. Besant speak in so inward and heartfelt a manner...." "Through Mrs. Besant I have found the way to H. P. Blavatsky." September to October, he gives a course of thirty-one lectures for a small group of esoteric students. In October, the annual meeting of the German Section of the Theosophical Society, which still remains very small, takes place. Rudolf Steiner reports membership has risen from 121 to 377 members. In November, seeking to establish esoteric "continuity," Rudolf Steiner and Marie von Sivers participate in a "Memphis-Misraim" Masonic ceremony. They pay forty-five marks for membership. "Yesterday, you saw how little remains of former esoteric institutions." "We are dealing only with a 'framework'... for the present, nothing lies behind it. The occult powers have completely withdrawn."

1906: Expansion of Theosophical work. Rudolf Steiner gives about 245 lectures, only 44 of which take place in Berlin. Cycles are given in Paris, Leipzig, Stuttgart, and Munich. Esoteric work also intensifies. Rudolf Steiner begins writing *An Outline of Esoteric Science* (CW 13). In January, Rudolf Steiner receives permission (a patent) from the Great Orient of the Scottish A & A Thirty-Three Degree Rite of the Order of the Ancient Freemasons of the Memphis-Misraim Rite to direct a chapter under the name "Mystica Aeterna." This will become the "Cognitive Cultic Section" (also called "Misraim Service") of the Esoteric School. (See: *From the History and Contents of the Cognitive Cultic Section* [CW 264].) During this time, Steiner also meets Albert Schweitzer. In May, he is in Paris, where he visits Edouard Schuré. Many Russians attend his lectures (including Konstantin Balmont, Dimitri Mereszkovski, Zinaida Hippius, and Maximilian Woloshin). He attends the General Meeting of the European Federation of the Theosophical Society, at which Col. Olcott is present for the last time. He spends the year's end in Venice and Rome, where he writes and works on his translation of H. P. Blavatsky's *Key to Theosophy*.

1907: Further expansion of the German Theosophical Movement according to the Rosicrucian directive to "introduce spirit into the world"—in education, in social questions, in art, and in science. In February, Col. Olcott dies in Adyar. Before he dies, Olcott indicates that "the Masters" wish Annie Besant to succeed him: much politicking ensues. Rudolf Steiner supports Besant's candidacy. April–May: preparations for the Congress of the Federation of European Sections of the Theosophical Society—the great, watershed Whitsun "Munich Congress," attended by Annie Besant and others. Steiner decides to separate Eastern and Western (Christian-Rosicrucian) esoteric schools. He takes his esoteric school out of the Theosophical Society (Besant and Rudolf Steiner are "in harmony" on this). Steiner makes his first lecture tours to Austria and Hungary. That summer, he is in Italy. In September, he visits Edouard Schuré, who will write the introduction to the French edition of *Christianity as Mystical Fact* in Barr, Alsace. Rudolf Steiner writes the autobiographical statement known as the "Barr Document." In *Luzifer–Gnosis*, "The Education of the Child" appears.

1908: The movement grows (membership: 1150). Lecturing expands. Steiner makes his first extended lecture tour to Holland and Scandinavia, as well as visits to Naples and Sicily. Themes: St. John's Gospel, the Apocalypse, Egypt, science, philosophy, and logic. *Luzifer-Gnosis* ceases publication. In Berlin, Marie von Sivers (with Johanna Mücke [1864–1949]) forms the *Philosophisch-Theosophisch* (after 1915 *Philosophisch-Anthroposophisch*) *Verlag* to publish Steiner's work. Steiner gives lecture cycles titled *The Gospel of St. John* (CW 103) and *The Apocalypse* (104).

1909: *An Outline of Esoteric Science* appears. Lecturing and travel continue. Rudolf Steiner's spiritual research expands to include the polarity of Lucifer and Ahriman; the work of great individualities in history; the

Maitreya Buddha and the Bodhisattvas; spiritual economy (CW 109); the work of the spiritual hierarchies in heaven and on Earth (CW 110). He also deepens and intensifies his research into the Gospels, giving lectures on the Gospel of St. Luke (CW 114) with the first mention of two Jesus children. Meets and becomes friends with Christian Morgenstern (1871–1914). In April, he lays the foundation stone for the Malsch model—the building that will lead to the first Goetheanum. In May, the International Congress of the Federation of European Sections of the Theosophical Society takes place in Budapest. Rudolf Steiner receives the Subba Row medal for *How to Know Higher Worlds*. During this time, Charles W. Leadbeater discovers Jiddu Krishnamurti (1895–1986) and proclaims him the future "world teacher," the bearer of the Maitreya Buddha and the "reappearing Christ." In October, Steiner delivers seminal lectures on "anthroposophy," which he will try, unsuccessfully, to rework over the next years into the unfinished work, *Anthroposophy (A Fragment)* (CW 45).

1910: New themes: *The Reappearance of Christ in the Etheric* (CW 118); *The Fifth Gospel* (CW 148); *The Mission of Folk Souls* (CW 121); *Occult History* (CW 126); the evolving development of etheric cognitive capacities. Rudolf Steiner continues his Gospel research with *The Gospel of St. Matthew* (CW 123). In January, his father dies. In April, he takes a month-long trip to Italy, including Rome, Monte Cassino, and Sicily. He also visits Scandinavia again. July–August, he writes the first mystery drama, *The Portal of Initiation* (CW 14). In November, he gives "psychosophy" lectures. In December, he submits "On the Psychological Foundations and Epistemological Framework of Theosophy" to the International Philosophical Congress in Bologna.

1911: The crisis in the Theosophical Society deepens. In January, "The Order of the Rising Sun," which will soon become "The Order of the Star in the East," is founded for the coming world teacher, Krishnamurti. At the same time, Marie von Sivers, Rudolf Steiner's coworker, falls ill. Fewer lectures are given, but important new ground is broken. In Prague, in March, Steiner meets Franz Kafka (1883–1924) and Hugo Bergmann (1883–1975). In April, he delivers his paper to the Philosophical Congress. He writes the second mystery drama, *The Soul's Probation* (CW 14). Also, while Marie von Sivers is convalescing, Rudolf Steiner begins work on *Calendar 1912/1913*, which will contain the "Calendar of the Soul" meditations. On March 19, Anna (Eunike) Steiner dies. In September, Rudolf Steiner visits Einsiedeln, birthplace of Paracelsus. In December, Friedrich Rittelmeyer, future founder of the Christian Community, meets Rudolf Steiner. The *Johannes-Bauverein*, the "building committee," which would lead to the first Goetheanum (first planned for Munich), is also founded, and a preliminary committee for the founding of an independent association is created that, in the following year, will become the Anthroposophical Society. Important lecture cycles include *Occult Physiology* (CW 128);

Wonders of the World (CW 129); *From Jesus to Christ* (CW 131). Other themes: esoteric Christianity; Christian Rosenkreutz; the spiritual guidance of humanity; the sense world and the world of the spirit.

1912: Despite the ongoing, now increasing crisis in the Theosophical Society, much is accomplished: *Calendar 1912/1913* is published; eurythmy is created; both the third mystery drama, *The Guardian of the Threshold* (CW 14) and *A Way of Self-Knowledge* (CW 16) are written. New (or renewed) themes include life between death and rebirth and karma and reincarnation. Other lecture cycles: *Spiritual Beings in the Heavenly Bodies and the Kingdoms of Nature* (CW 136); *The Human Being in the Light of Occultism, Theosophy, and Philosophy* (CW 137); *The Gospel of St. Mark* (CW 139); and *The Bhagavad Gita and the Epistles of Paul* (CW 142). On May 8, Rudolf Steiner celebrates White Lotus Day, H. P. Blavatsky's death day, which he had faithfully observed for the past decade, for the last time. In August, Rudolf Steiner suggests the "independent association" be called the "Anthroposophical Society." In September, the first eurythmy course takes place. In October, Rudolf Steiner declines recognition of a Theosophical Society lodge dedicated to the Star of the East and decides to expel all Theosophical Society members belonging to the order. Also, with Marie von Sivers, he first visits Dornach, near Basel, Switzerland, and they stand on the hill where the Goetheanum will be. In November, a Theosophical Society lodge is opened by direct mandate from Adyar (Annie Besant). In December, a meeting of the German section occurs at which it is decided that belonging to the Order of the Star of the East is incompatible with membership in the Theosophical Society. December 28: informal founding of the Anthroposophical Society in Berlin.

1913: Expulsion of the German section from the Theosophical Society. February 2–3: Foundation meeting of the Anthroposophical Society. Board members include: Marie von Sivers, Michael Bauer, and Carl Unger. September 20: Laying of the foundation stone for the *Johannes Bau* (Goetheanum) in Dornach. Building begins immediately. The third mystery drama, *The Soul's Awakening* (CW 14), is completed. Also: *The Threshold of the Spiritual World* (CW 147). Lecture cycles include: *The Bhagavad Gita and the Epistles of Paul* and *The Esoteric Meaning of the Bhagavad Gita* (CW 146), which the Russian philosopher Nikolai Berdyaev attends; *The Mysteries of the East and of Christianity* (CW 144); *The Effects of Esoteric Development* (CW 145); and *The Fifth Gospel* (CW 148). In May, Rudolf Steiner is in London and Paris, where anthroposophical work continues.

1914: Building continues on the *Johannes Bau* (Goetheanum) in Dornach, with artists and coworkers from seventeen nations. The general assembly of the Anthroposophical Society takes place. In May, Rudolf Steiner visits Paris, as well as Chartres Cathedral. June 28: assassination in Sarajevo ("Now the catastrophe has happened!"). August 1: War is declared. Rudolf Steiner returns to Germany from Dornach—he will travel back and forth. He writes the last chapter of *The Riddles of Philosophy*. Lecture cycles include: *Human and Cosmic Thought* (CW 151); *Inner Being of Humanity between Death and a New Birth* (CW 153); *Occult Reading and Occult Hearing* (CW 156). December 24: marriage of Rudolf Steiner and Marie von Sivers.

1915: Building continues. Life after death becomes a major theme, also art. Writes: *Thoughts during a Time of War* (CW 24). Lectures include: *The Secret of Death* (CW 159); *The Uniting of Humanity through the Christ Impulse* (CW 165).

1916: Rudolf Steiner begins work with Edith Maryon (1872–1924) on the sculpture "The Representative of Humanity" ("The Group"—Christ, Lucifer, and Ahriman). He also works with the alchemist Alexander von Bernus on the quarterly *Das Reich*. He writes *The Riddle of Humanity* (CW 20). Lectures include: *Necessity and Freedom in World History and Human Action* (CW 166); *Past and Present in the Human Spirit* (CW 167); *The Karma of Vocation* (CW 172); *The Karma of Untruthfulness* (CW 173).

1917: Russian Revolution. The U.S. enters the war. Building continues. Rudolf Steiner delineates the idea of the "threefold nature of the human being" (in a public lecture March 15) and the "threefold nature of the social organism" (hammered out in May–June with the help of Otto von Lerchenfeld and Ludwig Polzer-Hoditz in the form of two documents titled *Memoranda*, which were distributed in high places). August–September: Rudolf Steiner writes *The Riddles of the Soul* (CW 20). Also: commentary on "The Chemical Wedding of Christian Rosenkreutz" for Alexander Bernus (*Das Reich*). Lectures include: *The Karma of Materialism* (CW 176); *The Spiritual Background of the Outer World: The Fall of the Spirits of Darkness* (CW 177).

1918: March 18: peace treaty of Brest-Litovsk—"Now everything will truly enter chaos! What is needed is cultural renewal." June: Rudolf Steiner visits Karlstein (Grail) Castle outside Prague. Lecture cycle: *From Symptom to Reality in Modern History* (CW 185). In mid-November, Emil Molt, of the Waldorf-Astoria Cigarette Company, has the idea of founding a school for his workers' children.

1919: Focus on the threefold social organism: tireless travel, countless lectures, meetings, and publications. At the same time, a new public stage of Anthroposophy emerges as cultural renewal begins. The coming years will see initiatives in pedagogy, medicine, pharmacology, and agriculture. January 27: threefold meeting: " We must first of all, with the money we have, found free schools that can bring people what they need." February: first public eurythmy performance in Zurich. Also: "Appeal to the German People" (CW 24), circulated March 6 as a newspaper insert. In April, *Toward Social Renewal* (CW 23)—"perhaps the most widely read of all books on politics appearing since the war"—appears. Rudolf Steiner is asked to undertake the "direction and leadership" of the school founded by the Waldorf-Astoria Company. Rudolf Steiner begins to talk about the "renewal" of education. May 30: a building is selected and purchased for the future Waldorf School. August–September: Rudolf Steiner gives a lecture course for Waldorf teachers, *The Foundations of Human Experience (Study of Man)* (CW 293). September 7: Opening of the first Waldorf School. December (into January): first science course, the *Light Course* (CW 320).

1920: The Waldorf School flourishes. New threefold initiatives. Founding of limited companies *Der Kommenden Tag* and *Futurum A.G.* to infuse spiritual values into the economic realm. Rudolf Steiner also focuses on the sciences. Lectures: *Introducing Anthroposophical Medicine* (CW 312); *The Warmth Course* (CW 321); *The Boundaries of Natural Science* (CW 322); *The Redemption of Thinking* (CW 74). February: Johannes Werner Klein—later a cofounder of the Christian Community—asks Rudolf Steiner about the possibility of a "religious renewal," a "Johannine church." In March, Rudolf Steiner gives the first course for doctors and medical students. In April, a divinity student asks Rudolf Steiner a second time about the possibility of religious renewal. September 27–October 16: anthroposophical "college course." December: lectures titled *The Search for the New Isis* (CW 202).

1921: Rudolf Steiner continues his intensive work on cultural renewal, including the uphill battle for the threefold social order. "College" arts, scientific, theological, and medical courses include: *The Astronomy Course* (CW 323); *Observation, Mathematics, and Scientific Experiment* (CW 324); the *Second Medical Course* (CW 313); *Color* (CW 291). In June and September–October, Rudolf Steiner also gives the first two "priests' courses" (CW 342 and 343). The "youth movement" gains momentum. Magazines are founded: *Die Drei* (January), and—under the editorship of Albert Steffen (1884–1963)—the weekly, *Das Goetheanum* (August). In February–March, Rudolf Steiner takes his first trip outside Germany since the war (Holland). On April 7, Steiner receives a letter regarding "religious renewal," and May 22–23, he agrees to address the question in a practical way. In June, the Clinical-Therapeutic Institute opens in Arlesheim under the direction of Dr. Ita Wegman. In August, the Chemical-Pharmaceutical Laboratory opens in Arlesheim (Oskar Schmiedel and Ita Wegman, directors). The Clinical-Therapeutic Institute is inaugurated in Stuttgart (Dr. Ludwig Noll, director); also the Research Laboratory in Dornach (Ehrenfried Pfeiffer and Gunther Wachsmuth, directors). In November–December, Rudolf Steiner visits Norway.

1922: The first half of the year involves very active public lecturing (thousands attend); in the second half, Rudolf Steiner begins to withdraw and turn toward the Society—"The Society is asleep." It is "too weak" to do what is asked of it. The businesses—*Die Kommenden Tag* and *Futura A.G.*—fail. In January, with the help of an agent, Steiner undertakes a twelve-city German tour, accompanied by eurythmy performances. In two weeks he speaks to more than 2,000 people. In April, he gives a "college course" in The Hague. He also visits England. In June, he is in Vienna for the East-West Congress. In August–September, he is back in England for the Oxford Conference on Education. Returning to Dornach, he gives the lectures *Philosophy, Cosmology, and Religion* (CW 215), and gives the third priest's course (CW 344). On September 16, The Christian Community is founded. In October–November, Steiner is in Holland and England. He also speaks to the youth: *The Youth Course* (CW 217). In December, Steiner gives lectures titled *The Origins of Natural Science* (CW 326), and *Humanity and the World of Stars: The Spiritual Communion of Humanity* (CW 219). December 31: Fire at the Goetheanum, which is destroyed.

1923: Despite the fire, Rudolf Steiner continues his work unabated. A very hard year. Internal dispersion, dissension, and apathy abound. There is conflict—between old and new visions—within the society. A wake-up call is needed, and Rudolf Steiner responds with renewed lecturing vitality. His focus: the spiritual context of human life; initiation science; the course of the year; and community building. As a foundation for an artistic school, he creates a series of pastel sketches. Lecture cycles: *The Anthroposophic Movement* (CW 258); *Initiation Science* (CW 227) (in England at the Penmaenmawr Summer School); *The Four Seasons and the Archangels* (CW 229); *Harmony of the Creative Word* (CW 230); *The Supersensible Human* (CW 231), given in Holland for the founding of the Dutch society. On November 10, in response to the failed Hitler-Ludendorf putsch in Munich, Steiner closes his Berlin residence and moves the *Philosophisch-Anthroposophisch Verlag* (Press) to Dornach. On December 9, Steiner begins the serialization of his *Autobiography: The Course of My Life* (CW 28) in *Das Goetheanum*. It will continue to appear weekly, without a break, until his death. Late December-early January: Rudolf Steiner refounds the Anthroposophical Society (about 12,000 members internationally) and takes over its leadership. The new board members are: Marie Steiner, Ita Wegman, Albert Steffen, Elizabeth Vreede, and Guenther Wachsmuth. (See *The Christmas Meeting for the Founding of the General Anthroposophical Society* [CW 260]. Accompanying lectures: *Mystery Knowledge and Mystery Centers* [CW 232]; *World History in the Light of Anthroposophy* [CW 233].) December 25: the Foundation Stone is laid (in the hearts of members) in the form of the "Foundation Stone Meditation."

1924: January 1: having founded the Anthroposophical Society and taken over its leadership, Rudolf Steiner has the task of "reforming" it. The process begins with a weekly newssheet ("What's Happening in the Anthroposophical Society") in which Rudolf Steiner's "Letters to Members" and "Anthroposophical Leading Thoughts" appear (CW 26). The next step is the creation of a new esoteric class, the "first class" of the "School for Spiritual Science" (which was to have been followed, had Rudolf Steiner lived longer, by two more advanced classes). Then comes a new language for anthroposophy—practical, phenomenological, and direct—and Rudolf Steiner creates the model for the second Goetheanum. He begins the series of extensive "karma" lectures (CW 235–40); and finally, responding to needs, he creates two new initiatives: biodynamic agriculture and curative education. After the middle of the year, rumors begin to circulate regarding Steiner's health. Lectures: January–February, *Anthroposophy* (CW 234); February: *Eurythmy as Visible Singing* (CW 278); June: *The Agriculture Course* (CW 327); June–July: *Eurythmy as Visible Speech* (CW 279); *Curative Education* (CW 317); August: (England, "Second International Summer School") *Initiation Consciousness: True and False Paths in Spiritual Investigation* (CW 243); September: *Pastoral Medicine* (CW 318). On September 26, for the first time, Rudolf Steiner cancels a lecture. On September 28, he gives his last lecture. On September 29, he withdraws to his studio in the carpenter's shop; now he is definitively ill. Cared for by Ita Wegman, he continues working, however, and writing the weekly installments of his *Autobiography* and *Letters to the Members/Leading Thoughts* (CW 26).

1925: Rudolf Steiner, while continuing to work, continues to weaken. He finishes *Extending Practical Medicine* (CW 27) with Ita Wegman.

On March 30, around ten in the morning, Rudolf Steiner dies.

INDEX

R